STYLE CITY
HOW LONDON
BECAME A
FASHION CAPITAL

STYLE CITY
HOW LONDON
BECAME A
FASHION CAPITAL

Robert O'Byrne
CONSULTANT Annette Worsley-Taylor

F
FRANCES LINCOLN LIMITED
PUBLISHERS

The Publishers wish to thank
Wendy Dagworthy and
the Royal College of Art, and
also the British Fashion Council,
for their help and support
in the production of this book.

Frances Lincoln Limited
4 Torriano Mews
Torriano Avenue
London NW5 2RZ
www.franceslincoln.com

Style City: How London Became a Fashion Capital
Copyright © Frances Lincoln Limited 2009
Text copyright © Robert O'Byrne 2009
For copyright in the photographs and illustrations
see page 247

British Library Cataloguing in Publication Data
A catalogue record for this book is available from
the British Library

ISBN 978-0-7112-2895-5

Picture research Sian Lloyd
Fashion picture editor Kathryn Samuel
Designed by Maria Charalambous

Printed and bound in China

9 8 7 6 5 4 3 2 1

CONTENTS

Introduction:

THE WAY THINGS WERE

On the evening of 15 September 2008, 10 Downing Street, headquarters of the British government and home of the Prime Minister, was the setting for a reception celebrating a national industry annually worth more than £40 billion and a twice-yearly event worth £100 million to the capital's economy. The industry was British fashion and the event London Fashion Week. Both had come a long way over the previous three decades, from a time when they were barely noticed either at home or abroad to a point where Sarah Brown, the Prime Minister's wife, could assure her guests, 'the government will work with you to develop the creative talent. We want to work to make the UK the creative hub for the next twenty-five years and beyond.'

Britain's fashion industry is now acknowledged to be the most innovative and exciting in the world. Writing in the *Guardian* in February 2009, *Vogue*'s editor, Alexandra Shulman, affirmed that 'British fashion, unlike many of its counterparts, remains resolutely inventive, uncategorizable and challenging.' This is certainly true, but for much of its history British fashion has also been severely challenged, not least by an obligation to convince the British public of its own worth. It took a long time to do so.

In a witty feature on British style written for *Vogue* in June 1991, Sarah Mower had rhetorically asked, 'What does a Frenchwoman do when she buys a Saint Laurent jacket? She rushes home to show it to her husband. What does an Englishwoman do when she buys a Romeo Gigli jacket? She rushes home, feels ill, and hides it under the bed.' Mower went on to note that, 'In Britain buying expensive clothes is a vice. Where the French expect quality, the British suspect a rip-off. Where the Italians demand luxury, the British see vulgarity. Where the Japanese consume labels, we diagnose insanity. And where Americans buy clothing to give themselves class, the British argue, "but we have it already!"'

Mary Quant's name is synonymous with London fashion of the 1960s, although she had opened her original shop, Bazaar, on the King's Road in 1955 and continued to enjoy success and a high profile long after the sixties ended. 'I didn't think of myself as a designer,' she wrote in her autobiography. 'I just knew that I wanted to concentrate on finding the right clothes for the young to wear and the right accessories to go with them.' This shot taken in Embankment Gardens shows the designer with models wearing clothes from her autumn/winter 1972 collection.

When it came to clothes, British women had a tradition of being reluctant consumers. In August 1983 Malcolm McLaren – music impresario and former partner of Vivienne Westwood – told writer Georgina Howell, 'The British consider themselves above fashion. If you want to design interesting clothes you must make them in a bed-sit and sell them from a market stall …' Five years later, in his book *The Fashion Conspiracy*, Nicholas Coleridge amusingly came up with a list of other items on which the average British woman would rather spend her money – everything from a new horse trailer to her son's school fees – before concluding that, 'A dress, in the final analysis, is viewed as an indulgence, not a necessity. If you go to a ball in the same purple chiffon that you've worn for seven years, then chances are no one is going to notice, and if they do notice, and think less of you in consequence, then they're not the kind of people you wish to know anyway.'

Designers based in Britain had to learn the limitations of the domestic market. 'Fashion was never part of British culture, unlike in France or Italy,' says designer Roland Klein, a Frenchman who in 1965 moved from Paris, where he had worked with Karl Lagerfeld at Patou, to design for a small London ready-to-wear company called Nettie Vogue based in London. He has remained in Britain ever since. 'Fashion here was always pooh-poohed,' he adds. 'It was never considered the right thing for a woman to spend a lot of money on fashion.' To some extent, the situation remains unchanged today. 'In Paris and Italy, they take fashion seriously, it's a business,' remarks London-based milliner Philip Treacy, 'whereas here it's a bit of frivolity.'

In 1989, at the request of the British Fashion Council, Kurt Salmon Associates undertook a survey of the designer fashion industry. They found British consumers far less likely than their European counterparts to spend money on clothes by a named designer. At that time total designer and diffusion sales in Britain had an annual value of £265 million, while the equivalent figures for Italy and France were £1.85 billion and £1.4 billion respectively. A London-based fashion analyst bluntly informed Janet McCue of Cleveland's *The Plain Dealer* in October 1990 'They're hard to dress, the British … The middle-class woman doesn't buy designer clothes because she won't, or can't, pay designer prices.' The following March Martin Taylor, chief executive of Courtaulds Textiles, was equally frank when he informed the *Independent* 'British consumers are constipated about buying clothes.' A year later the same newspaper reported that five per cent of consumer spending was on clothing – just under half of what went on cigarettes and alcohol combined.

This attitude towards clothes on the part of the local consumer helps to explain why for much of its history the British fashion industry was so dependent on exports. The 1989 Kurt Salmon Associates survey showed that the indigenous market then accounted for only 35 per cent of British designer clothing sales, with Japan absorbing 16 per cent, Italy 14 per cent, the United States 12 per cent and Germany 9 per cent. Designer Edina Ronay is typical in reporting how at the height of her business during the late 1980s and early 1990s some 80 per cent of what she produced went abroad; for a period she even had her own shop in Los Angeles. Likewise, Betty Jackson estimates that over the same period '80 per cent of our business was overseas.' Even in the new millennium, designer John Rocha, for example, says that some 70 per cent of his own-label clothing (as opposed to the ranges he designs for the department store chain Debenhams) goes to retailers outside Britain.

Both a consequence and a cause of British parsimony with regard to fashion is the domestic consumer's historically symbiotic relationship with what is known as the high street: the chains of inexpensive clothing outlets found throughout the country and popularly exemplified by Marks & Spencer. 'British retail has an interesting profile,' says Harold Tillman, current owner of Jaeger and chairman since 2008 of the British Fashion Council. 'The density of the population in a relatively small country allows companies to penetrate the consumer market in quite a short space of time and make sure the branding of their product is out there.' High street businesses are able to produce large runs of inexpensive, albeit often not terribly imaginative, garments to satisfy domestic demand. Former fashion editor Sally Brampton comments 'There is no other high street like ours in the world. I think it comes down to psyche and temperament. You go back into the British psyche and look at how we buy clothes. In somewhere like Italy they've a different attitude to clothing, but they have a really rubbish mass market.' Her remarks are echoed by Betty Jackson: 'I do think you have to look at the market in Britain, which is totally reliant on what is happening on the high street. The British public demand cheap fashion.'

'In most countries,' noted an editorial on the state of the local fashion industry in the *Economist* in March 1987, 'the manufacturers are king, and small independent retailers – which account for the vast majority of shops – are happy to buy labelled goods.' However, this was not the case in Britain, 'where retailers are more powerful.' The piece went on to report that the C&A chain had 4 per cent of the total domestic market for clothing sales, the Burton Group 9 per cent, and Marks & Spencer no less than 15 per cent. Four years later Margareta Pagano and Richard Thomson examined the British clothing industry in the *Independent* and found that Marks & Spencer's share of the market had since grown to 16.5 per cent (£16.7 billion). Chain stores collectively accounted for 75 per cent of national clothing retail sales, compared with 50 per cent in France and Germany, 25 per cent in Italy and 20 per cent in Spain. 'Britain', the authors concluded, 'is a Mecca for good quality, reasonably priced, mediocre apparel.' Not much changed over the following decade. In 2002 the Malcolm Newberry Consulting Company produced a report on the UK Designer Fashion Industry for the British Fashion Council and the Department of Trade and Industry. Among its findings was the information that out of total annual sales of clothing of £30.75 billion, consumers in Britain spent just £3.45 billion – not much over 11 per cent – in independent clothing outlets, with chain stores in their various incarnations accounting for £23.19 billion. (And by that date, British consumers bought more clothes in sports shops and supermarkets combined – £4.07 billion – than they did from independent retailers.)

What was the reason for this curious state of affairs? Why was it that the British buying public displayed such reluctance to support the indigenous fashion industry? Might at least part of the explanation lie in the fact that for so long that same industry had no united voice and no central body to argue its case? Statutory and self-regulating bodies set up to promote and develop British clothing during the greater part of the last century tended to represent the vested interests of mass-market clothing manufacturers and high street retailers; most of them would eventually amalgamate to form the British Clothing Industry Association (BCIA). British fashion designers, on the other hand, had no organization even remotely equivalent to the Chambre syndicale de la haute couture, established in Paris in 1868 (ironically by an Englishman, the Paris-based couturier Charles Worth), as a means of regulating the French couture business and ensuring that the designs of its members were not copied without permission. By joining forces, designers in France exerted far more authority than would have been the case had they tried to resolve their difficulties individually.

Although Britain had a large and flourishing clothing industry – a 1928 survey estimated that in London alone 160,000 workers earned their living in clothes production – only in 1935 did some of the nation's designers come together to form the Fashion Group of Great Britain. Founded primarily to show its members' work to visiting journalists and buyers from the United

States within the context of group shows, three years later the Fashion Group broadcast its shows from Radiolympia and began to produce a quarterly magazine to maximize publicity. But it was fatally flawed by a problem that would hamper the development of the high fashion industry in Britain for a long time to come: lack of unity. While the group included many of London's couturiers, significantly Norman Hartnell, then by far the most famous designer in the country thanks to the clothes he designed for Queen Elizabeth, wife of George VI, was not among them.

Hartnell did, however, join the Fashion Group's successor, the Incorporated Society of London Fashion Designers, otherwise known as the Inc Soc, which was set up in 1942 by Harry Yoxall, managing editor of British *Vogue*, to promote the British clothing industry, in so far as this was possible in the midst of war. Government legislation introducing severe rationing of all goods had come into force the previous year and women were permitted sixty-six coupons annually for all clothing (by 1945 this number had fallen to just thirty-six). Inc Soc's ten members – including, as well as Hartnell, Captain Molyneux, Digby Morton, Victor Stiebel, Angèle Delange, Peter Russell, Madame Bianca Mosca and Hardy Amies – joined forces with the Board of Trade to produce thirty-four smart Utility Clothing designs, intended to show that a woman could dress well on a restricted budget. A selection of these garments was mass produced and did much to raise the profile of the new organization.

After the war the Inc Soc continued to promote British fashion both at home and overseas, and during the 1950s the organization represented Britain's best hope of surviving the peacetime resurgence of French fashion, especially following the emergence of Dior's New Look in 1947. British couture establishments tended to be considerably smaller than their French equivalents: in the mid-1950s, for example, Dior employed 1,200 staff, while on the other side of the English Channel Hartnell had a workforce of 400. And, tellingly, the Inc Soc never numbered more than a dozen couturiers (as compared to the forty-plus connected to Paris's Chambre syndicale). Ongoing shortages, plus government taxes (22 per cent on each quarter's sales) did not help matters, and in 1950 the Inc Soc annual report announced, 'The main aim of the Society is to promote the London Fashion Designers and British fabrics at home and overseas. Because of present-day conditions, the Society's activities are confined almost exclusively to developing the dollar market overseas.' Already a dependence on sales to the United States rather than to the rest of Europe was in evidence.

By its nature the Inc Soc was exclusive, and it acquired a justifiable reputation for remaining aloof from the greater part of the national clothing industry. Its board was dominated by society hostesses such as Lady Pamela Berry and Lady Rothermere, and not long after its demise *The Times*'s fashion editor, Prudence Glynn, observed how 'everyone connected with the Incorporated Society of London Fashion Designers seems to have had a title' (as it happens, in private life Glynn herself was Lady Windlesham).

An altogether more inclusive body, the London Model House Group, was formed in 1950 by eight of the country's leading clothing manufacturers. Like the Inc group, it synchronized shows for members' collections and acted as a collective promotional agency. Under the chairmanship of Leslie Carr-Jones, who owned the Susan Small label (in 1973 its head designer, Maureen Baker, would be responsible for Princess Anne's wedding dress), the London Model House Group, in fashion historian Christopher Breward's words, 'looked to the robust American fashion scene for inspiration; seeing in the corporate efficiency of Seventh Avenue's clothing giants a more appropriate model for modernization than the patrician elitism of the existing Incorporated Society of London Fashion Designers.'

However, the Model House Group was, in turn, superseded by the larger Fashion House Group of London, which, with an annual budget of £40,000 in 1958, began to market London Fashion Week as a twice-yearly platform for British designers to show their collections to interested buyers and members of the press. Like its predecessors, the Fashion House Group coordinated fashion shows and encouraged buyers and journalists from the United States and Europe to travel to London for these events. As well as Susan Small, members included other familiar names such as Frank Usher, Dorville and Polly Peck. The importance of the American market is demonstrated by a recollection of former chairman Moss Murray that in 1966 the organization arranged to cross the Atlantic 'with a party of eighteen model girls, manufacturers and twelve top British journalists. We were a wow! It simply wasn't done for a big store not to have British fashions.' Even by this date, however, the Fashion House Group had started to become somewhat out of step with the changes taking place within the industry. As journalist Alison Adburgham later remembered, many long-established members were unable to modernize fast enough to keep pace with trends exemplified by the rise of designers like Mary Quant. 'Indeed, one could say that the Group was fatally undermined, for in its London Fashion Week presentation to overseas buyers in May 1964, their collections fell between two styles: the one style stemming from the couture culture, the other influenced by the new kooky culture.' Nevertheless, though it had disintegrated before the end of the decade, according to Prudence Glynn the Fashion House Group 'was responsible for building Britain a fine reputation for well made, well priced, efficiently delivered and sympathetically interpreted top fashion.'

In the mid-1960s another relatively short-lived body, the Association of Fashion Designers, was established, primarily to promote exports among a younger generation of companies. Members included, among others, John Marks, Andre Peters, Wallis, and Victor Russell. They showed together in London at various hotels, as well as travelling abroad to fairs in Paris, Dusseldorf and Munich. 'English clothes were designed and sold at good prices,' says designer Anne Tyrrell who at the time worked for John Marks. 'There were queues of buyers round our stand at the Prêt-à-Porter in Paris to place orders.'

After 1965, British fashion designers were helped in their efforts to sell abroad by the Clothing Export Council established by the government in that year. The brief of the CEC was to provide a forum to discuss methods of promoting exports, to advise the Board of Trade, to encourage co-operation in the field of clothing exports and to arrange discussions on exports. Designer Jeff Banks, who at the time owned the fashionable clothes shop Clobber and was married to pop singer Sandie Shaw, recalls how he and a number of other youth-oriented British fashion labels including Stirling Cooper, Quorum and John Marks received help from the CEC to attend Paris's Prêt-à-Porter fair in September 1969. 'We were on a collective stand. We tore into the French and that was a real feather in everyone's cap at the time.'

The CEC was founded, at least in part, in response to the reputation London developed during the 1960s as a global leader in innovative fashion. It was no accident that the film often regarded as best embodying this era, Michelangelo Antonioni's *Blow-Up* of 1966, should have as its anti-hero a fashion photographer (whose behaviour and mannerisms are generally accepted to be closely modelled on those of David Bailey). At the time exciting fashion was one of London's distinctive characteristics. Its most famous exponent was Mary Quant – although it is worth remembering that she had opened her King's Road shop, Bazaar, as early as 1955. When *Time* magazine published its 'Swinging London' issue in April 1966 ('In a decade dominated by youth, London has burst into bloom. It swings, it is the scene.') Quant had already been in business for eleven years and had set up creative partnerships with American companies such as J.C. Penney. Other youthful labels like Foale and Tuffin, Gerald McCann and John Bates's Jean Varon were also well established by this date. Likewise, many London department stores had revamped their image, led by Woollands in Knightsbridge where in 1960 Martin Moss opened the influential 21 Shop, which was designed by Terence Conran and had twenty-two-year-old Vanessa Denza as buyer.

Despite its popularity and the publicity it attracted, Swinging London's fashion, while certainly less expensive than couture, on the whole was far from cheap. In 1967 a Mary Quant Ginger Group jersey dress cost eight and a half guineas, then approximately a week's wages for a young shop assistant. And in her memoirs, Barbara Hulanicki, the founder of Biba, wrote of going into Glass & Black (a King's Road shop opened by Kiki Byrne, who'd formerly worked in Bazaar) and buying a black dress there for twenty guineas, 'a fortune in those days'.

Bazaar, Biba and Glass and Black, along with Clobber, Hung on You, Granny Takes a Trip, Bus Stop and others were all independent boutiques set up during this period. These outlets played a key role in assisting the development of British designer fashion. *Get Dressed: A Useful Guide to London's Boutiques*, published in 1966, estimated there were at least eighty such premises in central London, many of them congregated around the King's Road, Kensington High Street and Carnaby Street. Typically, in 1962 Marion Foale and Sally Tuffin, not wishing to work for a manufacturer with no real interest in fashion, borrowed £200 and opened their own boutique on Carnaby Street, where the rent was cheap. Outlets such as theirs were an obvious way of reaching the consumer at a time when much of British retailing was staid and reluctant to sell the new styles of fashion.

However, as a rule these shops offered just their own clothes (sometimes made on the upper floors of the same building) and did not carry merchandise by other names. The designer-as-retailer phenomenon meant an outlet's fortunes were intimately connected with those of its own label; if the one went under, so did the other. It was only gradually that another sort of boutique emerged, the kind carrying stock by a number of different designers selected by the owner. This replicated the approach traditionally taken by department stores, but on a greatly reduced scale. Among the best known independents at the time were Elle on Sloane Street (run by Maureen Doherty, who would later open Egg), Chic in Hampstead, Lucienne Phillips in Knightsbridge and, far outside London in the Yorkshire town of Barnsley, Rita Britton's Pollyanna.

Retailers such as these were invaluable for designers who were starting their careers but did not want to open their own premises. Now professor of fashion at the Royal College of Art, Wendy Dagworthy used to make clothes for herself and for friends, one of whom introduced her to Joy Forrester, owner of a boutique called Countdown on the King's Road. 'She bought a few of my jackets and that's how it all started.' Soon Dagworthy was selling to a number of independent retailers, which were, she considers, 'the perfect outlet for a small design business like mine'. In those early days, she would go from one shop to the next with a carrier bag of samples and if she got an order she would make the clothes up on a sewing machine in the spare bedroom of her flat in West Kensington. As demand grew, she began employing machinists who would likewise work from home: 'My husband and I would drive around in the evenings, delivering bundles of cut-out shirts and taking back what they'd done the week before. Then we'd take those to the buttonholer before I'd sew on the buttons, iron the shirts and deliver them to the shops.'

The most celebrated of all the independent retailers was Browns, opened by Sidney and Joan Burstein as a single ground floor boutique at 27 South Molton Street in 1970 (and still today carrying the name of its previous owner, Sir William Pigott-Brown). Originally trading in underwear, the Bursteins had developed a string of shops across central London called Neatawear before their business collapsed. In 1968 they started again with Feathers, a boutique on Kensington High Street (where future shoe designer Manolo Blahnik worked for a time) before taking over Browns. The shop developed a reputation in the early years for carrying young French ready-to-wear designers such as Emmanuelle Khanh, Cacharel, Dorothy Bis, Daniel Hechter and Sonia Rykiel, and would later be among the first retailers to stock the new wave of Italian labels. However, from the start Browns also supported local designers, including Foale and Tuffin, Ossie Clark, Jean Muir and Anthony Price (then working for Stirling Cooper). 'Our philosophy', Joan Burstein explains, 'was to appeal to a small percentage of the public, to women who were fashion-conscious, focused on quality and originality, and wanted the current look.' Browns would become known for its advocacy of new British designers: Joan Burstein bought a wedding dress from Elizabeth Emanuel's graduation show in 1977 and the shop later bought the entire graduate collections of BodyMap (1982), John Galliano (1984) and Hussein Chalayan (1993). Linda Barron, who went to work at Browns immediately after leaving St Martins School of Art in 1970, remembers how influential the shop became (even as it expanded into neighbouring buildings). 'When American buyers came to London, we were their first port of call, because they wanted to know where to go and who to see.'

Increasingly those buyers wanted to see British ready-to-wear fashion, not least because the number of designers working in this area had steadily increased in the post-war era. That growth was thanks to the persistence of a number of women, notably Muriel Pemberton at St Martins and, at the Royal College of Art, former *Vogue* fashion editor Madge Garland and, after her, Janey Ironside. They battled to have fashion design taken more seriously, in particular fighting for academic acknowledgement. The struggle for this recognition was long and difficult. In 1967, for example, the Royal College of Art was granted university status and therefore permitted to award degrees, but fashion was specifically excluded from this qualification. After further campaigning, in 1969 the RCA finally considered fashion worthy of degree status and it was also granted to other art colleges and schools in 1972.

In her 1973 autobiography, Janey Ironside noted how 'One of the best results of the social revolution in Britain since the Second World War has been the release of many young designers to the world, whose potentialities would have been wasted before the war.' Previously, she wrote, 'the only openings for young people were as underpaid "hands" with almost no likelihood of reaching the designing stage.' From the mid-1960s onwards, British colleges began to produce large numbers of fashion designers; in June 1989 Kathryn Samuel reported that more than 1,500 fashion graduates would qualify at the end of the month. The high calibre of these new designers was soon internationally celebrated.

But before this could happen, they were forced to overcome a number of other hurdles, not least the problem of winning support from several key sectors. For a long time the development of the British fashion industry was hindered by the incomprehension designers encountered in financial institutions. Fresh out of college and keen to start a business, they usually found their initial challenge lay in persuading any bank to provide the necessary funding. When Tanya Sarne set up her first company, Miz, with a partner in 1978, she went to see her local bank and explained that a friend of her father had already lent £1,000 but she needed the same amount of money again. 'And I remember the man in the bank said to me, "You're a woman, what do you know about business?" I was a very angry woman.' Sarne's story has been replicated many times over. When Wendy Dagworthy needed funds to develop her business in the mid-1970s (she had already been loaned £300 by her mother), the first bank she approached 'wouldn't lend me a penny'; and in 1983 Malcolm McLaren told Georgina Howell, 'This country takes no account of talent – the banks won't give you the kind of financial backing you need to make your business international … all my bank manager wanted to know was whether I had a house I could mortgage.'

Unfortunately, the indifference to fashion displayed by banks was replicated in other areas. Today fashion receives so much coverage in print and broadcast media that it seems inconceivable that it was ever otherwise. Yet for a long time in Britain the subject was deemed by editors and publishers to be of minority interest only. In 1978 *The Times*'s Prudence Glynn compared the national press coverage of fashion to that in other countries and found Britain sorely lacking. 'The press in England,' she wrote, 'where fashion has a more tenuous hold on the intellect and a very tenuous hold on the pocket, all too often treats fashion as a "lightweight" to brighten up a serious day's news, as an opportunity to display as much naked flesh as possible under the cloak of an unexceptional heading, or as a commercial lure for advertisers who have been taught to expect editorial coverage as their due. Most damagingly for both the customer and the industry, coverage is relentlessly geared to cheap price.' (Some of Glynn's criticisms might still be applied to press coverage of fashion today.) Writer Sally Brampton remembers that when she joined the *Observer* as fashion editor in 1981, 'there was a corner of a page every Sunday, a kind of quarter-page, and then I would have a spread in the magazine every two or three weeks, and that was it.'

While women's interest magazines always contained fashion spreads, until the 1980s only *Vogue* consistently gave the subject ample space and made a point of promoting British designers. When Zandra Rhodes started her career as a clothes designer in 1969 (she had previously studied and worked as a print designer), she showed her collection to *Vogue* editor Beatrix Miller. The latter not only gave Rhodes a glowing reference to the relevant buyer at Fortnum and Mason in London but also an introduction to the editor of American *Vogue*, Diana Vreeland. Ten years later Jasper Conran started his career. He remembers how, 'with my second collection, Grace Coddington [the former model who had by then become a highly influential fashion editor at *Vogue*] came along and she took twenty pieces and I thought nothing more of it until around three months later when about ten pages of my clothes appeared in *Vogue*. Everything took off after that.' But *Vogue* was the exception. Elsewhere fashion was not a subject to be treated seriously, even though it had the potential to generate sums of money that could make a substantial contribution to the national economy.

That potential was even overlooked by the sector which ought to have been the fashion industry's closest ally: clothes manufacturing. Clothing made in Britain had an outstanding global reputation and certain sections of the industry enjoyed a long and celebrated history. By the last quarter of the twentieth century, many of the country's most respected companies had been in operation for more than a hundred years: Pringle since 1815; Aquascutum since 1851; Burberry since 1856; and Jaeger since around 1880. These and others like them were iconic names and had helped to create an image of traditional British style that could be summarized as revolving around either outdoor country pursuits or smart urban living. In the closing decades of the last century, such a strong image would be both a boon and a bane. Some fashion businesses, such as Paul Smith (founded 1970) and Mulberry (1971), were able to reinterpret it successfully in the closing decades of the twentieth century (and an American, Ralph Lauren, would eventually re-import it to Britain with astounding aplomb). The traditions of British dress had huge international appeal. In London Fashion Week in March 1987, Bernadine Morris of the *New York Times* wrote that 'Vivienne Westwood's Harris tweed connection and Alistair Blair's cheerful invocation of his Scottish heritage with his tartan plaids are probably the two most important long-range developments of the London fashion season as far as Americans are concerned. Both focus on aspects of classic British fashions which have always had appeal in the United States.'

At the same time, however, that traditional image could stultify innovation and creativity, as a tried and tested formula continued to be repeated long after it should have been jettisoned. Writing in the *Sunday Times* in March 1988, Charlotte du Cann commented on the recent London collections, 'Tweed jackets, pinstriped jackets, hacking jackets, hunting-shooting-fishing jackets ... oh dear yes, having recovered from the shock of the short skirt, British fashion is back where it feels safe: in the past.' The old design staples were a comfort blanket that was hard to shed.

Many manufacturers also found it difficult to let go of a reliance on orders from established high street businesses. This had unfortunate consequences for the successive waves of young designers who emerged from Britain's colleges from the early 1960s onwards. Producing a relatively insignificant number of items for them was of little or no interest to factories accustomed to receiving large orders from chain stores. 'The trouble with being little', says Caroline Charles, speaking from more than forty-five years' experience as a designer, 'is that nobody who can make you anything decent wants to do so in small quantities.' Having previously worked with couturier Michael Sherard and with Mary Quant, she launched her own label in 1963. 'There was no financing available in those days,' she says. 'The whole thing was run in a very loose and ad hoc way ...'

The reason for this state of affairs lay, once more, in the reluctance of the British consumer to spend money on clothes. The *Independent*'s Margareta Pagano and Richard Thomson worked out in March 1991 that the average manufacturer's profit margin on a Marks & Spencer suit retailing for £115 was £5. Given the large quantities of suits involved when producing for a chain store, this relatively low profit-per-item margin was worthwhile. The same could not be said when making a handful of goods for a designer: the return on capital expenditure was too small to justify the enterprise. Furthermore, clothes made for designers were often more complex in cut and time-consuming in manufacture than was the case with the basic goods required by high street stores. 'We could never use the big manufacturers,' says Wendy Dagworthy. 'I did go to one shirt factory, but they were so set in their ways that they didn't think our shirts were right, and their machines couldn't make them up anyway ... By the late seventies we were getting clothes made all over the place in small factories, jobbing factories, whatever we could find. But there was a problem with quality control: some of them weren't that good, and you had to check everything.'

Stephen Marks, the man behind the French Connection label, observed in 1988, 'British manufacturers who make large quantities are excellent, the ones who make anything vaguely complicated are useless. It's a question of quantity. Six thousand garments and you're away. Sixty and you're in trouble.' Designers who attempted to work with manufacturers in Britain agree that the challenges they faced often seemed insuperable. At the end of the 1970s designer Juliet Dunn decided to close down her business because she felt that the clothes she had manufactured in Britain 'just weren't made well enough.' As she told Kathryn Samuel in June 1980, 'Dealing with the factories as a small business had become a nightmare – you always went to the bottom of their list and the larger customers took precedence ... If you complained about anything – the quality of the making, late deliveries, absolutely anything, their reaction would be to tell you simply to take your work elsewhere.' Dunn subsequently started a new company producing luxury lingerie that was manufactured in Hong Kong where 'the Chinese are so helpful and willing to change anything that you don't like.'

In 1990, Gifi Fields, the manager of high street womenswear firm Coppernob, told Roger Tredre of the *Independent* that British designers were at a disadvantage because most of the country's quality manufacturers were geared towards producing for Marks & Spencer: 'In Italy, no retailer has that sort of stranglehold over the industry.' Faced with a choice between accepting an order for 50,000 shirts from a high street chain store, and one for fifty shirts from a young designer, any factory manager would understandably give the former precedence. Moreover, doing business with a large, long-established and dependable company like Marks & Spencer was obviously to be preferred over working with a fledgling design label with no track record and uncertain prospects. 'Marks & Spencer were brilliant payers,' says John Wilson of the British Clothing Industry Association (and former chief executive of the British Fashion Council), whereas young designers in a precarious financial situation could not be relied upon to meet pay their creditors promptly. 'The thing with young designers', remarks designer Anne Tyrrell, 'is that they have to pay for fabrics when setting out and there's always a difficulty with cash flow. Factories mightn't be paid for months and they're somewhat taking a gamble with a new designer.' In 1988 John Galliano grumbled to Nicholas Coleridge, 'It's a factory problem really, a Catch-22. You've got to get a certain number of orders for a factory to consider taking your docket. If you start accepting orders on a garment and you don't get enough, say sixty instead of a hundred, then you have to let everyone down.'

It took a long time for this to change. After retiring from Marks & Spencer, where he had been managing director of buying and deputy chairman, Clinton Silver was appointed chairman of the British Fashion Council in 1994. Of his four-year tenure in the position, he says, 'One of the things I tried to do – and I must say that I failed – was to help designers get their goods made by decent manufacturers in this country. One of the biggest issues I had when talking with designers was the question: where the hell do I get my goods made?'

It didn't help that most manufacturers, even those producing clothes under their own label (as opposed to making them for high street stores), had little interest in establishing a rapport with designers. There were, of course, exceptions, notably Quorum, which from 1968 onwards was owned by the large wholesale manufacturer Radley Fashions and at different times employed, among many others, Ossie Clark, Sheilagh Brown, Sheridan Barnett and Betty Jackson. Wendy Dagworthy also worked as a designer for Radley at the start of her career, while Anthony Price was with Stirling Cooper for several years. When Roland Klein took up his position with Nettie Vogue in the mid-1960s he found the experience so satisfactory that what was initially intended to be a six-month job continued through various incarnations until he finally established his own company in 1989. Clearly, there were some manufacturers who understood the merit of employing a designer.

They were, however, few and far between. At the time legislation on copying was far weaker than is now the case, especially between different jurisdictions (which explains why for so long French couturiers had strict rules about images of their clothes being reproduced). Often factories would simply produce imitations of popular styles, so they had no need to employ a designer. In 1978 Prudence Glynn wrote, 'There was, and is, a gulf between designers and industry, a suspicion and distaste of one for the other, which is part ideological and part political, and which the most strenuous efforts by individuals have only partly bridged.' Anne Tyrrell confirms, 'Manufacturers were not interest in designers. When I left college it was impossible to get a job. My first interview was with Jaeger and I got nowhere because I didn't have industrial training. The only job I could get was in a basement pattern-cutting and grading.' Although Tyrrell subsequently went on to have an outstanding career both with John Marks and under her own name, this was at least in part because she understood that 'technical skills are really important.'

Regrettably, for much of the second half of the last century far too many British designers did not appreciate the importance of acquiring those technical skills. While the nation's clothing producers can be considered remiss in their reluctance to form potentially profitable alliances with designers, the latter were also somewhat to blame for this scenario, since they tended to display little interest in the mundane, but critical, details of the manufacturing process. This had not always been the case. From the late nineteenth century onwards, trade schools were set up in London and elsewhere to provide skilled workers for the clothing industry with an emphasis on technical training. The London College of Fashion, for example, was originally established in 1915 as the Barrett Street Trade School, training its female students in every aspect of tailoring and dressmaking. By the 1930s, a number of art colleges taught dressmaking, but still with the focus on students acquiring technical skills rather than developing their creativity. A report commissioned by the Council for Art and Industry in 1939 (but only published in 1945) noted that in Britain the fashion designer was perceived within the industry as having no creative role. Instead the designer's function was to produce cheap versions of whatever was being made in Paris; the report commented that 'The possibility of any Art School, as at present constituted, turning out designers was generally dismissed by the manufacturers as fantastic.'

However, as heads of fashion departments started to promote fashion as an art rather than a technical craft, they were disinclined to encourage the acquisition of practical skills. Documentation from the offices of the Council for National Academic Awards in 1987 features material from various colleges offering fashion training at the time. One of these stated, 'The course does not propose to train students as pattern cutters', while another affirmed, 'As students are not being trained as machinists it follows that the selection of appropriate processes is more important than the skill with which it is executed.' Graham Fraser, one half of the Workers for Freedom label, commented to the *Independent*'s Roger Tredre in October 1990, 'The fashion colleges are churning out thousands of glamour-obsessed designers when they would be more useful if they produced merchandisers, fabric selectors, production people.' Four years later Andrew Purvie, a Scottish clothing manufacturer interviewed by Angela McRobbie, told her 'There is a shocking ignorance of the basics of production among design graduates. It's laughable how little they know.' While many successful designers in Italy gained valuable experience before launching their own labels by working with a clothing manufacturer for several years, with rare exceptions (Betty Jackson and Sheilagh Brown immediately come to mind), this did not happen in Britain. In other words, both designers and manufacturers had a degree of responsibility for the lack of understanding that often existed between the two parties.

None of this seemed to matter during the 1960s when a wave of young British designers embarked on what promised to be flourishing careers. However, when economic circumstances changed for the worse in the following decade, most of that generation found themselves on their own, lacking the support of a collective organization and obliged to survive as best they could, or else close down. Many of them suffered the latter fate and this helps to explain why London's 1960s fashion scene, seemingly so full of promise and attracting international renown, left a relatively modest legacy in terms of enduring labels. Nothing had been done to harness the era's remarkable creative energy and use it as the foundation for a more lasting British fashion industry. Instead it was like a fire permitted to burn itself out.

By the early 1970s London was home to only a handful of significant designers. Bruce Oldfield graduated from St Martins School of Art in 1973. 'When I started in this business,' he says, 'couture was really dead. The fashion establishment was Zandra Rhodes, Jean Muir, Gina Fratini, Bill Gibb, John Bates, Yuki and Thea Porter.' One might add to this number Ossie Clark at Quorum and Anthony Price at Stirling Cooper, as well as Biba, which, almost alone at this period, managed to be both innovative and inexpensive. This gives a total of ten names.

At the same time, the manufacturing sector had begun what would prove a long and inexorable decline. The national clothing industry had generally performed well during the post-war decades. The volume of clothing exports from Britain roughly doubled between 1954 and 1963, and then doubled again during the following two years to reach £50 million by 1965. The centre for activities in London was around Great Portland Street, running between Oxford Street and the start of Euston Road, where many companies had their premises and showrooms (and indeed where some continue to operate to this day).

The boom of the 1960s turned to bust at the start of the 1970s, a decade which is remembered for the terrible difficulties faced by all areas of British industry and indeed the national economy. Many explanations have been advanced for the collapse of manufacturing in Britain, but one of the most compelling is that too little was invested in modernizing plant and methods of production. 'We had some of the best factories in the world,' says John Wilson, 'making the most superb, high-quality product. But it was in long runs.' It was also, on the whole, within a limited range that failed to take changing tastes into account; British clothing manufacturers were inclined to fall into a rut and not to update their product, or, indeed, their machinery. They had not felt the need to do so. In 1978 *The Times*'s Prudence Glynn described British clothing manufacturing as 'for the most part under-capitalized, fragmented and dependent on the outworker system of labour far more than is desirable for consistent quality or efficient delivery'. Noting that wages had steadily climbed since the Second World War, she remarked, 'For an industry less endemically short-sighted, this ought to have been the moment to invest heavily in mechanization processes on the theory that labour was going to become ever more scarce and expensive.' This did not happen. Instead, manufacturers continued to rely on their established methods of working and failed to take changing circumstances into account. The result was that increasing numbers of factories were forced to close down; manufacturing fell from 34 to 30 per cent of gross national product between 1970 and 1977 and had dropped to 23 per cent by the end of the 1980s (in 2006 it stood at only 15 per cent). In 1971 one of the country's most renowned companies, Rolls Royce, had to be nationalized to save it from closing down. Between 1971 and 1974 the number of workers employed in all kinds of manufacturing in Britain fell by 2.2 per cent and it dropped by a further 6.1

per cent over the next three years. Already in the first quarter of 1972 national unemployment had reached a post-war high of 967,000 and it would continue to climb during the rest of the decade to reach more than 2.5 million by 1980.

The conservatism of manufacturers was matched by that of unions, which resisted change in work practices and demanded higher wages for members. Appalling industrial relations led to strikes so serious that on several occasions they threatened to paralyse the entire country (the number of days lost to strikes in 1969 was a little over seven million: by 1972 it had reached nearly twenty-four million). Over the winter of 1973/74, in the wake of a strike by the National Union of Mineworkers, Prime Minister Edward Heath's government had to declare a three-day working week in order to reduce electricity consumption and conserve dwindling coal stocks. Industrial relations hit a similarly bad patch during the so-called Winter of Discontent of 1978/79, when a series of strikes by key groups of workers led to schools being closed, ports blockaded, rubbish left uncollected and the dead left unburied.

It was during this period that Barbara Hulanicki's Biba, which had been one of the great fashion success stories over the previous ten years, ran into difficulty. As she wrote in her autobiography, following the company's move into the former Derry and Toms department store building on Kensington High Street in 1973, initially 'everything ran like clockwork ... Then came the miners' strike and the start of the three-day week of early 1974. At the same time the property market collapsed. Biba's sales, along with everyone else's, were badly hit and suddenly the complaints started to come pouring in.' The store would close for good in 1975.

At the same time, by the mid-1970s, manufacturers were asking the government to impose restrictive quotas to limit the flow of clothes into Britain. In the face of competition from cheap overseas imports, many clothing factories started to go to the wall. Their disappearance could hardly have come at a worse time for British fashion as it faced a severe economic recession. And yet it was precisely at this time that some of the country's designers initiated a venture which would have beneficial and long-lasting consequences for the entire industry.

After studying fashion illustration at Brighton School of Art, Barbara Hulanicki started a mail order business offering stylish clothes at low prices. It was such a success that in 1964 she opened her first Biba boutique in London's Kensington; its rapid turnover meant customers would come back week after week to see what new items were in stock. In 1973 – three years after this photograph was taken – Biba took over the former Derry & Toms department store in Kensington High Street. But financial problems caused by the mid-seventies recession forced the company to close down in 1975.

SEX, which specialized in fetishwear, was opened by Vivienne Westwood and Malcolm McLaren at 430 King's Road in 1974. Standing at the door is Jordan, who worked with Westwood for many years as a sales assistant.

PUNK EXPLOSION & NEW WAVE

Two events marked the end of the punk rock movement in its original impure incarnation: the discovery on 11 October 1978 of the corpse of Nancy Spungeon, girlfriend of the Sex Pistols' lead singer Sid Vicious (born John Simon Ritchie) in a bathroom of the Chelsea Hotel, New York, where she had been stabbed in the lower abdomen with a hunting knife belonging to Vicious; and the latter's own death four months later following a heroin overdose. Punk enjoyed a brief and largely inglorious history – the Pistols themselves only formed under that name in 1975 – but it had repercussions that continue to be felt to the present day.

The origins of punk were diverse and are still debated. However, what cannot be questioned is that it was rooted in the culture of mid-1970s Britain, an era of pervasive social dissatisfaction and bleakness in which the engine of state, unable to mount a successful opposition to widespread strikes and civil protest, appeared to be under threat of collapse. Punk was the most extreme and nihilistic expression of a grey cheerlessness that enveloped the nation, and while it may only have had a few hundred hardcore supporters, the spirit of punk reflected a more general malaise and discontent.

Writing about the phenomenon in 1989, Angela McRobbie perceptively emphasized the commercial aspects of the movement, based around the series of shops operated by Vivienne Westwood and Malcolm McLaren at 430 King's Road in London. 'Sociologists of the time ignored this social dimension,' observed McRobbie, 'perhaps because to them the very idea that style could be purchased over the counter went against the grain of those analyses which saw the adoption of punk style as an act of creative defiance far removed from the mundane act of buying.' Punk clothing was not cheap, any more than Mary Quant dresses had been in the 1960s: in 1977 a pair of bondage trousers from Seditionaries – as the Westwood/McLaren shop was then called – cost £50, which was twice the

Malcolm McLaren and Vivienne Westwood in 1977. The couple had originally met twelve years earlier and in 1971 together opened their first shop, Let It Rock. They would drift apart in the post-punk era.

average young person's weekly wage, and a parachute shirt
sold for £30. No wonder so many of punk's keenest supporters,
predominantly (although not exclusively) disaffected members
of the working class reliant on social welfare payments, resorted
to stealing from Seditionaries. It's also worth pointing out that
while punk was essentially a youth movement, punk fashion
was not: Westwood was thirty-five in 1976 and even McLaren
was thirty. These were no teenage rebels.

Westwood and McLaren had first met in 1965. At the time
she was married with a young child and working as a primary
school teacher while also making and selling jewellery in the
Portobello Road; McLaren remained a student at various art
colleges until 1971. By the latter date, the couple had already
established a presence at 430 King's Road. In the 1960s, the shop
had been a boutique run by Michael Rainey and called Hung on
You, before being taken over by Tommy Roberts and renamed
Mr Freedom. In 1970 it changed hands and names once more to
become Paradise Garage, selling used and new Americana; here
in a backroom McLaren and Westwood offered second-hand
1950s rock'n'roll records. They took over the business in 1971
and gave the premises yet another name, Let It Rock. In 1975
McLaren started to manage the band that was to become the
Sex Pistols.

Westwood and McLaren were to 1970s fashion what Mary
Quant and her husband Alexander Plunket Greene had been
during the mid-1950s and Barbara Hulanicki and her husband
Stephen Fitz-Simon in the mid-1960s: each acted as a catalyst
for the other and brought different qualities to their joint venture
in the world of fashion. McLaren was the confident impresario, whereas for a long time Westwood had limited faith in her
own abilities; these only gradually emerged and developed as
she gained more experience and confidence. Although she never
received any formal fashion training, Westwood began to make
clothes to sell in the shop, initially offering customers copies and
interpretations of fifties' Teddy Boy garments. From the start,
everything she produced was notable for the quality of materials used and the high standard of finish; even the rips in a T-shirt
were calculated beforehand. When in 1972 Let It Rock morphed

Punk revisited in a Vivienne Westwood retrospective show. The monochrome palette, the ripped garments, the aggressive slogans – all imprinted themselves on the public imagination.

into Too Fast To Live Too Young To Die, dealing in biker rock items, Westwood likewise switched styles, as she did again two years later following the shop's further transformation to become SEX, which specialized in leather and rubber clothing of the sort previously confined to fetishist groups. SEX in turn was reinvented as Seditionaries in 1977.

It was during the course of these various retail incarnations that punk style evolved into the form by which it would be remembered – and imitated – long after the movement had petered out in recrimination and death. The appearance of punk was critical to the impression it made at the time, since its followers so clearly looked different from the rest of society. Westwood's 1998 biographer Jane Mulvagh lists the various sources from which punk drew its visual inspiration and makes the point that, 'It was post-modern, borrowing symbols and clothing styles from other tribes to create its own collage.' At least some of the movement's imagery came from New-York-based musicians, in particular Richard Hell (born Myers) who, several years before the emergence

of punk, already wore slashed and safety-pinned clothing and had his hair razored into a shag cut. Jordan (born Pamela Rooke), who worked for many years in 430 King's Road as a sales assistant and appeared in Derek Jarman's 1978 film *Jubilee*, was also an important influence thanks to her extreme make-up and hair and her propensity for mixing militaristic and fetishist clothes. Dadaist and Surrealist elements were also appropriated, along with sartorial characteristics of Hell's Angel bikers and even the Nazi movement (although punk was never fascist in outlook). As Jane Mulvagh comments, 'Punk dress celebrated the sordid, the cruel, the inappropriate and the poor.' It was the style of choice for the self-elected outsider; one *aficionado* explained at the time, 'Punks just like to be hated.'

Widely reviled, punk nevertheless touched some kind of nerve with the general public. Although 'God Save the Queen', the Sex Pistols' single released in May 1977 to coincide with Elizabeth II's Silver Jubilee celebrations, was neither played on the major national radio stations nor stocked by any high street music retail outlet, it sold 150,000 copies within the first five days and reached number one in the charts. 'Such is the new-found and disturbing power of punk,' the *Daily Mirror* reported, 'that nothing can stop the disc's runaway success.' Aspects of punk dress would likewise infiltrate mainstream fashion. 'Far from fading away,' declared Kathryn Samuel in the *Evening Standard* in early August 1977, 'the punk movement seems to be attracting more devotees. Zandra Rhodes has designed a range of silk jersey punk dresses, slit, slashed and safety pin trimmed, which will be selling in her Grafton Street shop in October from approximately £270. I wonder how her normal jet-set customers will react?'

Not altogether well, as it turned out. Although Rhodes described what she was doing as 'Conceptual Chic' and worked with a palette of gorgeous pinks and reds far removed from punk's funereal black, 'It wasn't necessarily good for business,' she says. 'At the time I had to make sure the shop was still filled with the chiffon and stuff like that.' But, as she later wrote, 'There was a new parade on the King's Road. In the clubs around there and in Soho and Oxford Street, you could feel the tension.' Under those circumstances, what she had hitherto been producing felt irrelevant: 'In this atmosphere my floating chiffon butterflies were too delicate, too fragile, uneasy. I didn't feel right putting on any of the things I used to wear.' *Vogue* – which would not feature Westwood for several years to come (although it selected the Sex Pistols' Johnny Rotten as one of the 'Successes of the Year' in 1977) – photographed the Rhodes dresses and carried the pictures under the ironic caption 'What a Rip Off'.

Johnny Rotten of the Sex Pistols, in 1978.

'I didn't mind Zandra copying the punk rock thing,' Westwood told writer Valerie Steele in 1991, 'because she did it in her own way.' Other designers would display less imagination when it came to borrowing from her. The distance punk would travel from its anarchic origins is best embodied by the much-photographed Gianni Versace safety-pin dress worn in 1994 by actress and model Elizabeth Hurley to the London première of the film *Four Weddings and a Funeral*. But long before that date Westwood had moved into the mainstream; in both 1990 and 1991, for example, she was selected as British Designer of the Year.

Although little appreciated at the time other than by devotees, punk had the merit of focusing global attention on London just as the city's fashion scene was undergoing expansion thanks to the emergence of a new group of designers. Jasper Conran is the son of design maestro Sir Terence Conran and his first wife, writer Shirley Conran, and while the designer rightly emphasizes that these connections were of no benefit to him when it came to building a career, there can be no question but that he inherited his parents' entrepreneurial spirit and ambition. Returning from New York, where he studied at Parson's School of Design, Conran was given a job by Jeffrey Wallis (head of the long-established chain of Wallis shops who during the 1960s had bought the rights to reproduce Chanel designs for the high street), but found this arrangement not to his liking. 'So I left and I thought to myself, what should I do? Shall I be a waiter, or shall I start up my own business?' In 1978 Conran went for the second option: 'I bought myself a sewing machine and worked from home. Then at the Embassy nightclub I met a girl called Marysia Woroniecka who was doing PR at the time [she also looked after Vivienne Westwood] and it sort of developed from there … I had to learn all about production and at the start I was a one-man band. It was horrible.'

Conran benefited from the renewed international interest in British fashion evident in the growing amount of attention paid by non-national journalists and buyers with every passing season. The American market expanded

greatly during the late 1970s, with a number of transatlantic stores maintaining buying offices in London. In 1978 Gail Sackloff joined Gimbel Saks, which represented a stable of high-profile North American retail names such as Saks Fifth Avenue, Bergdorf Goodman, Neiman Marcus and Holt Renfrew. 'My job was to find all the new and wonderful people before the other stores did … American buyers would come into town and ask what had I got lined up for them.' In the 1970s, she says, 'All the evening-wear buyers came here. We were outstanding in that area because you couldn't get it anywhere else. The French only provided complete collections of day-into-evening and you had to buy the lot, and the Italians were more into sportswear and the like.' Similarly, Vanessa Denza, who had been buyer for the influential Woollands 21 boutique during the 1960s, opened a buying office in London for American retailers. 'Nordstrom was the only department store I represented, otherwise it was specialty independents. I'd go with them to designers when they came over. My buying power was pretty considerable: we were shipping about £1.5 million annually and that was important to the industry. We bought labels like John Bates, Katharine Hamnett, Ghost …'

In October 1977, Kathryn Samuel was able to report in the *Evening Standard* that while 'Beating the drum for the British fashion industry has been in the past something of a patriotic gesture, now there's been a great shake-up; last year exports rose by 51.1 per cent. And the signs are that the new summer collections could well reach £100 million.' A week later she told her readers how during London's just-concluded Fashion Week, 'The bumper turn-out of buyers from all over the world has exceeded everyone's hopes. More than 7,000 visited the three exhibitions at Olympia, the Inter-Continental and the Inn on the Park, on the first day.' Figures from the Department of Trade and Industry reported in *British Business* in December 1983 show how much the export business grew during the course of the 1970s. In 1973, the value of Britain's overseas trade in finished clothing was £86.9 million; by 1980 the amount had grown fivefold to £435 million. Much of the growth came from designer fashion, since during this period the national clothing industry was already in decline.

Below Here wearing Yves Saint Laurent in November 1977, Grace Coddington, the 1960s model who became a fashion editor on British *Vogue* and later creative director of American *Vogue*. One of the most powerful women in fashion, she exemplifies how British style has spread its influence across the globe.

It helped that for the greater part of the 1970s London's immediate rival, Paris, struggled to maintain its pre-eminent position in the fashion hierarchy. Paris's problems had begun in the previous decade and can be attributed in part to the emergence on the other side of the English Channel of a generation of adventurous ready-to-wear designers who seized the position of fashion innovators previously held by French couturiers. As Valerie Steele has observed in her 1988 survey of Paris fashion, 'The French had essentially no youth culture at the time. There existed no French equivalent to Elvis Presley, the Rolling Stones or the Beatles. Johnny Hallyday and Françoise Hardy, the most successful French pop singers, never obtained a truly international reputation.' The same was true of fashion. French haute couture looked staid, old-fashioned and out of touch with the social changes taking place during the 1960s. The story goes that when Coco Chanel offered to dress film actress Brigitte Bardot, the latter dismissed the proposal with the remark, 'Couture is for grannies.'

Some French couturiers attempted to emulate the fashions of London by promoting their own vision of the future; this is best exemplified by the 'space-age' dresses and suits produced by André Courrèges and Pierre Cardin. But even if these clothes were young and modern, they were still not affordable. French designers themselves recognized that the status quo impeded rather than helped them. 'Haute couture is dead,' declared model-turned-designer Emmanuelle Khanh in 1964. 'I want to design for the street . . . a socialist kind

Above Twiggy in a dress designed by Bill Gibb for the model-turned-actress to wear to the Los Angeles premiere of her first film, Ken Russell's version of the Sandy Wilson musical *The Boyfriend*, which opened in 1971. 'I felt like a princess,' she later said of these clothes.

Following pages Models on stage at the Royal Albert Hall in Bill Gibb's show of November 1977. One of the most successful and influential designers of the 1960s and 1970s, Scottish-born Gibb held this event in front of a five-thousand-strong audience to mark his tenth anniversary in business. Unfortunately, the following year the company foundered and Gibb failed to regain his pre-eminence in the British fashion hierarchy before his early death in 1988.

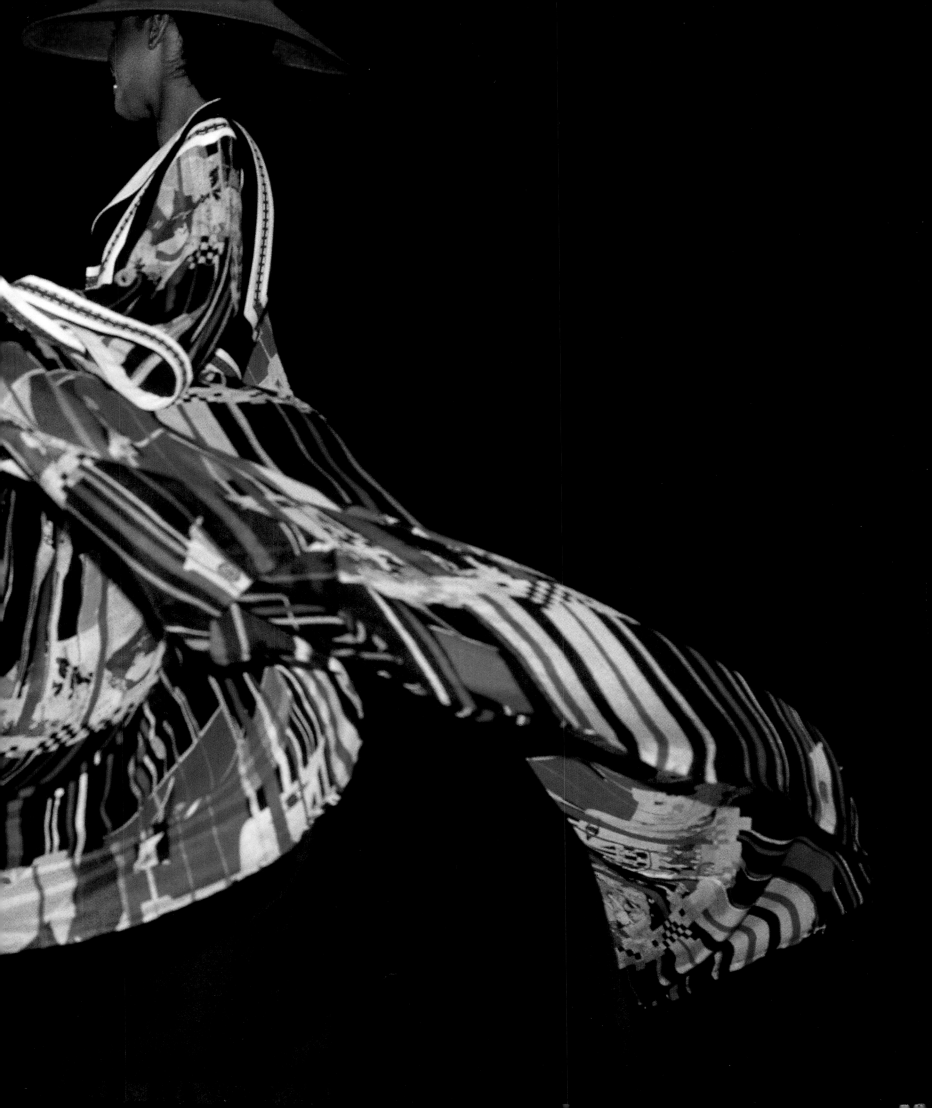

of fashion for the grand mass.' A year later Cardin proclaimed, 'My number one objective has always been … the whole world and not only fifty women.' Emanuel Ungaro, who opened his own house in 1965, agreed: 'Let's kill the couture. Kill it in the sense of the way it is now.' In 1968 the grand master of French couture, Cristobal Balenciaga, closed his atelier and retired. By then, the old order had already surrendered to the new: in September 1966 Yves St Laurent, the leader of the younger generation of couturiers, opened his first Rive Gauche boutique selling ready-to-wear clothes on rue de Tournon. Although efforts would be made to re-establish couture's hegemony – notably financier Bernard Arnault's underwriting of Christian Lacroix from 1987 onwards – it would never regain its former authority. (And in late May 2009 the house of Lacroix, by then owned by US group Falic, filed for voluntary bankruptcy.)

Nor, it seemed, was Paris itself likely to win back its crown, despite the efforts of some far-sighted individuals, notably Didier Grumbach. Managing director of Mendès, a family business that manufactured clothing lines including Yves St Laurent's Rive Gauche as well as Givenchy and Chanel, Grumbach founded Créateurs & Industriels in 1971. The organization's purpose was to promote ready-to-wear designers such as Emmanuelle Khanh and Jean-Charles de Castelbajac, giving them as much support and assistance as possible. This was something they could not expect from couture's Chambre syndicale, which continued to look down on ready-to-wear and thereby hindered its development in France (ironically in 1998 Grumbach became president of the Chambre's successor, the Fédération française de la couture). Créateurs & Industriels, which charged members a fee, took the trouble to stage for its designers proper runway shows with high production values. Acknowledging the superiority of British design in the field of ready-to-wear, in April 1971 Grumbach invited Ossie Clark to present a show in Paris. The occasion was an enormous success, with Clark's collection deemed *'divin, excentrique, érotique'*. The following October another London-based designer, Jean Muir, was offered a similar opportunity by Créateurs & Industriels and met with equal approbation; *Elle* magazine called her *'la nouvelle reine de la robe'*. For a period afterwards, some of Muir's work destined for the French market was made by Mendès.

But turning for help to non-national designers only confirmed the impression that French fashion was in decline, and the moment looked ripe for another city to seize what had hitherto been Paris's dominant position in the global hierarchy. Thanks to the likes of Clark and Muir, London appeared the obvious choice for this role. However, at least some of its thunder was stolen by an unexpected rival on the far side of the Alps. Milan's ranking as a

From the moment he emerged from the Royal College of Art in 1965 Ossie Clark was considered to be one of Britain's most exciting fashion designers and by the start of the following decade he had achieved international renown. But despite his outstanding abilities Clark's career, like those of so many of his generation, never realized its potential and eventually ended in disappointment. Here singer Jane Birkin is wearing a dress from Clark's spring/summer 1969 collection.

top fashion capital is now so firmly established that it seems inconceivable it could ever have been otherwise. Although a centre of innovative design, especially within the industrial sector, nevertheless, even as recently as 1970 the city had little fashion status either within Italy or overseas. Couture was based in Rome while, since the early 1950s, the centre for shows and trade exhibitions of ready-to-wear had been Florence. Various circumstances conspired to change this scenario: the development of high-quality exhibition facilities in Milan; the emergence of several new designers who chose to base themselves in the city; substantial financial investment in these designers by fabric and clothing manufacturers; and the failure of Florence to meet designers' needs. It also helped that many Italian cloth and clothing manufacturers were located around or close to Lombardy, of which Milan is the capital.

In 1969 a number of agents and commercial representatives of the clothing sector within Milan joined forces to launch a new exhibition called Milanovendemoda, which would quickly become a rival to the existing fair in Florence. One of the northern city's most powerful advocates was the designer Walter Albini, now largely forgotten but in the years prior to his death in 1983 considered a pivotal figure in the development of modern Italian ready-to-wear. Albini's links with Milan helped to attract other designers to the city, especially after the establishment of Milanovendemoda. Initially this event was held in the city centre Jolly Hotel, with each passing season attracting a growing number of exhibitors and designers, as well as journalists and buyers. Meanwhile, designers would stage their own individual runway shows in other hotels around the city. But during the first half of the 1970s, all those involved in the fashion business, not least the clothing manufacturers' association, came to understand that if Milan were to develop as a fashion capital then a purpose-built venue was required, one that could accommodate both a large trade exhibition and runway shows, so that visitors could avoid the strenuous and time-consuming process of moving from one location to another around the city. A powerful advocate of the campaign for such a centre was public relations expert Giuseppe 'Beppe' Modenese, who argued forcefully that the entire Italian ready-to-wear industry would benefit if local designers were able to stage their individual shows alongside a trade event. March 1978 saw the simultaneous launch in neighbouring pavilions on the outskirts of central Milan of two venues: Modit and the Centro Sfilate di Milano Collezioni. The first of these hosted fashion exhibitions and the second runway shows. The combination of both facilities in the one place was a winning formula (and one

A printed georgette balloon-sleeve smock with matching short skirt, tie and cap, from Jean Muir's spring/summer 1972 collection.

emulated by the French in March 1994 with the opening of the Carrousel du Louvre, which provided Paris with something similar).

The well-ordered character of Milan's fashion industry caught the attention of British visitors to the city even before the development of Modit and the Centro Sfilate. In 1974 Lindy Woodhead, who had been looking after public relations for Browns in London, left to set up her own PR business. She remembers being phoned by Aldo Pinto, whose wife, designer Mariuccia Mandelli, was the driving force behind the popular Italian label Krizia. 'He told me a number of the Italian designers had broken away from Florence to show in Milan but none of the British press were going there, so could I help?' From 1976 onwards Woodhead arranged to bring to Italy a number of influential fashion journalists such as Prudence Glynn from *The Times* and Barbara Griggs of the *Daily Mail* so they could see at first hand what was happening there. 'Milan was so well organized. I think the Italians know how to entertain and have a general love of hospitality; they did it all beautifully … There was such a sense of family in Milan, a real sense of pride. One of the differences between British and Italian fashion at the time was that the women in factories in Italy would wear the clothes they were making with pride at the weekends. Can you imagine their British equivalents doing the same?' In October 1978 *Newsweek* reported, 'Weary of French fantasy clothes and rude treatment on Parisian showroom floors, buyers were happy to take their order books next door.'

While Milanese designers could never hope to compete with Paris in the field of couture, they were prepared to take on the challenge of creating the world's finest ready-to-wear lines. In addition to already-established names like Missoni, Krizia, Basile and Callaghan, others now appeared. Having each previously worked for a number of other labels, both Gianfranco Ferré and Gianni Versace launched collections under their own names in 1978. Four years before, Giorgio Armani, then aged forty and with two decades of experience in the industry behind him, had set up business, first as a menswear designer but soon also producing womenswear. Armani's talents were immediately recognized, but the decisive moment in his career occurred in 1978 when he signed an agreement with the Italian clothing manufacturer Gruppo Finanziario Tessile (GFT). By the terms of this arrangement, the designer did not have to assume responsibility for the production of his clothes but instead was left free to operate a design studio. GFT entered similar agreements for the manufacture of high-quality ready-to-wear lines with many other fashion houses, both Italian and French, including Valentino, Louis Feraud and

Zandra Rhodes and Norman Parkinson partying in the mid-1980s. Popularly known as 'Parky', the tall, exceptionally thin Parkinson helped to revolutionize British fashion photography over more than half a century, beginning with his work for *Harper's Bazaar* in the mid-1930s. Renowned for his elegant insouciance, on one occasion in Africa he was taking a photograph of his model wife, Wanda, sitting astride an ostrich when the bird bolted. 'Marvellous, darling!' was his only response. 'Can I have just a little more profile?' Despite his apparent nonchalance, he was a consummate professional, observing 'I like to make people look as good as they'd like to look, and with luck, a shade better.'

Claude Montana. Other large clothing producers formed equivalent alliances with Italian designers: Ferré, for example, entered into just such an agreement with clothing entrepreneur Franco Mattioli. In a country with a centuries-old tradition of producing fine fabrics, it was a model which had already been shown to reap results. In 1968, for example, Ermenegildo Zegna, a company which had hitherto been the producer of fine fabrics, took the decision to assume responsibility for every aspect of the business, from the acquisition of raw material through the design and manufacture process to the dispatch of the finished garment to retail outlets (many of which were also operated by Zegna). In this way, quality control could be assured. Companies were already used to hiring designers to create collections. Walter Albini worked in this way for, among others, Krizia, Callaghan and Basile; Armani for Nino Cerruti; Ferré for rainwear company Sangiorgio; Versace for Callaghan, Genny and Alma. When a designer decided to go out on his own, he had a track record of producing commercially viable clothing and therefore represented an attractive proposition for manufacturers. The tie-in with a designer also encouraged many manufacturers to modernize their machinery and to update standards of production (something which, regrettably, did not happen in Britain).

It was, of course, not unknown elsewhere for a designer to join forces with a manufacturer to the benefit of both. After all, Christian Dior's meteoric rise

Fashion PR Lynne Franks with her husband, Australian designer Paul Howie, in November 1976 when they opened Mrs Howie, Covent Garden's first fashion store and designer studio.

in 1947, while owing a great deal to intrinsic talent, also depended on the backing he received from French textile entrepreneur Marcel Boussac who had been looking for a means to improve his own business in the aftermath of the Second World War. However, this example was subsequently not much emulated until it became the norm in 1970s Italy. The commercial advantages of a designer establishing a relationship with the producers of both fabric and finished clothing can be seen in the rapid development of Milan as a fashion centre from that time onwards. Once agreement had been reached on the division of profits between the various partners in the enterprise, manufacturers would not only assume responsibility for producing the fabric and the clothes, they would also pay for the marketing and promotion of the final goods carrying a designer's name, since by this means they could expect to better the return on their investment. A label carrying the words 'Made in Italy' was soon regarded as an almost infallible indicator of quality. By 1989 John Fairchild, the head of leading trade publication *Women's Wear Daily*, could pronounce, 'In one sense, the Italians have won the battle of fashion. The Italian monopoly is even more complete because, in addition to clothes, the Italians are responsible for designing and producing some of the most beautiful fabrics in the world.'

Meanwhile, back in Britain, not only was there no inclination among fabric or clothing manufacturers to collaborate with local designers, there remained what Vivienne Westwood described as 'an unbridgeable chasm' between the two. Manufacturers 'were quite good at tailoring,' says couturier David Sassoon, 'but if you gave them anything like a chiffon draped evening dress with boned bodice they weren't able to make it. They could make good basic high street clothes but that was the limit.' Designers who attempted to work with manufacturers in Britain confirm that the challenges they faced were often insuperable. Betty Jackson tried this approach after starting up her own label in 1981 but she found local producers 'were just resistant to doing things our way. They didn't see anything in it for them and thought they didn't want to work with us. In 1983 we went to Italy and had everything made in one factory.'

There was still no government organization or central agency to which British designers could turn for assistance. Nor had they any satisfactory venue where they could show their work to journalists and buyers during the twice-yearly periods that came to be constituted as London Fashion Week. Although runway shows have always received the greater part of media attention, the real selling of a collection to retailers takes place far away from the catwalk, in showrooms and on stands at trade exhibitions. By the 1970s Paris had Prêt-à-Porter, held in a purpose-built centre at Porte de Versailles, run by the Fédération française du prêt-à-porter féminin, and Milan had Milanovendemoda, likewise

A layered and beaded dress by Bill Gibb that featured in the designer's tenth anniversary show at the Royal Albert Hall in November 1977. Among the models on the night were many of Gibb's clients, including actresses Eileen Atkins, Zoë Wanamaker, Hannah Gordon and Millicent Martin.

Marie Helvin in a red sequin strapless dress from Bruce Oldfield's autumn/winter 1979 collection, shown in popular London restaurant San Lorenzo. In his autobiography, Oldfield remembers the time and effort that went into making such pieces: they required 'complicated techniques that really only lent themselves to couture'.

accommodated in its own centre and run by members of the national clothing industry. In Britain on the other hand, there were several different events, some of which overlapped with one another both in terms of the clothes being shown and the dates on which the exhibitions took place. All were owned by private companies with no direct link to the clothing industry and therefore no vested interest in promoting their country's fashion profile at home or overseas.

Dresswell Ltd mounted a London Main Season exhibition twice a year for producers of mid-to-upper range clothing, as well as a Midseason exhibition four times annually for producers of middle-range clothes; these shows all took place at the Kensington Exhibition Centre. Meanwhile Philbeach Events Ltd, the exhibition-organizing wing of Earl's Court and Olympia, hosted a twice-yearly London Fashion Exhibition at Olympia. In addition, Brintex Ltd staged a number of large-scale clothing trade exhibitions in Bristol and Birmingham, and in September 1978 they launched a new event, the Harrogate Fashion Show in Yorkshire. Separate arrangements existed for the exhibition and sale of menswear and childrens' clothes, involving other commercial organizations.

In addition to the problem of fragmentation, there was also that of scale. The average London exhibition ran to approximately 3,000 square metres of floor space (Harrogate was bigger at 8,500 square metres), while their equivalents in Paris and Milan were more than ten times that size and IGEDO in Dusseldorf covered an astonishing 110,000 square metres. Likewise, while a London show might do well to attract 5,000 trade, press and retail visitors, those in Paris and Milan could expect over 40,000 (by the mid-1980s Dusseldorf drew 60,000). As an example of the difference good organization could make, in 1961 Paris's Porte de Versailles event had only 100 exhibitors; ten years later that number had risen to 780. 'What struck me at the time', says Simon Ward of the British Fashion Council, 'was the difference of scale; my awareness was that we weren't actually big players on the global stage.'

For British designers, the greatest drawback to the existing situation was that indigenous exhibitions were quite unsuitable as a place in which to present their clothes to potential buyers and members of the press. When Betty Jackson established her business, in 1981, she showed at the Olympia fair, 'and there was nothing, no support at all; we had to get a sofa from our living room to put on the stand.' These events were very much aimed at the mid- and mass market, where clothing was manufactured and sold as cheaply as possible. Top-end ready-to-wear produced in small runs and at a relatively high price per unit looked out of place. As Bruce Oldfield later observed, the problem for designers who took a stand at one of these events was that 'they were always presented as an intrinsic part of the great rag trade. The result was that the

Above Ann Buck's sketch of her printed jersey outfit from the collection for spring/summer 1979 illustrates her gentle, feminine approach to design.

Left Two designs for spring/summer 1980: a black and white printed silk dress by Jan van Velden for Salvador; and a sugar-pink linen shift by Monica Chong.

buyers and press looked at their garments and were simply outraged at the prices … To understand the designer brands, it wasn't appropriate to show them in such a cheap and cheerful setting.' But things were changing.

'Really it was the need to export,' says Annette Worsley-Taylor, explaining how she became involved in the first New Wave show of designer fashion at the Ritz Hotel in April 1974. 'There were just very few British shops that bought our own designers, and we were in a recession.' Together with her business partner Tania Soskin, Worsley-Taylor had opened a shop in London called Tsaritsar in the 1960s; both women previously worked for Christian Dior. As well as their own line of clothing, Tsaritsar showcased the work of other emerging designers, including Bruce Oldfield. 'They had high expectations, bags of energy and inspiration and their fingers were right on the pulse,' writes Bruce Oldfield, who began producing collections for Tsaritsar within a year of his 1973 graduation from St Martins School of Art. In 1974, 'We decided that we had to get a bit more volume of sales, and thought that putting on a show and getting export orders was the only way forward,' recalls Worsley-Taylor. Initially Tsaritsar took space at a trade fair in the Grosvenor House Hotel organized by the Clothing Export Council (Katharine Hamnett with her first venture, a label called Tuttabankem she had started with Ann Buck, was on the neighbouring stand), but this proved unsatisfactory. 'London was full of international buyers, but they were coming for the cheaper things or more classic clothes and they weren't used to the idea that we had emerging ready-to-wear designer collections with beautiful fabrics that were more expensive.' Worsley-Taylor next thought of showing the Tsaritsar designers at Paris's Prêt-à-Porter, 'But Bruce said to me, "No, you can't, it's an enormous trade fair, you'd never get noticed there. You've got to put on an exhibition here and get the buyers to come to it."'

Having taken the decision to do this, Worsley-Taylor and Lindy Woodhead met the Clothing Export Council's executive director, Peter Randle, who agreed to provide a limited amount of funding – 'enough for the hire of the room and the PR'. The CEC had assisted such ventures before, notably a show mounted in 1970 by eleven designers – Mary Quant, Ossie Clark, Alice Pollack, Thea Porter, Gina Fratini, John Bates, Christopher McDonnell, Janet Lyle, Leslie Poole, Caroline Charles and Hilary Floyd – who came together in a group called the London Designer Collections, which, however, rather rapidly petered out.

The manager of the Ritz was coaxed into allowing the show to take place on his premises. 'He was called Mr Graham,' Worsley-Taylor remembers, 'and I badgered him to let us in, which he eventually did very reluctantly.'

Held in the hotel's Marie Antoinette suite, the three-day event featured eight young designers: Ann Buck; Jane Cattlin; Juliet Dunn; Bruce Oldfield; Tania Soskin; Carlos Arias; Ritva Westenius; and Sue & Helen. 'The Clothing Export Council was amazed to find it was actually going to happen. I persuaded them to use their petty cash to buy a bunch of violets for every stand.' In addition to the static buying exhibition, it was agreed that the group, to be known as the New Wave, would stage a fashion show, scheduled to take place in the basement of the Ritz at 6 p.m. on Friday, 5 April. Lack of money meant friends were inveigled into providing their services for free and the designers were expected to supply their own models: Bruce Oldfield persuaded Grace Coddington, who by then had left modelling to work as fashion editor at *Vogue*, to return to the catwalk for him. 'The Ritz provided gilt chairs,' says Worsley-Taylor, 'and I knocked up a running order.' *Vogue* fashion editor Mandy Clapperton took on res- ponsibility for producing the event.

To help promote the show and ensure it was well attended by the press, Worsley-Taylor turned to Percy Savage, an ebullient Australian who during the 1950s and 1960s worked in Paris as publicist for the fashion houses of Lanvin and Nina Ricci. Savage had moved to London in the early 1970s and is remembered by Worsley-Taylor as 'the most exuberant man you could ever meet; if there were four telephones, he'd be on all of them at the same time.' As the hour for the show approached, Peter Randle and other representatives of the CEC began arriving to take their seats in a room designed to accommodate around a hundred guests. 'Then Percy arrived with about five hundred people behind him. The place filled up and there was no space for anyone.' Bruce Oldfield would recall how 'The manager of the Ritz was having a fit,

but more chairs were produced, more drinks laid on and somehow the whole thing happened.'

Indeed Mr Graham of the Ritz was so piqued that he later presented the Clothing Export Council with a substantially larger bill than had originally been agreed. Nevertheless, the New Wave show was a success for all the participants and led to increased orders for their work. 'But the show had far greater significance than that,' Oldfield wrote afterwards. 'It was the seed from which something much bigger and very important for British fashion would emerge.'

A second New Wave show was held in October 1974, this time in the Chesterfield Hotel. The number of participants expanded from eight to eleven, the new names being Anna Beltrao, Wendy Dagworthy and Yuki. Peter Randle told the press that 'more than 800 American buyers are expected for the show; that is 40 per cent up over the last show's attendance.' With Tony Porter rather than Percy Savage responsible for public relations, another catwalk show was staged, at the Coq d'Or restaurant on Stratton Street; it was afterwards described by *Women's Wear Daily* as being 'better in every way than the first presentation in April. It started on time, was snappier and had a stronger message.'

Things might have continued along similar lines indefinitely had the Clothing Export Council not announced a change of policy. It had been lobbied by members of the manufacturing sector who were unhappy that the organization should put money into a small exhibition for a select band of designers when large trade shows for clothing already existed in London. Bowing to pressure, the Clothing Export Council decided that if it were to continue supporting the New Wave group, then the latter must move into and become part of the Earl's Court exhibition run by Philbeach Events Ltd. What the Council hadn't counted on was resistance from the designers. 'We'd already discovered in a painful way,' says Worsley-Taylor, 'that to join in an exhibition full of mass-market goods was counter-productive and didn't present us in the right way to the right people. Fashion is as much about atmosphere and context as anything else and it was important to show the designers' clothes in the right setting and in a way sympathetic to what we were trying to do.' Many of those who had shown at the two New Wave occasions felt the same way and they met to discuss how they might avoid being subsumed by the Earl's Court show. 'Anna Beltrao was married to a Brazilian diplomat,' Bruce Oldfield recalls, 'and our meetings were held in their plush apartment in Park Mansions where, accompanied by a maid and canapés, we plotted the new organization in style.'

A padded waistcoat over printed cotton shirt and trousers, by Michiko Koshino for spring/summer 1979. Born in Japan, after graduating from Tokyo's Bunka Fashion College in the mid-1970s Koshino moved to London, where she soon became a member of the London Designer Collections. Sketch by Krystyna.

That new organization was to be a designer collective, the members of which would be responsible for deciding who else could join. Funded by contributions from its membership, the collective would take charge of twice-yearly exhibitions where participants could show their clothes without having to rely on commercial events. In addition it would provide a forum for pooling shared resources and knowledge of the business. 'The members wanted people around them who were working in the same kind of market,' says Worsley-Taylor. 'And people who could deliver, so as not to damage the reputation of the group.' Between them, the initial members came up with a name for their group: the London Designer Collections. Obviously this was quite a different organization from the one which flourished briefly in 1970, and it was to have a much longer history.

The new London Designer Collections made its debut at the Montcalm Hotel in April 1975. Not everyone who had previously shown with the New Wave opted to take part in that first exhibition. Wendy Dagworthy, for example, unsure of the group's viability, chose instead to take advantage of the Clothing Export Council's offer and planned to show at Earl's Court. But on the day before that exhibition was due to open, the set builders went on strike. 'I delivered my clothes to an empty space,' Dagworthy remembers. 'There weren't even stands because the unions wouldn't allow anything to go ahead.' A panic ensued as those designers who had planned to exhibit at Earl's Court sought space elsewhere, with many of them – including Dagworthy – taking suites in the Montcalm Hotel, where the London Designer Collections was already installed and where a visit from key buyers and journalists could be guaranteed.

After this auspicious beginning, the following season the London Designer Collections moved to the Inn on the Park, which, with occasional exceptions, would remain its twice-yearly home for the next five years (after which it took space at the Hyde Park Hotel). The Montcalm had been a small venue and this had imposed certain limitations; the larger Inn on the Park allowed a greater number of designers to

Silk, cotton and linen separates from Wendy
Dagworthy's spring/summer 1979 collection
mix print and texture in her trademark style.
Sketch by Ros Terrill.

join the LDC. During this period, Annette Worsley-Taylor assumed responsibility for the organization, at first working from an office in Covent Garden that she shared with Percy Savage (who was once more in charge of public relations). The success of the October 1975 Inn on the Park exhibition – writing about it afterwards *Women's Wear Daily* declared that 'The Great has been put back into Britain' – led more and more designers to apply for membership of the LDC. It was understood that by showing as part of a group in this way, individual businesses had more clout than operating on their own. In addition, a link with the LDC acted as an informal guarantee of quality: a strict vetting process before membership was granted meant the organization's standards were kept high. The alternative – the admission of all applicants – might have led to the LDC show's becoming indistinguishable from those already hosted by commercial companies in venues like Olympia and Earl's Court. A number of parties were involved in applicant evaluation, including whoever had been elected the LDC's chairman and *Vogue*'s Mandy Clapperton. According to her recollection, criteria for membership of the group included an expectation that the proposed member be reasonably young, evidently talented and unlikely to run into immediate financial difficulties. Companies engaged in mass market manufacturing were not allowed to join and it was always considered essential that all members' businesses be headed by a designer.

Exclusivity gave the London Designer Collections a certain cachet; buyers and journalists expected to see only the best designed British ready-to-wear clothing when they visited the exhibition or watched one of the organization's runway shows. 'The LDC meant that buyers could come and look at clothes in London seriously,' remarks Caroline Charles. 'It had been amusing to find a designer in a rickety old basement or attic in the sixties, but not in the seventies. It generally made the whole thing more professional than it had ever been before.' Jasper Conran agrees that the LDC 'had the right kind of buyers coming along. It was a very good forum for us.' Similarly Wendy Dagworthy says, 'I think the London Designer Collections gave us a lot more exposure. It opened up many more shops to us – they used to come from all over the world – and showing together in the Inn on the Park gave all of us a better profile.' Bruce Oldfield remembers, 'We used to play up being the new kids on the block, you know it was a real Judy Garland/Mickey Rooney "let's put on a show" thing. There was quite a dichotomy between the two things: the radical nature of the group and the wearable clothes being produced.' Indeed, in the second half of the 1970s London did not have the reputation it would later acquire for being the *enfant terrible* of the fashion world. Nor was that what the

LDC wanted; the organization's *raison d'être* was to provide an opportunity for talented young designers to show their work in a sympathetic, professionally managed environment otherwise not available in London.

The LDC's committee would meet once a month and the full membership would attend at least two meetings every season when major policy decisions would be taken. 'The designer intelligence side of things was really important,' says Worsley-Taylor. 'The more established names helped the younger ones. We had a credit control system where members could check who was a good or a bad payer. There was information on what was required for shipping and a standard order form for everyone with all the right terms checked by a lawyer.' It was at one such meeting at the end of 1975 that Percy Savage proposed the LDC expand and run a second exhibition for those not showing at the Inn on the Park – in effect a 'Salon des Refusés'– to be held in another hotel, the Intercontinental. Although the group's members turned down his proposal, Savage went ahead with it anyway, ended his ties with the LDC and the following spring ran the first of what would be a twice-yearly fashion exhibition called the London Collections at the Intercontinental; these continued until his business went into receivership in 1981.

Around this time another organization offering help to young designers also made its debut. Lesley Goring had worked in fashion retail and also with Lynne Franks before setting up her own PR business in 1976. 'A lot of my clients wanted to show somewhere during London Fashion Week,' she remembers, 'but they didn't have a place.' Together with textile and print agent Wendy Booth, she set up the Individual Clothes Show, an exhibition space in a hotel on Curzon Street where selected designers could present their collections to buyers and press in a professional setting and with the support of Goring and her staff. Later the venue changed to the Athenaeum Hotel. 'We held the exhibition twice a year, promoted it, invited press and buyers and looked after our clients,' remembers Goring. 'We charged each designer for the stand space, but our rates had to be at rock bottom to keep it affordable for everyone. People came to us by word of mouth. There was a very informal committee that decided who should be in and who shouldn't.' Among those who exhibited at the Individual Clothes Show were such luminaries as Betty Jackson, Ally Capellino and John Richmond.

In March 1980 the organization was invited to take part in the London Fashion Exhibition, a twice-yearly trade event run by Philbeach Events Ltd at Olympia. 'They offered us a deal we couldn't refuse,' Goring explains. 'A space of our own that we could design as we wished. Plus they gave us

Right Glowing colour and witty attitude from the joint Sheridan Barnett and Sheilagh Brown spring/summer 1978 collection.

Below Key members of the London Designer Collections Sheridan Barnett and Sheilagh Brown, photographed in 1978. The two designers worked together between 1976 and 1980, both having previously been employed by Quorum. In the following decade they each had their own label, with Barnett also designing for Jaeger and Reldan. In 1990 Brown was appointed head of womenswear design at Marks & Spencer and in that role can take the credit for persuading Britain's best-known high street store that it made sound commercial sense to work with established fashion designers.

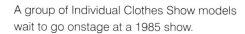
the Pillar Hall where we could stage our own catwalk show; we felt this was really important in order to raise our profile. We got sponsorship from a freesheet called *Miss London* and others as well, so the show was self-financing.' Certain concessions were demanded of Philbeach, not least that the Individual Clothes Show be accommodated as a separate group within a designated area. So too was another body of twelve design companies including Strawberry Studio and Miz (the sportswear business Tanya Sarne ran prior to setting up Ghost) which went under the collective name of The Exhibitionists. In addition, there were sponsored catwalk shows by the likes of Vivienne Westwood and Zandra Rhodes, which helped to attract members of the press to the exhibition.

Meanwhile the London Designer Collections – now formally established as a not-for-profit company – continued to expand, operating from an office first in Bridle Lane (in a building that belonged to designer Salvador) and later Beauchamp Place. Familiar names in British fashion who joined the organization during this period included Janice Wainwright, Benny Ong, Paul Howie (husband of publicist Lynne Franks), Michiko, Maxfield Parrish, Monica Chong and Jasper Conran. *Vogue* editor Beatrix Miller wrote an an introduction to the LDC's April 1976 brochure in which she announced, 'Not since buyers and press from all over the world zeroed in to witness a phenomenon called Swinging

Previous pages A group shot taken by David Bailey for the London Designer Collections spring/summer 1978 brochure. The designers shown include Anna Beltrao, Ann Buck, Benny Ong, Chatters, Cherry Frizzell, Christian, Chris Trill, Clutch Cargo, Esther Pearson, Paul Howie, Jane Cattlin, Julia Fortescue and Yvonne Langley at Collection 'O', Juliet Dunn, Kay Cosserat, Marisa Martin, Michiko, Roger Saul of Mulberry, Patricia Roberts, Patti Searle, Pauline Wynne Jones, Salmon and Greene, Salvador, Sheilagh Brown and Sheridan Barnett, Shuji Tojo, Virginia, and Wendy Dagworthy.

Left A menswear designer of the 1960s and 1970s, Michael Fish achieved notoriety through creating attention-grabbing looks for musicians such as the Rolling Stones and David Bowie, as well as the kipper tie, notable for its extreme width and garish hue.

Below Caroline Charles in 1980. Charles set up her own business in 1963, after working first for couturier Michael Sherard and then for Mary Quant. In the years that followed she designed Ringo Starr's wedding outfit and dressed performers including Petula Clark, Lulu, Marianne Faithfull and Mick Jagger. 'I do have tremendous drive,' she once said.

London has there been greater potential for creating a vital new fashion image and putting Britain firmly back on the world fashion map. The fresh talents that have been developing have their own individuality, inventiveness and quality, unmistakably British style.'

The seasonal brochures would always carry a group portrait of the full LDC membership, and these were taken by some of the most famous photographers of the time: Norman Parkinson; David Bailey; Patrick Lichfield; Barry Lategan. From April 1979 onwards, a more substantial magazine was produced, thanks to the efforts of – among others – Mandy Clapperton and art director Tim Lamb, whose wife was fashion editor Liz Shirley. One outcome of these various initiatives was that British designers started to achieve a higher international profile. In April 1977 Eric Hall, who worked with Salvador, arranged for a group of LDC members to go to New York, where they showed together at 1 Penn Plaza. Seven months later, the LDC went on tour to South Africa at the invitation of department store chain Greatermans. 'We had a wonderful time,' Wendy Dagworthy remembers. 'We flew to Johannesburg and were met off the plane with huge bunches of flowers. We did a big show in a hotel ballroom there and then went on to Cape Town and Durban. It was a big production, all very grand. They bought our collections too and did so for a while afterwards.'

Obviously there were also runway shows, organized by the LDC and featuring its members' new collections. Shows during Fashion Week were important because they attracted press coverage. Exhibitions, no matter how smartly arranged or well attended, simply didn't produce the same volume of publicity. While some of the LDC's members were happy to take part in a

Below Design guru Anne Tyrrell has worked in every fashion market during her career. From 1974 to 1995 she was senior tutor at the Royal College of Art, nurturing many current British designers, and from 2000 to 2007 she was vice-chairman of the British Fashion Council. She is now chair of the British Fashion Council Colleges Committee and continues to run her own international design consultancy with clients that have spanned Nike, Next, Royal Ascot and the Orient Express.

group runway show, others opted to stage their own presentations. But a runway show always required considerable funds, as Bruce Oldfield explains: 'In those days, a show could add anything between £5,000 and £10,000 to your costs, depending on the location, the models, the accessories, the staff and whatever extras you laid on for the clients, with another £3,000 for an exhibition stand of your own.' A report in *Drapers Record* in mid-April 1983 quoted buying consultant Vanessa Denza on the importance of runway shows. She noted, 'It is a lot to expect the designers to capitalize the shows on their own. It is not their fault that all they can afford as a venue is a gallery or restaurant.' In the same article Annette Worsley-Taylor complained that owing to financial limitations, 'It is frustrating that we can only do half the job. The cost of putting on just one designer show in Paris amounts to 50 per cent of our total expenditure.' No wonder a lot of designers decided to forgo organizing their own live presentations.

A further and necessary step in the promotion of London as a style capital occurred at the start of the 1980s when the LDC arranged its first parties during Fashion Week. To a degree this was due to awareness of how much Milan had benefited from providing visitors to the city with memorable extracurricular social activity. Although Lindy Woodhead was then employed as a publicist by Italian fashion houses such as Missoni, Krizia and Walter Albini, she also did her best to promote British fashion and received a small retainer from the LDC for this purpose. 'I would go out flying the flag for Great Britain in Milan,' she remembers. 'If I saw a buyer from Barneys or Saks, or a fashion editor, I would say to them, "You *are* coming to London, aren't you?"' Returning to London, she

Left Princess Margaret on an official visit to the London Designer Collections at the Inn on the Park in 1976, receiving a bouquet from Annette Worsley-Taylor. Behind the Princess, Frank Buck, first chairman of the London Designer Collections, is talking to lady-in-waiting Mrs John Wills. Before Lady Diana Spencer became Princess of Wales in 1981 royal involvement with British fashion was a rarity.

provided invaluable assistance to the LDC, not least by reporting on what had recently taken place in Milan: in particular, she was able to explain the difference a well organized social calendar had made.

In March 1981 it was decided that the LDC should throw its own party during London Fashion Week. *The Times*'s Prudence Glynn, who by that date had visited Milan on a number of occasions, suggested that Sir Jack Lyons, a noted cultural philanthropist as well as one of Britain's most successful clothing retailers, might be persuaded to host a party in his Holland Park house. He agreed to the proposal and Michael Fish, noted menswear designer and man about town, was asked to help with the guest list. The night itself was not without incident: when members of the band Spandau Ballet arrived at the house, Lady Lyons, receiving guests in a Hartnell couture gown and white evening gloves, attempted to turn them away before Michael Fish stepped forward to explain who they were. But otherwise the event – with Funkapolitan playing in the garage and Jasper Conran bobbing about in the swimming pool amidst daffodil-shaped lights – was deemed a great success. It was followed by other parties, not least one the following season in the Leighton House Museum where jazz singer Annie Ross performed.

Among the most significant such occasions of the early 1980s was that held in March 1983 in the King Street premises of auction house Christie's, jointly hosted by the London Designer Collections and Lady Henderson. Mary Henderson was married to Sir Nicholas Henderson, recently retired as British Ambassador to the United States. She was known as a stalwart promoter of

her country's cultural activities; during the Hendersons' four years in Paris prior to going to Washington, she had regularly arranged shows of British fashion in the Embassy. And while in the United States, she invited a number of leading British interior designers each to redecorate one of the rooms of the Ambassador's residence, making the house a showcase of national design. Her reputation, among both British and American journalists and retailers and indeed with the government of Mrs Thatcher, was of enormous benefit to the promotion of British fashion, and the Christie's party (which Bruce Oldfield had recommended she co-host) attracted some seven hundred guests; another at Sotheby's in October 1983 drew a similar attendance. Lady Henderson was to prove a valuable ally in the drive to improve standards in the national fashion industry. She was a friend of many key figures within the business, including both *Vogue* editor Beatrix Miller and designer Jean Muir. Before long these three women were to join forces and play an important, albeit largely unacknowledged, role in the formation of the British Fashion Council.

Above Key figures in the London fashion world during the 1970s and 1980s included publicist Percy Savage and Knightsbridge retailer Lucienne Phillips (left); photographer David Bailey and fashion icon Tina Chow (centre); and designer Bill Gibb, here with singer Lynsey de Paul (right).

Left Mary Henderson (far left, with her husband, the diplomat Sir Nicholas Henderson) and *Vogue* editor Beatrix Miller (left) were key figures in the drive to improve standards within the British fashion industry during the early 1980s and deserve credit for working behind the scenes to ensure that the fledgling British Fashion Council received government support.

THE NEW ROMANTICS

On 29 July 1981, twenty-year-old Lady Diana Spencer married the Prince of Wales in St Paul's Cathedral before a worldwide television audience of over 700 million people. By the following morning, copies of her wedding dress – a vast cumulus of ivory silk taffeta with endless ruffles and bows as well as a twenty-five-foot train – were available for sale on London's Oxford Street. If the rest of her wardrobe over the next sixteen years did not spawn quite so many imitations, it was certainly just as much photographed, criticized and analysed.

The wedding dress had been designed by David and Elizabeth Emanuel, a couple only a few years older than the Princess herself. Both had graduated from the Royal College of Art in 1977 and they then set up their own business on Brook Street. From the start, the Emanuels were known for their elaborate evening and wedding dresses. In an era otherwise dominated by punk, they were precursors of the early 1980s New Romanticism exemplified by the fanciful costumes worn by bands such as Adam & the Ants, Spandau Ballet and Duran Duran. Frilly shirts and heavily flounced skirts eventually became the fashion norm but when the Emanuels made their debut, almost no one else was designing clothes in this style. Writer Meredith Etherington-Smith remembers buying one of the couple's dresses from their RCA graduation show: 'It was a huge lilac satin ballgown to the ankle, with ruffles and a lace trim. I wore it to the first Berkeley Square Ball in July 1977 and people thought I was really weird.'

The Emanuels' lush romanticism gradually caught on: Joan Burstein bought a wedding dress from Elizabeth's graduation show and displayed it in the window of Browns on South Molton Street where, Mrs Burstein later recalled, it evoked much admiration. Her support greatly enhanced the designers' prestige, as did the calibre of their early clients: Bianca Jagger; Princess Michael of Kent; the Texan socialite Lynne Wyatt.

Even so, Lady Diana was taking something of a gamble when, rather than going to one of the established London couturiers, she invited the Emanuels to make her wedding dress. Having worn an Emanuel blouse for her official engagement photograph, she contacted them looking for something to wear for

The royal wedding, 29 July 1981. Lady Diana Spencer became Princess of Wales wearing a fairytale dress of ivory silk taffeta designed for her by David and Elizabeth Emanuel.

Below Prince Charles and Lady Diana Spencer attending a recital at Goldsmiths' Hall shortly after the announcement of their engagement. The future Princess's strapless black dress, designed by the Emanuels, caused a sensation.

the first public engagement to which she accompanied the Prince of Wales: a recital at Goldsmiths' Hall in the City of London in early March 1981. Emerging from the Prince's car in a black strapless taffeta dress, she created a sensation – not least because, to the delight of the waiting paparazzi, far too much cleavage was on display.

Diana's dress sense was much criticized over the next decade or so, especially during the early years of her marriage when she had little confidence in her own taste and was keen to conform to the style norms of the British royal family. The Queen is five foot four, while her sister, Princess Margaret, stood only an inch over five foot. Both had become accustomed to wearing bright colours and strong shapes on public occasions so that they might easily be identified in a crowd. Diana, however, was five foot ten, as well as extremely good looking. She did not need to rely on startlingly bright dresses or big hats. Nevertheless, during the initial period of her marriage, Diana was anxious to dress like a traditional royal wife, even when the results were less than flattering. 'She was very determined to do what she wanted to do,' says Anna Harvey who, as a senior fashion editor at *Vogue* in the 1980s, advised the Princess on what to wear.

Even before the wedding, Diana – whose two older sisters had both briefly worked for the magazine – had begun turning to *Vogue* for assistance. In the beginning accompanied by her mother, she would arrive at a rear entrance of Vogue House and take the lift to the fifth floor, where racks of clothes had been assembled for her inspection. Designers are used to sending items to magazines like *Vogue* for fashion shoots, so a phone call from Anna Harvey's office would not have caused comment, although after a while

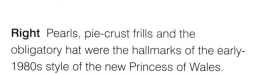

Right Pearls, pie-crust frills and the obligatory hat were the hallmarks of the early-1980s style of the new Princess of Wales.

Below David and Elizabeth Emanuel. The couple met at Harrow School of Art, married in 1976 and went on to study design at the Royal College of Art. In 1977 they opened their own business.

it became quietly understood when these occasions were being organized for the Princess's benefit. According to Harvey, despite being offered every help and guidance, right from the start Diana 'was anxious to make her own decisions and be her own person; she didn't want to be a *Vogue* clotheshorse. One mightn't have liked all of her choices …' She recalls once being quizzed on the subject by Patrick McCarthy of *Women's Wear Daily* and, when Harvey explained that she didn't choose everything the Princess wore, back came the response, 'Ah, but Anna, everybody thinks you do.' Indeed, in 1986 *Harpers & Queen* magazine named Harvey as the twenty-third most influential person in Britain (ironically, Diana only came in at number thirty-one).

The Princess's wardrobe during the first half of the 1980s displayed a kind of sartorial schizophrenia: she veered between extremes in which the only consistent features were a lurid palette and a penchant for frills. In 1985, *W* magazine cruelly but correctly remarked that Diana 'exhibits all the symptoms of a fashion victim, a sufferer of the all-too-common disease of grabbing at every new look and trend, whether it suits her or not.' For a tour of Italy that year, she had abandoned *Vogue*'s assistance and devised her own wardrobe; the outcome was generally regarded as a disaster. Admittedly some of what would now be derided as fashion crimes can be put down to the taste of the time. 'For heaven's sake,' Anna Harvey points out, 'everyone was wearing those pie-crust shirts then.' And of course before her marriage Diana, who had worked as a kindergarten assistant, dressed in the same way as other girls of her class and age: in jeans, frilly shirts, floral-print skirts and V-neck lambswool jumpers. It was hardly to be expected that she would instantly develop an understanding of what most became her. Designers who worked with the Princess during this period privately agree that she was unsophisticated in her approach to clothes.

One of Diana's main concerns was that the items under consideration would appeal to her husband. Another was that her wardrobe be sourced locally. Although before her early death in 1997 she had started to patronize foreign designers, this was emphatically not the case in the early years of her marriage. 'She did make the decision almost from Day One that she'd back British fashion,' Anna Harvey confirms. 'She was a free PR machine for a lot of designers.' Some of them did very well from the royal association, notably Bruce Oldfield, as well as Jasper Conran, Jan van Velden, Jacques Azagury, Victor Edelstein, Roland Klein and Murray Arbeid. As Oldfield notes in his 2004 autobiography, *Rootless*, 'Of course the best ambassador I had was the Princess of Wales – the most photographed woman in the world. The press were rapaciously interested in what she had worn, what she would be wearing, what she might be wearing.' Royal protocol prohibited designers from notifying the media when Diana bought clothes from them; only after she had publicly appeared in something were they permitted to confirm whether or not it had come from their atelier. Breaking this rule meant exclusion from the chosen circle. 'Everyone was sworn to secrecy,' confirms Harvey. 'I have to say the whole British fashion industry was impeccable in that respect. It was all so discreet.'

Did individual designers benefit from the Princess's patronage? Obviously they did. Directly, because for her many public functions she needed to buy a lot of new clothes each season. When she went to Australia with the Prince of Wales on an official tour in spring 1984, for example, her suitcases contained forty-five outfits by seventeen different British designers. And she was a high spender: the *Daily Star* estimated that the Princess paid £100,000 for her new wardrobe for the 1985 Italian tour. But that was only the beginning. A week after Diana's death at the end of August 1997, Amy Spindler of the *New York Times* correctly assessed that what the Princess had done for the 'more sedate designers' she favoured was 'to create an environment in which British society could eschew French couturiers and shop at home instead'. Diana's patronage certainly helped to raise the profile of favoured designers. 'I remember she wore something of mine to the British Fashion Banquet,' says Bruce Oldfield, 'and the next day Ira Neimark of Bergdorf Goodman was on the phone placing

The cover of the London Designer Collections autumn/winter 1984 brochure: a black maribou- and sequin-embellished lace dress by Jacques Azagury. Born in Morocco, Azagury attended both the London College of Fashion and St Martins School of Art before starting his own business, specializing in glamorous eveningwear. Since the 1960s, London has enjoyed an international reputation for producing high-quality ready-to-wear evening clothes of the kind designed by Azagury.

LONDON DESIGNER COLLECTIONS

AUTUMN/WINTER 1984 £1.50

The Princess of Wales and Bruce Oldfield at a ball held for Barnardo's in London's Grosvenor House Hotel in March 1985. The Princess's silver lamé dress was designed by Oldfield.

his order.' At the same time, Oldfield points out, Diana was 'at the couture end of the market' and the kind of clothes she ordered from him and other designers were simply beyond the means of most consumers. And for some designers there could be a downside to providing clothes for the Princess. 'I used to make a lot of things for her,' Jasper Conran remembers. 'Mine were the more subdued items, many of them things she wore at home. Ironically, that used to cost us a lot of money because they had to be made specially for her in our workrooms and that would hold up everything else, all the other orders would have to wait.'

'She was like a gorgeous loss-leader,' Oldfield suggests. 'I think she certainly raised the general consciousness of British fashion because she was an ambassadress. Whether that turned into pounds, shillings and pence I can't really say.' 'Oh, I think the Princess in the 1980s did give a tremendous boost to British fashion,' says David Sassoon of Bellville Sassoon, another business that regularly dressed Diana during that era. 'This gauche young girl became a style icon . . . Not that she was a trend-setter or particularly fashionable, but nobody in the fashion world had the same kind of pull.' Likewise Gail Sackloff, who for thirty years was employed to look after American store buyers coming to

London, comments, 'The Princess of Wales was great for me because I could tell my clients she had been wearing David Sassoon or Murray Arbeid the night before and they loved that.' And Anna Harvey has no doubt that the Princess 'cannot but have been good for British fashion as a whole.'

In the end it will always be impossible to quantify just how beneficial she was. On the other hand, the sheer volume of global press coverage generated by the Princess during this period had to be to the advantage of the domestic fashion industry. 'The Princess of Wales was *the* public face of British fashion,' Zandra Rhodes agrees. 'She hooked people in here even though the clothes she wore were often old-fashioned.' As Nicholas Coleridge commented in his 1988 book *The Fashion Conspiracy*, Diana's enthusiasm for clothes and the media's enthusiasm for Diana inevitably meant that attention was paid to British fashion, both at home and abroad: 'The Princess has raised the fashion temperature of the country to such a degree,' Coleridge wrote, 'that no newspaper editor can sleep soundly in his bed at night unless a photograph of her newest backless evening dress is draped across four columns.' In fact, when the Princess desperately wanted journalists to focus their attention on her work for certain charities in the early 1990s she found this to be a near-impossible challenge. Dickie Arbiter, Buckingham Palace's Press Chief at the time, remarked, 'The media put the emphasis on fashion and we've been working pretty hard to get the emphasis off fashion.'

Eventually, as her marriage disintegrated and her self-confidence grew, the Princess would develop a sleek, pared-down style quite different from that which she had projected in the 1980s. She would also give her business to a smaller number of designers, many of them non-British. When Diana sold eighty of her dresses at Christie's for charity in June 1997, all of the lots were by London-based designers and the majority of them dated from the 1980s. It was as though she were shucking off that era in her life.

But before this shift in direction occurred, aside from wearing British-made clothes she had helped the development of the indigenous fashion industry in a number of other ways. Although no innovator in terms of style, Diana was the first member of the British royal family to socialize regularly with fashion designers. She was perfectly happy to go to charity parties organized by the members of the fashion industry. In March 1985 the Princess accepted Bruce Oldfield's invitation to be guest of honour at a fund-raising dinner for Barnardo's at the Grosvenor House Hotel to which she wore a backless silver lamé dress he had designed. Photographs of Oldfield and the Princess sitting beside one another that night – subsequently described by Nicholas Coleridge as 'the most important London fashion party of 1985' – were published around the world. 'I realize that it was a quite extraordinary moment,' Oldfield would later write in *Rootless*. 'I certainly can't imagine a scenario where Norman Hartnell would have sat next to the Queen.'

In addition, the Princess was prepared to lend practical support to British fashion. On a number of occasions during London Fashion Week she turned up at the exhibition and spent time touring the stands. Joanne Davis, who organized this event at Olympia in west London throughout the 1980s remembers, 'We'd worked out in advance which stands she'd go to, but she kept veering off to one that had fluffy sweaters.' And Gail Sackloff recalls that she and an American buyer were with Murray Arbeid when Diana and her entourage arrived at his stand. 'The buyer asked which was her favourite piece and the Princess tactfully replied, "They're all my favourites."'

Following the formation of the British Fashion Council, Diana was better able to give official support to the industry. In October 1986, for example, as part of London Fashion Week the Council organized a banquet for 170 guests at Fishmongers' Hall at which the Princess presented Jasper Conran with the Designer of the Year Award. According to *Women's Wear Daily*, 'Hi-Fi Di', as the magazine was then calling her, 'left fashion pros agog when she made her bare-shouldered entrance in a torso-hugging purple panne velvet gown' – once more designed by Bruce Oldfield – her exposed flesh covered 'in glittering disco spray'. Commenting on the occasion, the *International Herald Tribune*'s Hebe Dorsey noted that the Princess was seated between the government's Minister of State for Industry, Giles Shaw, and Ira Neimark of Bergdorf Goodman, 'emphasizing that the United States is Britain's principal fashion market, with £162 million in 1985 exports'. Neimark was only one of a large number of American retailers present, all of them enchanted at the idea of meeting the night's guest of honour. As Dorsey observed, 'The British are right in using Princess Diana, for she is fashion dynamite.'

The Princess showed herself entirely willing to be used in this way. In March 1988 she hosted her own reception for 150 national and international members of the fashion industry at Kensington Palace. Dressed in an egg-yellow suit by Catherine Walker, by then confirmed as her London designer of choice, she received guests accompanied by her five-year-old son Prince William. Again, the American visitors were the night's most enthusiastic attendees, with vice-president of Saks Fifth Avenue Helen O'Hagan telling the *Philadelphia Enquirer*'s Jill Gerston, 'The highlight of my trip was meeting the future King of England.'

Once more dressed by Catherine Walker, the Princess presented Graham Fraser and Richard Nott of Workers for Freedom with the British Fashion

Jean Muir photographed in February 1979 sitting in her favourite chair. As she grew older, Muir's designs grew increasingly spare and she became known for the purity of her work.

Left, above The Princess of Wales sits with Anna Harvey of *Vogue* while they wait for a show to begin during London Fashion Week in March 1995.

Left, below The Princess of Wales with Jasper Conran at a banquet organized by the British Fashion Council at Fishmongers' Hall in the City of London in October 1986. The Princess has just presented the twenty-six-year-old Conran with the Designer of the Year Award.

Council's Designer of the Year Award at a ceremony in the Royal Albert Hall in October 1989. Thereafter, as her own personal circumstances began to change and her official role as a member of the royal family diminished, she came to have less public involvement with the national fashion industry. Though the public interest in her appearance never dimmed, she no longer felt the need to represent British fashion in the same way. The last occasion on which she did so was as guest of honour at a London Fashion Week reception in early October 1994 at Lancaster House. By now officially separated (although not yet divorced) from the Prince of Wales, she still excited as much interest as ever, especially among the American visitors presented to her such as Stephen Elkin of Bergdorf Goodman, Bert Tansky of Neiman Marcus and Scott Bowman of I Magnin. 'When she'd finished working the line of store buyers,' recalls Clinton Silver, who at the time was Chairman of the British Fashion Council, 'there was a rush for the door. I was curious to know what was going on: they were all outside on their mobile phones talking about Diana.'

Even at its height, however, it must be noted that the Princess's representation of British fashion was by no means universal. Though she wore clothes by too many different designers during the early 1980s, some high-profile names of the period were entirely overlooked, not least Jean Muir.

In the pantheon of British fashion, Jean Muir occupies a special niche. Sinty Stemp, who worked with the designer from 1987 onwards and wrote a biography of Muir following her death in 1995, believes she was unfairly neglected not just by the Princess of Wales but by the industry as a whole. Muir never, for instance, received the accolade of Designer of the Year, although she was given a Hall of Fame Award in 1994.

Self-taught, Jean Muir began her career as a designer in 1956 when she joined Jaeger. Six years later she began designing for Jane and Jane, one of the seminal labels of the time, and then in 1966 she established her own business. Thereafter for almost thirty years, she followed a distinct path untroubled by transitory trends and famously focusing on difficult materials such as silk jersey and suede. In September 1991 she told *Vogue*'s Sarah Mower, 'Twenty-five years ago I made a very conscious decision to avoid fads.' As her husband and business partner, Harry Leuckert, told Iain R. Webb of *The Times* not long after her death, Muir 'made beautiful clothes which women like to wear and feel good wearing. Jean was never hung up on silly fads, she was not distracted by "fashion". She disliked that word ...'

Sinty Stemp comments that Muir thought of her work not as art but as a craft, a technique that had to be learnt and refined over a long period of time. She attracted a consistently loyal admiration among both clients and such members of the press as Bernadine Morris of the *New York Times*, who in 1979 described Muir as 'The superstar of London. Her clothes have a pared down manner. Nothing superfluous is going on.' A decade later, Morris called Muir, 'England's most professional designer', and described her clothes as 'unpretentious, beautifully crafted and a distinguished part of the British fashion scene'. American *Vogue*'s European Editor, Hamish Bowles, has remarked that Muir's style 'seemed the distillation of modernity', and that her clothes 'are perfectly judged, perfectly formed, perfectly simple and simply perfect'.

That her collections did not receive as much notice during the 1980s as many produced by lesser talents was due to a

A knitted wool dress from Jean Muir's spring/summer 1988 collection (left) and (below) an orange wool crepe coat and green dress from her autumn/winter 1986 collection. The timelessness of Muir's work is generally acknowledged.

number of factors, not least their understated refinement and Muir's disinclination to court publicity. In addition, by the time Lady Diana Spencer became Princess of Wales, Jean Muir had been working in the business for more than a quarter of a century; the experience of age and an illustrious career counted for little in an era more interested in the young and the new. Because if there was one outstanding trait of British fashion during first half of the 1980s, it was a preoccupation with youth and novelty, a fixation that has characterized the national industry ever since.

'I think England's obsessed with always being the Next Big Thing – just so long as it's different, never mind the quality,' remarks Bruce Oldfield. While a number of factors were responsible for this development, the most important was the burgeoning influence of popular culture on British fashion. Traditionally it had been the responsibility of the designer to propose how consumers would dress each season, which styles and colours and fabrics would be worn, whether skirts were to be short or long, and so forth. Their decisions would gradually trickle down through the clothing market's sundry layers and so fashion evolved from one year to the next. Naturally the system was not infallible, and sometimes the consumer refused to do as bidden, but overall it was accepted that the designer be fashion's ultimate arbiter. In Britain, this balance of power had already begun to shift during the 1960s, and it fundamentally moved with the advent of punk, especially after October 1977, when Zandra Rhodes offered her own interpretation of the populist movement's ripped and safety-pinned clothes: here was a blatant instance of street fashion influencing the designer rather than the other way around.

In March 1987 Bernadine Morris observed that it had been 'the street scene with the spiky hair and eccentric costumes that brought American retailers back to London in the 1980s'. The impact of young street culture on British fashion was to grow steadily stronger over the course of the decade, aided by the appearance of new publications mixing fashion photoshoots with features on music and cinema. Again, there had been such magazines since the 1960s when the likes of *Petticoat*, *Honey*, *Nova*, and even *Vogue* – under the incomparable editorship of Beatrix Miller – provided their readers with just such a blend of material. But *Petticoat* and the rest were aimed squarely at a female audience. The first fashion-oriented magazine to attempt appealing equally to both sexes was *Ritz*, which made its debut in 1976 and had much of the character and style of Andy Warhol's *Interview*, first published in New York seven years before. However, although it carried the right mix of elements and had been co-founded by the defiantly cockney photographer David Bailey, *Ritz* was

unashamedly patrician in outlook (its first gossip columnist was Old Etonian society decorator Nicholas Haslam) and never commanded a large audience; even at its peak in 1981 monthly sales were just 25,000 copies.

1980 saw the arrival of three magazines which would play a far more influential role in the future development of British fashion. *The Face* was published for the first time in May that year, and both *Blitz* and *i-D* appeared in the next few months. Although *The Face* always provided extensive fashion coverage, tellingly its founder, Nick Logan, had already created the popular music magazine *Smash Hits* and had also been the editor of *New Musical Express* during the previous decade. The brainchild of Carey Labovitch, *Blitz* was a lifestyle magazine targeted at consumers in their twenties, initially published quarterly, then bi-monthly and finally monthly during the four years before it closed in 1991. *i-D*, which at the start appeared in the form of a hand-stapled fanzine with text produced on a typewriter, was the creation of designer and former *Vogue* art director Terry Jones. While *Blitz* was engaged by mainstream

Above Polka dot dresses from Adrian Cartmell's spring/summer 1981 collection. During the late 1970s and the following decade, Cartmell's elegant clothes were much admired. He was, however, unwise to summarize one collection as embodying 'throwaway chic'. In the *Sunday Times* Michael Roberts retorted, 'Some of it is indeed chic, much should be thrown away.'

Below Two outfits from Janice Wainwright's spring/summer 1983 collection. Wainwright started her career in 1965 as a designer working for the Simon Massey clothing company and then, after some time freelancing, established her own label in 1974. In the years that followed she enjoyed exceptional success thanks to her creative use of high-quality fabrics such as matte jersey and crepe. Her business closed in 1990 and Wainwright clothes, especially those from the 1970s, are now considered highly collectable.

fashion (in 1986 it commissioned twenty-two designers, including Katharine Hamnett, Jean Muir, Rifat Ozbek, Zandra Rhodes and Vivienne Westwood, to customize Levi jackets; the results, along with the original artwork, were then exhibited at London's Victoria and Albert Museum), neither *The Face* nor *i-D* was especially interested in showing their readers what established designers and the clothing industry had come up with for the season ahead. Instead, aided by forward-thinking photographers such as Juergen Teller, Nick Knight, Wolfgang Tillmans and Terry Richardson, they preferred their fashion pages to reflect what readers were wearing on the streets and in the numerous nightclubs that sprang up during this period. Setting the tone for what lay ahead, the first issue of *i-D* declared, 'Style isn't what but how you wear clothes. Fashion is the way you walk, talk, dance and prance.' The success of these magazines meant the clothes and styles they featured would soon reach a broad audience. *The Face* and *i-D* were unquestionably far less demure and respectful towards fashion than any existing publications – but then so too was their target market, much of which was composed of students surviving on tight budgets but with ample determination to make an impact. Fashion, in this instance, became another aspect of popular culture, alongside music and cinema.

Above all, music and its performers were a primary source of inspiration, and the most visible evidence of current street fashion. This had been the case since the time of Punk in the mid-1970s, when Malcolm McLaren was simultaneously managing the Sex Pistols and running Seditionaries with Vivienne Westwood. The New Romantic movement of the early 1980s further strengthened the links between pop music and fashion in Britain, since many of the bands involved had emerged from London's club scene of the time. When Vivienne Westwood staged a runway show for the first time, at Olympia in March 1981, her New Romantic 'Pirates' collection was promoted by McLaren's latest band, Bow Wow Wow, while the clothes themselves were soon seen

Previous pages Dresses from the finale of Zandra Rhodes' spring/summer 1982 collection. Although she flirted briefly with sophisticated punk during the previous decade, the elaborate romanticism of the 1980s was altogether more to her taste, and it gave full rein to her talent for mixing fabrics and colours.

Left Adam Ant first came to public attention when he appeared in Derek Jarman's 1977 film *Jubilee*. His band, Adam & the Ants, was managed by Jordan, who worked in Vivienne Westwood's King's Road shop, and Westwood made some of the clothes he wore on stage and in videos. The group subsequently altered its image in tune with the emerging New Romantic movement, enjoying huge success between 1980 and 1982.

Right Vivienne Westwood in her studio in 1982. In March of the previous year, the designer had presented her first catwalk show, the influential 'Pirates' collection, seen below, which was held in the exhibition hall at London's Olympia.

on Adam Ant in the video accompanying his single 'Stand and Deliver'. Before long the music/fashion bond had become common currency not just in youth magazines but throughout the media. In 1983 McLaren told Georgina Howell, 'When I went into the music business no one wanted to know about the fashion connection. Now it's the biggest plus you can have ... As long as the group has the right look today, the music doesn't matter too much.' Writing in the *Evening Standard* at the start of London Fashion Week in March 1984, Robert Elms noted that a recent seminar on style at the Institute of Contemporary Art had concluded, 'Our pop industry is our fashion industry.' Elms went on to observe that during the previous summer, when there had been eighteen British records in the United States Top 40 chart, the American fans had been buying 'a slice of British youth culture, a piece of the most vibrant fashion scene in the world. Fashion sells our pop industry.' He finished by stating that London's nightclubs, 'where so many of the new looks are first paraded', were then filled with overseas fashion photographers 'frantically snapping our startlingly stylish young things'.

In the 1980s fashion and music most commonly intermingled in London's clubs. As Betty Jackson notes, 'If you didn't go out three times a week to a club you were nobody.' Clearly, popular clubs such as Blitz in Covent Garden, hosted by Steve Strange and frequented by the likes of Boy George and the androgynous Marilyn (they both worked in the cloakroom), were a world away from receptions given by the Princess of Wales in Kensington Palace. Both, however, were important in the development of British fashion and especially in its promotion overseas. In 1985 *Women's Wear Daily* described

London as 'a teeming fashion marketplace buzzing with ideas. They bounce off the streets and out of the prodigious art colleges.' In particular colleges with fashion departments were responsible for producing many of the most assiduous nightclub attendees. Their engagement with the world of clubs was often actively encouraged by the institutions. As one college lecturer told Angela McRobbie in 1998, 'Fashion students need to observe what's going on around them … They have to have an interest in the outside world and the club scene is part of their research.' John Galliano, who studied at St Martins School of Art from 1981 to 1984, would later remember how, 'Thursday and Friday at St Martins, the college was almost deserted. Everybody was at home working on their costumes for the weekend. Honestly, it took two days to get ready.' From the late 1970s (when Rusty Egan and Steve Strange opened Club for Heroes in Soho) through to the late 1980s, clubs sprang up around the capital, and often just as quickly disappeared again. Even after he had graduated, Galliano continued to be what he termed 'a club demon', frequenting the likes of Taboo, which was opened in January 1985 by Australian designer and performance artist Leigh Bowery and his erstwhile lover Trojan (born Guy Barnes). 'The club scene fed me,' Galliano would observe. 'Being with other creative people like Boy George was a crucial experience for me.' As late as 1997, although based in Paris for the previous eight years, Galliano's design assistant Steven Robinson would declare, 'More and more we need to take in London. We visit London six to eight times per year, to get its spirit. We use the streets, the clubs, the libraries.'

Right Andy Warhol and Tina Turner pictured at the 1986 opening of Club Parisienne at the Café de Paris, one of the venues that was briefly but intensely fashionable in the eighties.

Following pages In the early 1980s no London club was more fashionable than Blitz, which first opened in Covent Garden in February 1979. Co-hosted by Steve Strange and Rusty Egan, lead singer and drummer of the group Visage, the venue attracted a crowd that was as interested in fashion as in music and exerted considerable influence in both fields. Here the members of Visage stand outside the club entrance, with Strange and Midge Ure (subsequently frontman of Ultravox) to the far right and Rusty Egan far left.

Fashion born within the club environment did not remain there, but rapidly moved out to reach a broader constituency. As designer Helen Storey remarked in her 1996 autobiography, *Fighting Fashion*, 'From Leigh Bowery and Rachel Auburn to Stephanie Cooper and Christine Arherns, it seemed that anyone who could floor the pedal of a sewing machine was jumping into the party that was London.' Recalling the period more than a quarter of a century later, fashion critic Sarah Mower wrote, 'In the 1980s I was absolutely certain what made British fashion great. It was rebelliousness. It was young people kicking up against the class system. It was teenagers forced into ever more inventive extremes of creativity by the strictures of school uniform regulations. It was music. It was clubs and fanzines; punk, New Wave, New Romantics ... It was a roar from the British streets and how it was amplified in the amazing, new, glossy style press of the Designer Decade.'

Michael Clark, dressed by BodyMap, in 1987.
The outstanding dancer of his generation,
Clark trained at the Royal Ballet School and
joined Ballet Rambert before forming his own
company in 1984. It was around this time
that he became associated with the rising
fashion label BodyMap and with London's
burgeoning club scene. He appeared on the
catwalk at BodyMap shows and performed for
BodyMap at Fashion Aid in November 1985.
(One of the BodyMap duo, Stevie Stewart,
continues to work with him.)

The history of BodyMap exemplifies how during the 1980s fashion could make the transition from club to catwalk – and demonstrates the difficulties this switch often caused for all concerned. The company's two founders, David Holah and Stevie Stewart, first met at Middlesex Polytechnic where both had enrolled as fashion students in 1979. Even while still undergraduates, they had begun to make an impact both within the college – Mikel Rosen, their tutor at the time, would later produce the BodyMap shows – and within the broader London scene. They also demonstrated entrepreneurial flair by taking a stall at weekends at Camden Market where they sold dyed army surplus pyjamas. Meanwhile, through nightclubs of the period, they had begun to meet like-minded individuals outside the immediate world of fashion, including Boy George, as well as the dancer Michael Clark (Stewart would later design the costumes for many of his productions) and future filmmaker John Maybury. 'We'd a work hard/play hard ethic,' Stewart remembers. 'It was Taboo every Thursday night, and dressing up and showing off. It was the eighties and all different fields of music, film, theatre, dance were working together. There were interconnections being made between different worlds.' By the time the pair left Middlesex Polytechnic in 1982, they had already been marked out for success, especially after their entire graduation collection was purchased for Browns by the store's far-sighted buyer, Robert Forrest.

Forrest in turn introduced Holah and Stewart to Susanne Bartsch, the Swiss-born club promoter who in 1981, following many years' residence in London, had moved to New York. There on Thompson Street in the SoHo district she opened a shop specializing in new British fashion. 'It was the size of a shoebox,' she remembers, 'but full of clothes like nobody in New York had ever seen before. I'd BodyMap, of course, and Rachel Auburn, Stephen Jones, Dexter Wong, Richard Tory, John Richmond and John Galliano after he graduated.' At the time, American fashion was considerably more staid than it would later become and the advent of new names from London caused a sensation: 'The *New York Times* gave me a full page even before we'd opened. And then people would come in on buses just to look at the windows. We were the talk of the town.' To promote the enterprise further, in April 1983 Bartsch decided to stage a fashion show and given her London background, it was inevitable this should be held in a nightclub: the Roxy on 18th Street. A cultural festival, Britain Salutes New York, was taking place at the time and although this had no official fashion element, Bartsch's event – New London in New York – was included. 'Everyone wanted to be in it,' she says. 'I had models like Janice Dickinson and Beverly Johnson, and I showcased about

twenty-four different British designers, some of them still at college.' With invitations by Leigh Bowery and Trojan, and sets by Michael Kostiff (subsequently co-host with his wife Gerlinde of another famous London nightclub, Kinky Gerlinky), the show was a success even before it began; though the Roxy could hold several thousand guests, 'we had a queue going twice round the block,' remembers Bartsch. Somehow the occasion came together, despite being 'a total shambles. I'd never done anything like this before, there was no sound-proofing, we had to screen off part of the space to make a changing room and the wrong people went out at the wrong time ...' Two further shows were held during the following seasons, both at another club, the Limelight on Sixth Avenue and featuring sixteen and eighteen British designers respectively.

In 1984 Bartsch, after being approached by Akira Mori, son of the Japanese designer Hanae Mori, also organized three days of fashion shows for young British talent in Tokyo 'It was considered scandalous,' she recalls. 'Leigh Bowery came out wearing aprons with exposed backsides.' Bowery's friend Sue Tilley would later write that, 'The Japanese were at first horrified at Leigh's show and didn't know what to make of it at all, but once they saw the other English designers laughing and clapping they dared to titter embarrassedly behind their hands.'

In New York, thanks to support from a financier, Bartsch was able to move her shop to larger premises on East Broadway and also began to act as a wholesaler for design companies like BodyMap. 'They exploded in New York. I think we sold $750,000 worth of merchandise in the first season.' When the financier pulled out of the enterprise in 1987, she closed the business and instead became a club impresario.

The first BodyMap runway show, called 'Cat in the Hat Takes a Rumble with the Techno Fish', held in March 1984. Almost all the clothes shown were in black and white cotton and were designed to be worn in a layering of prints and textures to create a loose, unstructured look. The show was a critical and commercial success.

Back in London, BodyMap's business soon began to grow as British retailers like Joseph and Whistles sought to carry the company's clothes. In December 1984, the *Creative Review* proposed that thanks to companies such as BodyMap, 'the revitalized British fashion industry is entering a golden period such as it enjoyed in the mid-sixties. In the sixties, of course, it was the Beatles and the "alternative" marketing and fashion philosophy of the ill-fated Apple shop. In 1984 it is the mutual influence of stars like Boy George and Frankie Goes to Hollywood and designers like Katharine Hamnettt and BodyMap that is in evidence on video and on the high street.'

BodyMap was highly innovative in its approach to pattern-making and garment construction, the two designers working with a factory in Sweden on the creation of new stretch fabrics incorporating Lycra; this is now commonplace but at the time it was revolutionary. A measure of the label's success is how quickly and often the BodyMap style was copied by other fashion businesses; Holah and Stewart sued several well-known companies but in the end received no compensation. In fact, despite its rapid expansion, BodyMap remained something of a cottage industry. Since Holah and Stewart were without financial backing, they continued to work from her home, the two of them making the clothes and Stewart's mother helping with deliveries. 'We put all the money back into the company,' Stewart remembers. 'David and I lived on about £35 a week and in the winter we used to go to Italy and freelance for the Genius Group in the Veneto area to make more cash; we got lots of practical experience there, seeing how a successful business operated.'

Meanwhile, in March 1984 BodyMap participated in London Fashion Week for the first time with a catwalk show called 'Cat in the Hat takes a Rumble with the Techno Fish'. Before the event Holah and Stewart were interviewed for the *Evening Standard* by a clearly bemused Angus McGill, who reported, 'The clothes are almost all black and white and made of cotton I now learn is called sweatshirt. They are all pull-on, comfortable (said the model), crumpled, the girls with lots of holes and baggy, ballooning tops and skirts that suddenly flare, the boys distinctly Genet. People who know recognize these clothes as BodyMap at a glance.'

The ability to translate London's club look on to the catwalk and thence into shops meant 'Cat in the Hat' was a huge success, but one that left Holah and Stewart with a problem. 'Afterwards,' she explains, 'we had £500,000 in orders but no money to make the clothes. So we went to the bank, mortgaged my mother's house and took out an enormous overdraft.'

Demand for BodyMap kept on growing, and in early September of the same year, the duo signed a licensing agreement with an American company, Design Consortium, for the latter to manufacture and market BodyMap clothing for distribution within the United States. It was also agreed that there would be an additional, less expensive range named B-Basic. All seemed set fair, but unfortunately BodyMap's second catwalk show, staged that autumn and given the title 'Barbie Takes a Trip Round Nature's Cosmic Curves', was far less well received than its predecessor. The anarchic presentation, complete with bare-breasted models and boys in skirts kissing each other, led the American *Daily News Record* to wonder whether what had been shown was 'an outrageous pretension or merely a pretentious outrage'. Although BodyMap recovered from this setback and presented further collections in 1985, already Holah and Stewart seemed ultimately doomed to failure, not least because the scale of what they were trying to achieve was beyond their capabilities. They had no management training or skills (and indeed no manager) and brought their clubland sensibility with them wherever they went. Nicholas Coleridge's *The Fashion Conspiracy* includes an entertaining description of the two young designers making a presentation to besuited and baffled Japanese clothing executives from the department store Isetan in Tokyo, 'Stewart in an orange flannel hat with purple cake frill, crimson lips and Rajasthan earrings, Holah in cantilevered tortoiseshell spectacles and a black turtle-neck jersey.' The cultural chasm between the BodyMap duo and their hosts appeared unbridgeable, especially after models appeared wearing lime-green flares and turquoise leggings. At the beginning of June 1986, *Women's Wear Daily* reported, 'BodyMap, the British design team of Stevie Stewart and David Holah, has gone into "liquidation" because of cash flow problems, and is seeking to reorganize.' Stewart explains: 'All of a sudden our American licence ended up owing us a lot of money. Then a Swedish distribution company owed us money and we'd production problems with one fabric. It was a horrible

Right Although she had no formal training in fashion, Margaret Howell established her own business in 1971, producing a range of accessories and later shirts. She has since become renowned for clothing collections that contemporize the traditional English look, as seen in this 1984 outfit, worn by Andie McDowell.

Far right After a varied early career that included interior design and music, Nigel Preston began designing clothes for performers including Suzy Quatro and the members of Emerson, Lake and Palmer. This in turn led to his establishing Maxfield Parrish, which specialized in producing the finest quality suede and leather garments such as the skirt and shirt Andie McDowell is wearing here, in 1982.

Left In 1972 Patricia Roberts established her own business specializing in hand-knits. These were initially sold through shops such as Browns in London and Bloomingdales in New York, but within four years Roberts had opened the first of her own premises in Knightsbridge. Others soon followed, as well as a series of yarns and pattern books. By the early 1980s she had become one of the most influential figures in knitwear, an area of design in which Britain had always enjoyed a pre-eminent position. This sweater, called 'Beano', worn by Catherine Bailey, dates from 1981.

thing and all happened in the same season. Then the bank pulled the plug. We'd grown so quickly that we were underfunded.' There were attempts to revive the business, 'We kept going in a small way, we had a concession in Hyper Hyper,' and over the next five years there were periodic reports that BodyMap was making a comeback; in a feature on the preparations for London Fashion Week in March 1990, the *Independent*'s Roger Tredre described Stewart and Holah putting the finishing touches to their latest collection in her mother's north London home – but the business never regained its former position and finally folded altogether in the early 1990s.

For indisputably gifted but inexperienced designers like David Holah and Stevie Stewart of BodyMap, the decade ended with far less optimism than it had begun. Many years later, a chastened Stewart told fashion writer Tim Blanks that she and Holah would have become more commercially minded had they only been given the time to do so: 'We often say if we knew then what we know now, we would probably still be doing BodyMap and have all the accessories and the handbags and the fragrance and the lifestyle.' BodyMap is merely the best-known name from an era that began in expectation and ended in disillusion, and that would see the rise and fall of many other young designers.

The BodyMap saga has since been replicated many times over. During the following two decades, it became a familiar tale. Young and clearly talented designers would emerge from one of Britain's fashion colleges and be encouraged to set up business immediately, before they had time to acquire any management experience, training or support. A rush of orders and seeming

Gina Fratini is the pseudonym of designer Georgina Butler, who was born in Japan of English parents. She studied fashion under Madge Garland at the Royal College of Art in the early 1950s and launched her own label in the 1960s. In 1971 she was chosen to design the dress worn by Princess Anne for her twenty-first birthday. This shocking pink silk moiré evening coat comes from Fratini's autumn/winter 1984 collection.

A silk satin evening dress with ruched cummerbund and deep pagoda-style sleeves filled with black silk flowers designed in 1984 by Bellville Sassoon. This couture house was originally founded in 1953 by Belinda Bellville; David Sassoon joined the business five years later. After more than half a century, it continues to flourish, with the collaboration of Irish-born designer Lorcan Mullany.

success would soon follow but, relying on a modest bank loan that demanded monthly repayments, the business would remain chronically underfunded and barely able to survive from one season to the next. Then came a single setback – a retailer would fail to pay on time or a manufacturer would deliver the finished collection too late – and, with no financial safety net in place, the whole flimsy structure fell apart. Thereafter the talented young designer would be regarded by financial institutions as a bad credit risk and fail to find further backing. As Colin McDowell has written in his monograph on John Galliano, 'London fashion in the mid-eighties was a complicated cocktail of hope and hype; idealism and cynicism; volatility and predictability. As seasons passed, one of the most predictable of all developments was that young talents would be overstretched; they were all given too much too soon, and ended up burned-out and rejected.'

At the beginning and for a very brief moment, the anarchy associated with Britain's young designers had seemed charming, but it rapidly grew tiresome once retail buyers and members of the press found they were unable to do their jobs satisfactorily because of poor organization. Inevitably this did little to help the fledgling designers' cause. 'London was very funky then,' remembers Anna Harvey. 'Everything was late and that was thought funny and we would queue in the rain and that was all right, and then you'd get into the tent and it would be filled with groupies who'd no right to be there.' At the BodyMap show in March 1986, a 'seething throng of hangers-on' forced the *Guardian*'s Sarah Mower 'into a grovelling position on the floor, to see what I could from a viewpoint on a level with the photographers' backsides.' Elsewhere there were 'threadbare, gimmicky, badly controlled' shows where journalists found their seats taken by gatecrashers who refused to move and some buyers were unable to gain admission into the venue at all. Friends and supporters of young designers, college contemporaries, nightclub associates and passing acquaintances, believed they had as much, if not more, right to attend the event than those actually in receipt of an invitation.

Too often the party atmosphere was allowed to prevail, as though there were no difference between a fashion show and a night club. 'We were definitely more unruly,' Lynne Franks accepts, 'but it was harder to be autocratic than was the case in Paris or Milan ... we'd a hell of a lot less money to play around with, unlike the French and the Italians, and we were horribly understaffed. We did have a lot of very young, inexperienced designers putting on shows that were under-funded. It was our creativity everyone came for, but chaos comes with that level of creativity.' In any case, it could be argued that things were ever thus in British fashion. Writing in 1978, *The Times*'s Prudence Glynn commented that 'Designers have always liked to make a performance out of their collections, and anyone putting together a directory of rudeness could write almost the whole thing from the memoirs of journalists who have had to cover the big shows.' Nevertheless, in 1980s London youthful enthusiasm was deemed a poor substitute for professional competence, especially when competing in the international market place. Anna Harvey correctly points out, 'This is a business, not a party, and it should be run like a business.'

Furthermore, bad management was sometimes coupled with inadequate standards of finish on garments. Writing in *The Times* in October 1983, Suzy Menkes regretfully noted 'that London designers use our so-called "creativity" as a duster coat to cover up bad make, sloppy details and poor accessorizing.'

MONTY DON

I renew myself at the fountain of the past. FRANÇOIS TRUFFAUT

Today one of Britain's best-known gardeners, Monty Don previously ran a highly successful costume jewellery business, begun in 1981 with his wife, Sarah, who had trained as a designer. These pieces come from the autumn/winter 1984 Monty Don collection and are teamed with a black cashmere dress by Benny Ong. Unfortunately, three years later, following the stock market crash of October 1987, Monty Don Jewellery suffered widespread cancellation of orders from American clients and never recovered. 'Our collapse was spectacular,' he has since commented. 'We were all along pretending to be businessmen and now our cover had been blown.'

After tersely declaring that London's newer names deserved to fail while 'hems trail and threads dangle', Sally Brampton commented in the *Sunday Times* in late March 1986, 'It is luxury to encourage or even allow young designers to show clothes that would not have stood comparison with a student show, let alone pass the acid test of eyes that have, the week before, criticized the likes of Armani, Ferré and Versace.' Her judgment was echoed by overseas visitors such as Pat Waxman, who had four shops in California and who told *Drapers Record* during the same season, 'There is so much talent in London that it is a shame when designers do not live up to their potential in terms of business ability.'

The disparity between commerce and creativity lasted longer than it should have done and tarnished all aspects of the business. The inevitable downside to this situation was that buyers, especially those from the all-important American market, were reluctant to place orders with London design labels just starting out in business and desperately in need of support. While a few small outlets such as that run by Susanne Bartsch in New York would stock newer names, there were not enough of them to make a real difference to the turnover of a fledgling company. Meanwhile, bigger stores in the United States were understandably cautious about venturing into unknown territory, especially when the designers seemed to possess so little understanding of what was needed to achieve commercial success, such as staging well-presented shows. 'There was a lot of conservatism about at the time,' agrees Gail Sackloff, who had trouble persuading American buyers to consider investing in younger British designers. 'I don't think my clients were ready for that look and that approach. Business dropped a lot except for eveningwear and knitwear. Americans would look but they wouldn't buy.'

Thankfully, this scenario was not allowed to continue for long. As the 1980s progressed increasingly professional levels of organization were introduced to London's fashion arena.

THE BUSINESS
OF FASHION

If the Princess of Wales was the most photographed woman in Britain during the 1980s, Margaret Thatcher ran her a close second. Prime Minister from May 1979 to November 1990, Mrs Thatcher could hardly be said to have a particular preoccupation with fashion (aside from a fondness for wearing 'Tory' blue) or to being a sartorial role model (except for women who favoured blouses with pussy-cat bows at the neckline). Writing of the Prime Minister in the *Correspondent* magazine in April 1990, Georgina Howell observed, 'Rather like the man who knows nothing about art but knows what he likes, she has groped her way from the fashion nadir of Bri-nylon, little scarves and plonking brooches to the perfectly good suit for all occasions.' At the start of her term, members of Mrs Thatcher's team did speak to the staff of *Vogue* about helping with her appearance (as they would do with the Princess of Wales a couple of years later) but this never came to anything; a woman of such strong opinions was unlikely to take advice on any subject, even one apparently outside her immediate field of interest.

At the same time Mrs Thatcher was more engaged by the subject of the British fashion industry than any of her predecessors had been – or any of her successors would be. Asked during an interview broadcast by the BBC World Service in mid-March 1984 whether the domestic fashion industry should be helped by the state, the Prime Minister replied, 'It needs to be seen to have government support ... When I go overseas, you know, I go to a lot of countries where governments really regard fashion as a very important industry. We haven't regarded it as anything like as important as we should ... It is big business. It is important to business. It has repercussions for many, many other industries and you know being British we tend perhaps sometimes to think of it as a little bit, what should I say, frothy or not quite so important because it is fashion.'

It was presumably the business aspect of fashion that particularly interested the Prime Minister. During her tenure Mrs Thatcher gave evidence of her interest in the subject by hosting a number of receptions for members of the fashion industry and by encouraging relevant ministers in her government to do likewise. The first such party she gave at No. 10 Downing Street,

The highly political designer Katharine Hamnett upstaged Margaret Thatcher when she wore one of her own slogan T-shirts to an evening reception at No. 10 in March 1984. Wearing a T-shirt was unusual enough, but the slogan, following recent polls indicating public opposition to the siting of American medium-range missiles in the UK, was explosive. The photograph was gleefully published worldwide.

in March 1984, was also the most memorable, although for reasons not of the Prime Minister's choosing. Among those representing the design sector was Katharine Hamnett, whose political sympathies could never have been aligned with those of Mrs Thatcher. In 1979 after the closure of the Tuttabankem label Hamnett had started a business under her own name and was by now well known for producing oversized T-shirts on which were printed large block-letter slogans, often with a political content. Not long before the Downing Street reception, a consignment of her T-shirts proclaiming 'U.S. GO HOME' had been rejected by retailer Joseph Ettedgui, who felt they would not be acceptable to his clientele. So Hamnett, together with her PR consultant and friend Lynne Franks, drove to Greenham Common, Berkshire, where for the previous two and a half years a group of women had been peacefully protesting at the deployment of Cruise missiles by an American air force unit based on the site. There they distributed the T-shirts, which, Hamnett remembers, after some initial hesitation the protestors chose to wear when 'they ringed the fence around the base at sunset and sang; all the soldiers came out and looked at them in silence.' Hamnett was to cause even more of a stir at Downing Street, although initially she had no intention of attending the Prime Minister's reception. The previous year Mrs Thatcher's government had emerged victorious from the short Falklands War against Argentina and, Hamnett remembers, 'As Jasper Conran said to me, "Why should we drink a glass of warm white wine with that murderess?" so my decision to go to the party was pretty last minute.' The designer arrived at Downing Street wearing one of her T-shirts on which was emblazoned the message '58% DON'T WANT PERSHING',

Above Margaret Thatcher showed enthusiastic support for the British fashion industry and also hosted several parties for designers, buyers and press. Here she is presenting Rifat Ozbek with the British Fashion Council's Designer of the Year Award in October 1988. Ozbek remembers that Mrs Thatcher, having noticed the old docksiders on his feet, remarked, 'Well, I'm sure you'll be able to afford a decent pair of shoes now.'

Right, above John Galliano receiving his award as Designer of the Year from Lord Young, Secretary of State for Trade and Industry, in October 1987. Galliano would win the award again in 1994 and 1995 (and share it with Alexander McQueen in 1997).

Right, below Cyril Kern and Edward Rayne at the British Fashion Awards in January 1986. Later that year, Rayne would take over from Kern as chairman of the fledgling British Fashion Council.

a reference to recent polls showing public opposition to the siting of American medium-range ballistic missiles in the UK.

'It was a dark practical joke,' says Hamnett. 'I never imagined it was going to go as far as it did.' If Mrs Thatcher was disconcerted when confronted with a message-bearing T-shirt (according to Hamnett, 'she squawked like a chicken, "Oh, we haven't got Pershing here, we've got Cruise missiles"'), she managed to look her customarily serene self in globally syndicated photographs of the two women standing beside each other in Downing Street. On the other hand, the designer was not invited to the next reception Mrs Thatcher hosted for the fashion industry ('Lady Henderson said, the message is no messages, please'). But despite, or perhaps because of, the incident, that same year Hamnett won the Designer of the Year award at the first-ever British Fashion Awards; there is, it seems, some truth in the maxim about no publicity being bad publicity.

Ministers in Mrs Thatcher's government gave receptions in 1985 and 1986, while in March 1987 the Prime Minister once more opened 10 Downing Street to the fashion world, hosting a reception 'to celebrate London Designer Week'. According to the *Evening Standard* the hostess went against the prevailing preference for black and wore 'a Tory blue self-patterned jacquard dress' in which she proceeded to inform her guests, 'The trouble with black is that everyone looks the same.' Mrs Thatcher was no more reticent about expressing her views on fashion when she next invited members of that milieu to Downing Street, in October 1988. Marylou Luther of the *Los Angeles Times* reported that the Prime Minister, this time dressed in a brown silk and wool houndstooth check two-piece by Aquascutum, told the assembled company that she 'had no idea what a power suit looks like, prefers cocktail suits to ballgowns, gets "fed up" wearing dull colours all the time and believes "fashion adds a great deal to the quality of life."' The *coup de grâce* was Mrs Thatcher's advice to *Daily Express*'s fashion editor Jackie Modlinger that her Yves Saint Laurent skirt was too short ('Tell him it must be lengthened, and tell him I told you to do it.'). On this occasion she had agreed to present Rifat Ozbek with his award as Designer of the Year but whoever was responsible for briefing the Prime Minister had done a poor job, since she described the thirty-five year old as 'almost a toddler', and was incorrect in naming both his city of birth (which was Istanbul, not Liverpool) and place of training (London, not Milan). At the same reception, fashion PR Rosalind Woolfson recalls, 'I was standing with the fashion editors of the *Guardian* (Brenda Polan) and the *Observer* (Sally Brampton). Denis Thatcher wandered over, glass in hand, and asked where we came from. When he was given the names of the two papers, he turned on his heel and marched away without another word.'

Though she gave no more fashion parties at Downing Street, Mrs Thatcher did attend a government reception at Lancaster House during London Fashion Week in March 1990, again wearing Aquascutum, this time a floor-length skirt suit of wine brocade, and telling Janet McCue of *The Plain Dealer*, 'I love this because it also has a short skirt which makes it nice for dinners when I'm travelling. And I love the long jacket – it makes the eye move quickly past the waistline.' The Prime Minister also made a point of visiting the London Fashion Week exhibition several times, usually in the company of Lady Henderson. On just such an occasion in October 1987 she asked several designers, 'Why aren't you people making clothes for people like me any more?', before finally telling Bruce Oldfield, 'Not too short. Not too short. You've just got it right.' As Lisa Anderson commented in the *Chicago Tribune* in October 1987, 'Onlookers were surprised that Thatcher sandwiched in a fashion visit, with only a day to spare between her victorious address to the Conservative Party conference in Blackpool and her departure for the Commonwealth Summit in Vancouver this week.' Asked why the Prime Minister should have taken time out for such an expedition, Lady Henderson simply replied, 'She likes it.'

But there were other and more important ways in which Mrs Thatcher's government assisted the development of British fashion during the 1980s, not least through its involvement in the establishment of the British Fashion Council. The organization's origins lie in efforts made at this time to resolve problems which had long bedevilled every attempt to promote and develop the national fashion industry. Its lack of an official organization caused difficulty when it came to co-ordinating dates for London Fashion Week within the European schedule. From 1977 onwards Joanne Davis worked with Philbeach Events and was responsible for organizing its Olympia exhibitions. She remembers that meetings to agree the seasonal calendar 'were dominated by the French and Italian show organizers. London was simply squeezed in – from their viewpoint the afterthought.' In November 1983, *Drapers Record* reported that, 'The dates, and in some cases even the venues, for London Fashion Week in March, hang in the air this week as exhibition organizers grapple with the problem of fitting their shows into a packed and changing European calendar.' It didn't help that in London the larger static exhibitions were not organized by a central authority representing the interests of designers and manufacturers, as happened elsewhere in Europe. Instead, as has been noted, they lay under the control of commercial businesses with no interest in the development of British fashion.

Joanne Davis, who worked with Philbeach Events, helped bring together many disparate organizations and individuals to create the British Designer Show, which made its debut in March 1984.

Annette Worsley-Taylor was largely responsible for organizing the original New Wave fashion show held at the Ritz Hotel in April 1974. A year later she founded the London Designer Collections, which she went on to run for the next twenty years. From 1993 to 2006 she was creative and marketing director of the British Fashion Council, and consultant to the BFC for Fashion Week.

'The whole scene was being driven by exhibition organizers at places like Earl's Court and Olympia,' explains Gerry Saunders, who from 1980 served as both editor and publisher of the trade journal *Drapers Record*. 'These people were competing among themselves for the largest slice of the money and holding exhibitions at exactly the same time each season.' Clearly this situation was in nobody's best interest and eventually representatives of the manufacturing industry approached Saunders, who remembers, 'the trade was incandescent with rage about the whole thing.' As someone who was non-partisan and yet familiar with every aspect of the business and its key players, Saunders was asked if he could find a solution to the problem. His first step was to call a meeting in mid-May 1981 at the Regent Street Polytechnic to which everyone with an interest in the matter was invited. 'When I went along that evening, I didn't know what was going to happen. In fact, two or three hundred people turned up and we had a very vociferous meeting.' Many representatives of the clothing industry vented their frustration with existing circumstances, not least the fact that British designers were attracting more and more press attention despite being relatively insignificant in economic terms when compared with their manufacturing equivalents. One of the latter, Israel Rondel, managing director of Topcoat, expressed the fundamental lack of understanding between the two groups when he remarked of designers, 'Why do we waste our time discussing the tail end of this industry?' Nonetheless, at the end of the evening it was agreed to establish a new body, the Fashion Industry Action Group (FIAG). This, in turn, appointed a twelve-strong committee that numbered among its members not just clothing manufacturers such as Topcoat and John Marks but also Lynne Franks and Annette Worsley-Taylor of the London Designer Collections, as well as designers Murray Arbeid and Tanya Sarne, and Lesley Goring of the Individual Clothes Show. Financial support came from seventy-plus companies which each contributed £50 to the organization, while the three main womenswear exhibition organizers, Brintex, Dresswell and Philbeach, donated £5,000 apiece.

In the short term, the purpose of the Fashion Industry Action Group, as reported in *Drapers Record* the following November, was to establish 'a united London Fashion Week'. There was also the idea that the organization would liaise with other bodies to obtain maximum government support for London Fashion Week, and that it would 'support all initiatives to secure the future of the British fashion industry'. 'We met every few weeks,' remembers Gerry Saunders. 'There was always something we wanted to talk about but we didn't have any formal agendas or keep minutes.' While no doubt helpful in creating a more convivial atmosphere in which matters of common interest could be discussed, the ad hoc nature of FIAG soon turned out to be unsatisfactory, particularly since the fundamental problems which had led to its creation remained unresolved. Furthermore the new body had no official standing so no real credibility when it came to negotiating with organizations which did possess this advantage. For the same reason, it was hardly in a strong position to approach the government for help. 'FIAG was seen as a thorn in the side of officialdom,' Gerry Saunders admits, 'because it wasn't an Establishment body. Anyone could join and we never even really had a formal committee.'

It is hardly surprising, therefore, that a number of the larger clothing manufacturers contacted the Minister for Trade and Industry, Norman Lamont, to express their frustration at the existing situation and to enquire what the government might do to help. One of those most active in trying to achieve improvement for the entire sector was businessman Cyril Kern, who ran a long-established family clothing business, Reldan (in the 1950s it had teamed up with the designer Digby Morton to create a line of stylish but affordable women's fashion marketed as 'Morton for the Masses'). Kern agrees that 'there was a lack of structure in FIAG and that wasn't very satisfactory. I volunteered that I would allocate an office and a secretary in my own premises on Regent Street.' John Wilson recalls that Kern 'put aside time for knocking heads together. There were a lot of very big people in the industry and he helped pull them all together.' In October 1983, Kern told the *Evening Standard*'s Liz Smith that the experience had been 'like trying to bring together different tribes. They hardly said a word to one another at first.' Gradually an entente was achieved.

Everyone involved in the process agrees that Norman Lamont was keen to find an acceptable solution to the absence of an official organization for British fashion, FIAG being seen as merely a stop-gap. Kern remembers, 'It was decided there was a need for an all-embracing organization to be linked to the Clothing Export Council (CEC), to make the most of export development and manufacturer participation in government-sponsored "British Weeks" and UK trade exhibitions.' As far as he was concerned, 'the only way to stop the talking was to form an umbrella council' which could be linked to the CEC and would represent the interests of the various groups in clothing design, manufacture and retail when making contact with the government. To this end, in March 1983 the British Fashion Council was set up with Cyril Kern as its first chairman and Gerry Saunders as deputy chairman (and subsequently treasurer until 1998). It was, Kern told *Drapers Record*, 'A most welcome first step towards a healthier UK fashion industry'. Yet in its initial form, the British Fashion Council was almost as amorphous an organization as FIAG had been:

In the early 1980s, as part of a programme to raise the international profile of London fashion week, the London Designer Collections organized a number of parties, including, in March 1984, a black tie dinner jointly hosted with Harvey Nichols and *Harpers & Queen* at which Sir Terence Conran and model Marie Helvin were guests.

it had no legal standing, no funds or staff, and no public profile. Operating under the auspices, and from the premises, of the Clothing Export Council, the BFC's chances of long-term survival looked no better than those of FIAG.

Meanwhile, the fashion design sector had been having its own internal debate about how best to present a united front to the rest of the world. Entirely financed by the contributions of its members, the London Designer Collections had been providing the funds for international press accreditation and co-ordination of show schedules at the twice-yearly Fashion Week, but it was becoming increasingly difficult to manage without assistance. Roger Saul of Mulberry, then serving as chairman of the LDC, was eager that it should become 'the professional marketing body for the fashion designer industry' as a whole. In order to do this, the LDC would have to change from being, in his words, 'a small, self-sponsored elitist body', into 'a far wider, powerful, sponsored organization with genuine responsibilities for all aspects of our designer industry', tackling everything from helping college students to looking after international marketing. This appeared unlikely to occur in the short term – not least because the LDC lacked the means to take on such a major role – and Saul resigned as chairman in October 1983. By then, of course, the British Fashion Council had been inaugurated and while it would seem to have provided the solution everyone sought, designers remained unhappy because they felt the new body was primarily run by, and for, the manufacturing sector. The BFC, they believed, would have little interest in representing them or championing the cause of fashion design in Britain.

Coincidentally, during the same period *Vogue* editor Beatrix Miller brought together a small group of interested and well-connected individuals – designer Jean Muir; shoe manufacturer Edward Rayne; retail entrepreneur Sir Terence Conran; Sir Roy Strong (then Director of the Victoria and Albert Museum); and Lady Henderson – to address precisely this question: how could the interests of British fashion and its designers best be advanced? As Liz Smith reported in the *Evening Standard* in October 1985, the 'self-appointed fashion think tank' sought 'both to harness the creative energy London can undoubtedly claim and to win the financial support of the industry's biggest clothing manufacturers and retail groups'. To this end, the Gang of Six – as it was popularly known – met Norman Lamont at the Department of Trade and Industry on a number of occasions to discuss the matter with him. Jasper Conran suggested that representatives of the LDC should meet with the Gang of Six, and Roger Saul, Meredith Etherington-Smith and Annette Worsley-Taylor duly did so, in mid-May 1984. On that occasion Terence Conran reported that the Minister's own main objective was to find an organization to which he could offer government funding and which, in turn, would carry enough weight and influence to support and assist the industry, thus preventing it 'from being manipulated, as in the past, by other international designers and their dates'. The problem from the perspective of British designers was that the British Fashion Council in its current incarnation was not that organization.

Annette Worsley-Taylor had been hoping to transform the London Designer Collections into a broader body that would be more effective in supporting British designers. Initially named the Federation of British Designers, later the British Designer Executive, this would need central government funding were it to have any real substance. In June 1984 she met Norman Lamont and outlined her concept to him, after which he wrote, 'I can assure you that the proposals will be looked at carefully and sympathetically.' Following further discussions, it was agreed that Worsley-Taylor would produce a detailed paper on the subject of the British Designer Executive.

Presented under the auspices of the LDC, that document was delivered to the Department of Trade and Industry in November 1984 before being circulated to other interested parties. It argued that a specific organization was required to look after the interests of the country's fashion designers because 'High fashion womenswear has always been presented and marketed in a different way from the rest of ready to wear clothing.' Anyone wishing to promote indigenous fashion design at the time had 'no single organization to contact for expertise and assistance', whereas the suggested British Designer Executive 'would be able to act as a central organization for stores, boutiques, manufacturers, agents, press and promoters who require information about or wish to work with British designers.' At the same time, the Executive could serve as an information centre for the designers themselves, 'giving them assistance on all aspects of the fashion business with particular reference to the future expansion of their companies'. It would also coordinate activities during the twice-yearly London Fashion Week. While much of the money to pay for the organization would come from fees levied during London Fashion Week on all exhibitors (both manufacturers and designers) as well

In the 1970s, London-based Meredith Etherington-Smith worked as a consultant for Bloomingdales of New York to seek out new concepts and names. Later one of the most influential fashion journalists of her generation, she was London editor for French *Vogue* and the first woman editor of the American edition of *GQ* magazine, before becoming, in 1983, deputy editor of *Harpers & Queen*.

as from commercial and trade sponsorship, the document advocated that the Department of Trade and Industry contribute pump-priming funding of £100,000 over a two-year period in the form of two tranches of £50,000.

It was probably this element as much as any other that led to the scuppering of the scheme. While there were merits to the idea that the rapidly expanding fashion design sector have its own official representation, the government noted the recent establishment of the British Fashion Council which, as far as those outside the fashion world were concerned, was ideally placed to perform whatever tasks the proposed British Designer Executive might undertake. Setting up a second body looked like expensive duplication.

So, although the scheme was backed by the likes of Terence Conran, it was not to be. In early January 1985 Norman Lamont asked that Cyril Kern, the British Fashion Council's Chairman, be sent a copy of the Worsley-Taylor document and that representatives of all relevant groups should meet to consider its contents. Kern in turn wrote to the London Designer Collections stating that at the next meeting of the British Fashion Council, 'discussions will be centred on the necessity of the Industry avoiding "fragmentation" of effort, whether organizational or promotional.' Following meetings between the various bodies and the Department, in April 1985 it was agreed that the British Designer Executive concept be developed within the British Fashion Council, the latter to have a Designer subcommittee with a certain amount of autonomy.

Inevitably there were those who felt disappointed that Britain's fashion designers did not get their own independent representation. Instead, by linking their fortunes with the British Fashion Council, they considered themselves yoked to a national manufacturing industry that was, at best, indifferent to the design sector. 'It was a compromise,' says Worsley-Taylor, 'which in some ways I've always regretted because the British Designer Executive was meant to have focused on designers and promoted just their business.' Given the different aspirations and histories of the parties involved, the new Council could never hope to win universal support, and it took a long time for some designers to accept that the organization might be working with their best interests in mind. All the same, its establishment represented a major achievement and the end of London's inability to present a united front in the face of competition from other fashion capitals. Furthermore, it meant there was now an organization recognized by the government and therefore eligible for funding.

Before that could happen, however, the Department of Trade and Industry sought further information on the state of designer fashion in Britain and commissioned a report on the subject from John Wilson of the British Clothing

Parachute silk sportswear-inspired separates from Katharine Hamnett's autumn/winter 1984 collection. Following the closure of Tuttabankem, a business she had started with fellow designer Ann Buck, Hamnett launched her eponymous label in 1979 and quickly rose to international prominence, particularly after her clothes stamped with political slogans were worn by bands such as Wham! and Frankie Goes to Hollywood. She was the first recipient of the Designer of the Year award in 1984.

Industry Association. This he delivered in February 1986. His document once more emphasized the need for unity and co-ordination of effort within the national clothing industry, as well as such practical measures as the provision of a central office that would provide relevant information during London Fashion Week, along with assistance throughout the year on manufacturing, finance, marketing, exports, and so forth. Just then a new British Apparel Centre was being set up as home to groups like the BCIA and the Clothing Export Board. Wilson suggested: 'What needs to be done can be achieved by a properly constituted and resourced British Fashion Council within the overall ambit of the British Apparel Centre.' Indeed this is where the BFC found a home. Wilson also recommended the BDE's proposal of November 1984 – that the government provide pump priming funding of £100,000 spread over two years – now be put into action. Though Norman Lamont had since moved to another ministry, the Department of Trade and Industry continued to be sympathetic and agreed in principle to provide the funds provided the BFC raised the same amount – £100,000 –from commercial sponsors. All that remained was for the Council to become a legal entity in its own right. On 1 September 1986 the BFC was registered as a company limited by guarantee. Its new chairman was Edward Rayne, who had occupied the same position in the Incorporated Society of London Fashion Designers twenty-six years earlier.

Rayne remained at the helm of the new organization until 1990. In October 1988 he informed Colin McDowell (writing in the *Guardian*) that, 'The BFC has advanced the cause of British fashion immeasurably and we are a *very* sensible organization.' It had to be sensible not least because of the commitment to raise £100,000 from private sources before the Government would release the same sum. Rayne's position as the head of a successful shoe manufacturing company naturally meant that he was well placed to turn to other businesses for support. In March 1987 Sheridan McCoid of the *Daily News* reported that Rayne had announced 'There was to be industrial sponsorship in the form of donations to the fashion industry from leading manufacturers and companies involved in fashion.' Ten companies were sought, each of which would make a donation of £10,000; those persuaded to do so at the start included Coats Viyella and Courtaulds, as well as retailers such as Harrods, Selfridges and Marks & Spencer. Condé Nast and the National Magazine Company were among the publishers who also supported the endeavour. Rayne had clear ideas about how the funds raised should be used to encourage but not to

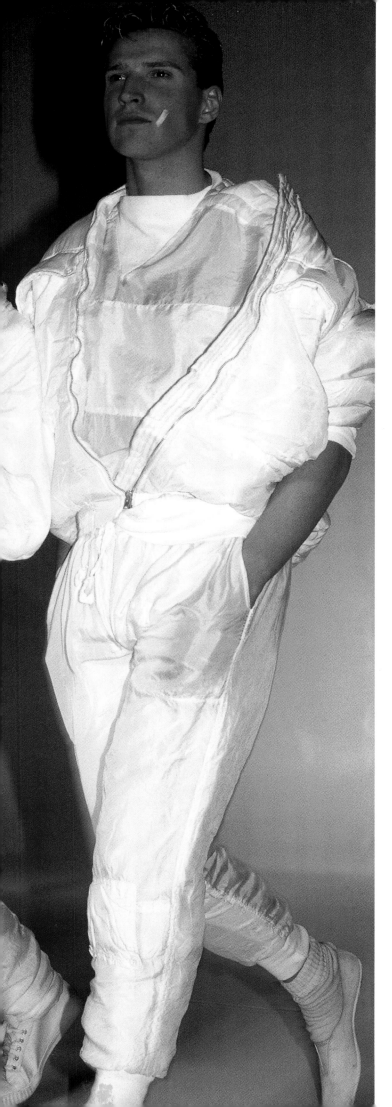

underwrite designers. 'Life is about talent,' he informed Colin McDowell, 'and money does not necessarily bring talent to the fore. I am a believer in market forces but I am prepared to subsidize talent in the short term. However, in the long term, designers must learn to stand on their own feet. Yves Saint Laurent and Armani do not expect subsidies, I am sure. British designers are not ambitious enough.' It would seem the Thatcherite concept of enterprise reaping its due reward was as applicable to fashion as any other area of business.

Nevertheless, the British Fashion Council did try to give as much help to designers as its rather limited means would allow. Committees were established covering such areas as exhibitions and press and in addition a Designer Bureau was set up. This consisted of three elements: a Register of Apparel and Textile Designers, intended to link designers and manufacturers together for specific projects and attempt to break down the ongoing antipathy that existed between the two entities; a Customer Information Service, which would allow designers to gain in-depth information on new customers prior to the confirmation of any orders; and an Advisory Service which was to provide assistance for designers on a broad range of subjects such as copyright, labelling requirements, basic import/export procedures, sourcing, contracts and so forth. The Council also arranged a number of seminars, such as that held in June 1988 dealing with government advice and assistance available to clothing exporters. Inevitably some designers felt that what the BFC provided was not relevant to their needs and that it ought to have been more specifically focused on raising money to support them for undertakings such as fashion shows. But overall the arrival of the Council was perceived as beneficial, if only because it helped to bring better order to what had previously been a rather muddled state of affairs. As early as October 1986, the *Guardian*'s Sarah Mower, who had written harshly about London Fashion Week over several previous seasons, remarked favourably on the new environment, commenting that 'there's been a distinct change of mood, both on the catwalk and amongst the audience. No chaos, no hordes of gatecrashers, no collapsing sets, no fake photographers. The shows have even started on time in a brisk schedule which has left the audience nothing to criticize save the lack of time to eat – and the clothes.'

Red or Dead began in 1982 when founders Wayne and Gerardine Hemingway took a stall at Camden Market to sell second-hand clothes. Soon Red or Dead had sixteen stalls and an outlet in Kensington Market selling their own designs, and within a decade they had stores throughout Britain and overseas. This outfit was part of the autumn/winter 1991 collection.

The emergence of the British Fashion Council coincided with an upsurge in the number of new designers entering the marketplace and for this Mrs Thatcher and her government can once more take some credit. The Prime Minister was a fervent believer in the power of self-help. During her period in office, she introduced a large number of measures designed to encourage entrepreneurship and the development of new businesses, which, if they performed well, could expect to benefit from lower taxes. As her Chancellor of the Exchequer, Nigel Lawson, explained, 'If you reward enterprise, you get more of it.' Among various government initiatives to swell the ranks of budding entrepreneurs were the Business Expansion Scheme, devised to stimulate investment by offering tax relief up to £40,000 to individuals investing in non-public British companies; the Loan Guarantee Scheme, facilitating bank borrowing by small companies; the Enterprise Allowance Scheme, providing £40 a week for up to a year to unemployed people who wanted to start businesses; and the establishment of local enterprise agencies to advise small businesses on marketing, design, business planning, information systems, etc.

The result was an upsurge in the number of new ventures: from 1979 onward, Britain saw an average net increase of 500 new companies every week. In 1987 alone, at the peak of the decade's boom, 45,000 businesses were started. By the following year, some three million people – 11 per cent of the British workforce – were self-employed, an increase approximately six times greater than the rise in self-employment during the previous three decades combined. Between 1983 and 1988 the Business Expansion Scheme helped more than 3,000 companies to raise £750 million. The Enterprise Allowance Scheme assisted 325,000 individuals to become self-employed. And in the years 1981 to 1987 the Loan Guarantee Scheme aided more than 19,000 businesses by providing £635 million in loans.

More than a few of those businesses were in the area of fashion. The number of designers emerging from colleges had been steadily rising since the early 1970s – by 1989 the annual figure stood at 1,500 – but since clothing manufacture, in which designers had never been especially welcomed anyway, was by now in terminal decline, there was little likelihood of their securing employment within the existing industry. As Mrs Thatcher demonstrated during her government's twelve-month battle against the National Union of Mineworkers over the strike that began in April 1984, she had no interest in propping up industries, regardless how long established or how important to the local economy, if they were unable to adapt to the new world of self-enterprise. Clothing manufacturers had to move with the times or close; most of them closed. The obvious choice for a young fashion graduate, therefore, was to take advantage of government-backed schemes and start up a business. Of course, even before this period many designers had been self-employed but they had perforce to set themselves up without any state support. Once this became available in the 1980s, an unprecedented boom in new fashion labels followed as more and more designers assumed they could do no better than to become their own bosses.

Seeking an outlet for the clothes they were producing, many of these young British fashion graduates opted to take space in a market. This, after all, is

Wayne Hemingway of Red or Dead.

what Holah and Stewart of BodyMap had done at the start of their careers. 'It was here in the street markets,' Angela McRobbie has suggested, 'where new fashion ideas mingled with the second-hand dresses, that a good deal of the groundwork in creating British fashion design was carried out.' In *Time Out* at the end of September 1983, Lindsey Shapero wrote, 'In the past few years, a whole new breed of stall-holders has been appearing. They sell new clothes, designed by the stall-holders themselves, and always one jump ahead of, if not dictating, the current fashions ...'

As a typical example of how such businesses started, one of the best-known fashion names of the 1990s, Red or Dead, began after founders Wayne and Gerardine Hemingway took a stall at Camden Market dealing in second-hand clothing and footwear. That was in 1982 and the following year Gerardine Hemingway opened an outlet in Kensington Market selling clothes she had

Opened in 1983, Hyper Hyper was a retail premises on Kensington High Street divided into more than seventy units. Each of these could be rented for a year at a fixed rent, and they became very popular with young designers. Shown here are scenes from one of Hyper Hyper's typically exuberant shows – this one was held in 1985.

designed and made. From these seemingly inauspicious beginnings grew a business that within a decade had stores throughout Britain and overseas. 'Buyers from Macy's New York were seduced by London's youthful cultural vibrancy,' wrote Wayne Hemingway in 2008, 'and visiting our little stall in Kensington Market, where Gerardine would sit sewing individual items on her little machine, they placed Red or Dead's first big export order ...'

The rise of the street market was yet another instance of 1980s Thatcherite enterprise culture. One especially popular location was Hyper Hyper, a retail premises on Kensington High Street owned by Loren Gordon, whose family business, Atlantic Estates, had a long history of running public markets (including that at Camden, which had started in 1974 and where Holah and Stewart, as well as the Hemingways, had begun their respective careers). Hyper Hyper was internally divided into more than seventy units, each of which could be taken for a year at a fixed rent. From the time it first opened in 1983, the formula was a success with young designers, and a waiting list for available units soon formed; among the names associated with Hyper Hyper are Ghost, Nigel Hall, Pam Hogg and Dexter Wong. It continued to occupy the original site until 1996, when leasehold problems forced a move to another location on the same street under the new name of Hype DF. This in turn closed down in late 1999, by which time the London retail scene was radically different from what it had been sixteen years before.

Hyper Hyper was not alone; many similar markets flourished during the period, providing an outlet for new fashion ventures. In 1984, for example, sisters Helen David and Judy Purbeck and their friend Claire Angel started selling their label, English Eccentrics, from a stall in Kensington Market. These rather ad hoc venues attracted more publicity than their tenants' modest turnovers would seem to justify. As Val Baker told Angela McRobbie in August 1994, 'Hyper Hyper gets huge amounts of press coverage, from the *Evening Standard*, *Elle*, from *i-D* and *The Face* to *Vogue*. So we get people coming in all the time looking for something they've seen in one of the magazines.'

The spirit of the 1980s was firmly in favour of self-enterprise. Handbag designer Anya Hindmarch set up her own company in 1987 after borrowing money from her father, 'which I had to pay back, with interest'. She remembers, 'there was that whole mood in London at the time – an extraordinary confidence in the air. All these businesses were starting out with a sense that you were in charge of your own destiny.' But it wasn't just emerging young designers who took advantage of the government initiatives. Sheilagh Brown had more than ten years' experience designing for both Stirling Cooper and Quorum and then in partnership with Sheridan Barnett before finally launching her own label in the 1983. Her venture was supported by a group of investors. 'They were called the Leading Ladies' Fund, and they got tax relief for investing in my business. What was good was that it wasn't just about them giving you money but also solid support beyond the pounds, shillings and pence – it went through to business advice at all levels.'

Caroline Coates trained as a school teacher but then, in 1981, she read in the *Guardian* of the government's schemes to nurture new small businesses. She joined a state-sponsored course designed to lead to the establishment of her own company, 'and towards the end of it I came up with the notion of working with a group of designers to put on a fashion show and help the participants start their own labels. I'd *no* fashion experience so for two years I trawled around courses and colleges specifically looking for designers who'd just graduated.' Coates then established a business called Amalgamated Talent. 'I got a small office in Great Portland Street and was a sole trader; I persuaded loads of people to come

and work with me for nothing. I think the naïveté really helped; I thought, if I'm going to make something of my life, why not now? What I severely underestimated was the amount of money I'd need.'

Amalgamated Talent staged its first show in the Brewery in the City of London in February 1983. The event featured twenty designers and cost £12,000; 'I lost £8,000 but I was completely hooked. My dad, bless him, said he'd give me £4,000 and a bank loan.' Fortunately, Gifi Fields, the clothing manufacturer who owned high street company Coppernob, saw the potential in Coates' business and put £8,000 into the second show, while Stephen Quinn, then publisher of *Harpers & Queen*, paid for an advertisement in the programme, 'and the prestige of the magazine meant others followed. From the second show I recouped quite a lot of the money I'd lost in the first one.' Coates next met with representatives of the London Enterprise Board, an organization established to promote new businesses. This raised some £40,000 for her from independent investors. In order to receive the money, Amalgamated Talent became a limited company, 'and each of the backers had a representative on the board. Some of the risk went out of the undertaking, but it opened even more doors.'

Around this time, Coates started to collaborate with designer Helen Storey who, after working for Rome-based fashion houses over a number of years, had returned to London and established her own label. In a further display of free enterprise that would have delighted Mrs Thatcher, the two women started to seek and find commercial sponsors to help underwrite the cost of Storey's shows: her very first, for example, was backed by BP. Although another designer, Karen Boyd, was involved in their venture for a while, eventually Coates and Storey would work exclusively together. The former explains, 'I'd worked out that for longer-term success I needed to consolidate and focus on those fashion designers who had a chance of real success.' Amalgamated Talent was dissolved before the end of 1985 with no debts, while Storey's business went on to expand at home and abroad during the late 1980s and early 1990s.

Storey and many other designers of the time were beneficiaries of the mid-1980s economic boom that effectively wiped out all memory of the previous decade's misfortunes and was fuelled by the easy availability of consumer credit and a cult of conspicuous consumption exemplified by the mannerisms of comedian Harry Enfield's 1988 creation 'Loadsamoney'. Yuppies – Young Upwardly Mobile Professional Persons – were a phenomenon of the age and could be identified as much as anything else by their dress: this was, after all, the period which saw the emergence of both the Power Suit and 'Designer Fashion' (indeed, the word 'designer' used as an adjective and attached to any imaginable product). This social tribe was preoccupied, as have been similar groups since that time, with lifestyle branding and the visible display of status. Obviously fashion could play a key role in the achievement of this objective. In his 1991 book *Consumer Culture and Postmodernism*, Mike Featherstone wrote that the yuppified middle class was 'fascinated by identity, presentation, appearance, lifestyle and the endless quest for new experiences'. In a city like London which, according to cultural historian Professor Frank Mort, could be considered 'the centre for a national orgy of material excess', the urge to buy new clothes grew ever stronger. Recalling the period in the *Financial Times* in November 1992, fashion journalist Brenda Polan wrote of how during the 1980s, 'It was fashionable to appear wealthy and an army of the fashion-aware would break the bank to own the correct accessories, to signal that they belonged to a club based on wealth and taste.'

The growth in consumer spending led to a boom in retail. The spectacular rise of the Joseph brand during this period provides an interesting example. A French-Moroccan by birth, in the 1960s Joseph Ettedgui had opened a hairdressing business called Joseph Salon 33 on the King's Road in London. Gradually he began to offer items of clothing for sale. 'Women would come in,' he recalls, 'and tell me they couldn't find a good white shirt anywhere, or good grey flannel trousers. So I had a little corner of the salon selling these things.' Bit by bit the corner grew and hairdressing was phased out in favour of clothing; the same thing happened in a second outlet he ran on Gloucester Road. Like Browns, Joseph specialized in French ready-to-wear, carrying names like Dorothy Bis and Castelbajac. In the early 1970s he opened a shop on Knightsbridge Green, followed by two more on South Molton Street, one of them devoted to British designer Margaret Howell. During this decade, the expansion of Joseph was steady but slow; the real growth took place in the 1980s, especially after the launch of his flagship store at 6 Sloane Street, designed by Norman Foster. 'When we opened Sloane Street, the area was mostly banks and financial institutions. Suddenly it became a destination point, so we were in a position to open one shop after another.' Over the next few years, he came to own nineteen shops across London

The first Joseph store opened in 1974 and the chain expanded rapidly during the economic boom of the 1980s, offering both the pick of international designer names and the Joseph own label collections of knitwear and chic casual classics. His shows at London fashion Week during the late eighties were must-sees, often wittily choreographed by Michael Roberts. Shown below are pink silk knits worn backstage at his spring/summer 1987 show.

(plus outlets in Paris and New York and a licensing arrangement in Tokyo). In addition to the wildly popular Joseph label, launched in 1984, these premises offered clothes by British designers such as the Richmond-Cornejo team and Rifat Ozbek, as well as emerging Japanese names like Kenzo and Yohji Yamamoto. There were three small shops called Chinese Laundry and selling designs by Katharine Hamnett, and even two restaurants, L'Express and Joe's Café.

Joseph shops were not only filled with covetable merchandise, they were also attractive places to spend time. The design of a retail outlet would become steadily more important as shopping developed into a leisure activity, no longer undertaken simply as a necessary task but instead perceived as a social pursuit. During the 1980s British retail design grew in influence and provided inspiration for markets overseas. 'One of the shops my American buyers always wanted to visit was Joseph,' Gail Sackloff remembers, 'to see how he was merchandising, because he had a special way of putting things together.'

In this enterprise he was joined by his brothers Maurice and Franklin, the latter a former banker. 'For us,' says Joseph, 'up to the eighties we weren't in the background but we were just building up the company from the financial and image point of view. Then came the explosion. It was a very dynamic period, the early eighties. The minute we discovered something and thought it was good, we opened a shop. Nothing was marketed in advance, nothing planned. It was a time when we just did what we felt was great; it was less organized than now.' Joseph customers represented the new consumer, happy to spend money in order to look fashionable and, after he launched Joseph Pour La Maison, prepared to take equal trouble over the decoration of their homes. 'Where Joseph has been so clever,' another retailer told Nicholas Coleridge in 1988, 'is finding a completely new market. They're entirely self-made and have excellent modern taste ... They haven't inherited anything from their parents – whom they've often stopped seeing – so they aren't weighed down by "things". There's no clutter. They're starting from scratch.'

Starting from scratch meant that these consumers had a lot of catching up to do. Fortunately, thanks to the economic boom of the mid-1980s, they also had more money than ever before to spend, not least on clothing. Garment sales in Britain rose by 70 per cent between 1983 and 1988. In October 1985 Liz Smith told *Evening Standard* readers that the nation's entire clothing industry was worth £3.7 billion annually. Three years later, Marylou Luther of the *Los Angeles Times* reported that the figure had climbed to £4.5 billion.

And business didn't just boom at home. As early as April 1983, the *Daily Express*'s Jackie Modlinger quoted a spokesman for the British Clothing Industry

After working freelance for several seasons, in 1984 John Richmond joined forces with Maria Cornejo (seen, left, in November 1986) to create the label that bore both their names. Although the pair only remained a business duo for three years, they attracted admiration for their sure skill in combining biker chic, rock sensibility, interesting detail and brilliant tailoring, as seen in these outfits from their spring/summer 1987 collection (right). Richmond continues to enjoy a successful career based in Italy, while Maria Cornejo works in the United States.

Association saying that between 1978 and 1982 the value of clothing exports had gone from £670 million to £840 million. Modlinger also spoke to an (unnamed) American department store buyer who declared of British fashion, 'It's as though you've got a second wind ... a chance to do it all again but better.' Between 1984 and 1986, exports of clothing rose by 18 per cent to £1.17 billion. Betty Jackson, who started her business in 1981, informed *The Sunday Times* five years later that at least 40 per cent of everything she produced went to American retailers. By March 1988 Suzy Menkes was writing in the *Independent* that 'It is not unusual for British big name designers to export 60 to 70 per cent of each collection to the United States.' Menkes further noted that even the European market for British clothing had grown in the two years since 1986: up by 200 per cent to the Netherlands; 150 per cent to Spain; 120 per cent to Germany; 'and in the chauvinistic French market by 100 per cent'.

Growth was by no means confined to the upper end of the market. The expansion of Joseph and the opening of other outlets across London devoted exclusively to labels like Armani and Hamnett were evidence of trends that the mass market ignored at its peril, especially since even by the late 1970s there was a visible decline in spending at traditional high street stores. The mould was broken by a number of imaginative retail initiatives, such as Jigsaw and Monsoon, both of which were established in 1972.

Likewise, Jeff Banks was a pioneer in recognizing that the old high street model could not be sustained, that uninspiring clothes sold in drab surroundings had no appeal for a new generation of consumers. In 1976 he opened the first Warehouse shop on Duke Street; a second branch appeared on Oxford Street the following year and a third on the Brompton Road before the end of 1977.

The idea behind the brand was simple: small runs of attractively designed clothing offered at an affordable price in smart surroundings. In other words, the kind of merchandise now seen in abundance on every British high street but at the time rarely found outside a handful of independently owned shops like the recently deceased Biba. Banks worked with a small team of designers and the clothes for Warehouse were made by his own manufacturers both in Britain and abroad. 'We tried to get exactly the same quality as you would in a store like Harrods, but by cutting out the middleman and giving the product directly to the consumer we could keep our prices down. There was a single margin; it wasn't going through a wholesaler. There were range reviews every Tuesday and new stock always going through.' The interiors of Warehouse shops, their layout, even their window displays, were given as much attention as the clothes on sale.

The difficulty for Warehouse, Jigsaw, Monsoon et al was that they were privately owned and self-financed. No matter how successful they were, limited access to capital inhibited their growth and restricted the number of outlets they could open. This was not a problem for a retail group that made its debut in 1982 and became synonymous with the decade's consumer boom. J. Hepworth & Son, Gentlemen's Tailors, was founded in Leeds in 1864 and over the next century expanded into a nationwide menswear retail chain, especially after the company went public in 1948. In 1981 Hepworth's acquired the womenswear chain Kendalls, which had eighty shops in key sites across the country, but, like so many other long-established brands, it had grown tired and was in need of an overhaul. Led by chairman Terence Conran, Hepworth's chose to reinvent itself, beginning with the appointment of a new chief executive, George Davies. It was Davies' idea to keep Kendalls trading in womenswear but to focus its shops on the sale of in-house designed and branded merchandise. This would be available under a new name and within a new retail store concept called Next. The original seven Next shops opened in former Kendalls locations in February 1982 and the sales figures for their first year of trading were two and a half times what the company had anticipated. By the end of 1982, more than seventy Kendalls branches had been converted into Next outlets and the brand had a turnover in excess of £82 million. That figure had climbed to £108 million by 1984, when some of the old Hepworth & Son stores began to be turned into Next for Men shops; at the end of the following year there were 130 of these. Next then branched out into multi-department stores offering womenswear, menswear and homeware, the last of these under the Next Interiors label. Finally, in 1986, the Hepworth brand disappeared altogether with the adoption of a new company name, Next plc.

Although this was not the first company to present high street consumers with attractively designed clothing in smartly decorated premises, the sheer quantity of its outlets and the scale of their success made Next the exemplar of mass-market retailing in the 1980s and led to a revolution in this sector of the business. Like Warehouse and the others, Next answered a growing demand among consumers for improved standards of design in both clothing and retail display; the Next interior was not dissimilar to what could be seen inside the Joseph, with pale wood floors, matte black display units and chrome fittings. Since Next oversaw the production of the goods it sold, the business was able to exercise a high level of quality control at every stage of the process from raw material to finished garment. This helped it to win a loyal following. Consumers unable to afford the prices charged at the likes of Joseph but with a hankering to stay in fashion were able to find inexpensive equivalents of the latest trends at Next.

Meanwhile, increased demand for clothes acted as a stimulus to British designers either to open a new business or to expand an existing one. Edina Ronay was in the second category, having been selling knitwear to an ever-growing market since the mid-1970s. But in the following decade, her company

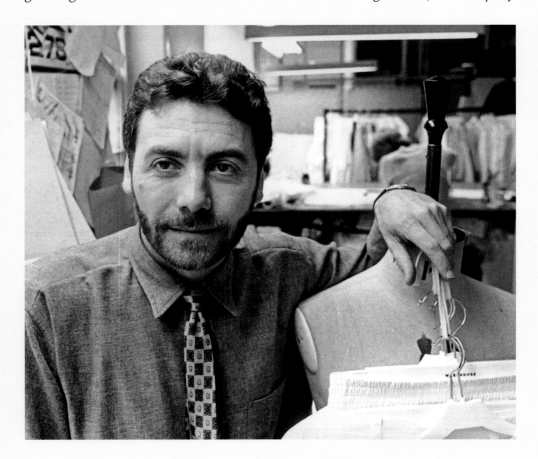

Left Seen here in 1983, Jeff Banks had launched the first Warehouse shop seven years earlier; using stocks of fabrics from warehouses across Europe, the outlets offered British consumers a constantly changing range of well-designed clothing at affordable prices, presented in attractive surroundings. This was a new approach to retailing that would become the norm in the following decade.

Right Tanya Sarne launched the Ghost label in 1984, after her first business, Miz, which specialized in sportswear, had 'ended in tears'. At the heart of Ghost's success was the discovery of and focus on the Italian machine-washable viscose with a crinkled texture that has since became a staple in so many women's wardrobes. Andrea Sargeant was the original, crucial designer of the Ghost look, which was directed by Sarne's realistic attitude to how women wanted to dress.

underwent phenomenal growth, to the point where at the twice-yearly exhibition during London Fashion Week, 'we had to close our stand to anyone who hadn't made an appointment. Not because we wanted to be difficult, but it was just that so many people came, we couldn't look after them if they hadn't booked to see us first. Looking back on it, one was very much part of a successful British scene.'

Tanya Sarne started the Ghost label in 1984 after her first business, Miz, had folded. The break-up of her marriage to singer Mike Sarne and the need to support two young children acted as a spur, as did her perception that there was a gap in the market for clothes that understood the female form. In September 1999 she explained to the *Independent on Sunday*'s Susannah Frankel, 'A woman's body is soft and rounded. Her weight fluctuates. She can lose or put on half a stone in a week. As a woman, I know how to cater to that.' Sarne's breakthrough came when she discovered a machine-washable viscose produced by a north Italian mill; she used this to manufacture a range of dresses and separates that were versatile, easy to wear and attractive. Ghost underwent rapid development during the eighties. 'I first showed at the Olympia exhibition in September 1984. All the Americans were here then and it was absolutely a boomtown – they all stayed in places like Claridges or the Ritz. I had three pretty models on my stand and it was the first time anyone had seen this fabric, this crepe. I remember Mark Keller who had a shop in Detroit, he stood on my stand shouting "It's money in the bank, folks." I got so many orders I had to get some girls from the local market in Portobello to help me. We stayed up all night sewing hems. There wasn't so much competition then, you could bring out something novel and it would work.'

In fact, 1984 appears to have been a particularly good year for the launch of new fashion businesses, since it also saw the debut of, among others, Rifat Ozbek and Workers for Freedom, labels that would pick up Designer of the Year Awards in 1988 and 1989 respectively. Turkish-born Ozbek had worked with Walter Albini at the start of his career, but he chose to settle in England, where he was employed as in-house designer by Monsoon, before establishing his own company, with backing of £40,000 from a Pakistani businessman. He based himself in London, he says, 'because I wanted to live here. I'd studied here, I spoke English, I thought it was a very liberal place, you could express yourself. I never thought of the downside; they never occurred to me, the practicalities. I just thought it would be great to start building up my own business.' In this enterprise, Ozbek and others were helped by the feeling of confidence then permeating every area of the British fashion industry.

One area that certainly experienced improvement in its circumstances during this period was London's exhibition scene. The fragmentation of operations among different commercial companies in the mass-market sector had become untenable and was actively damaging London's chances of competing in the international arena. In addition, an ever-expanding number of companies run by fashion designers needed a showcase for their work. A solution now emerged that allowed for the creation of one exhibition area for the entire designer industry in Britain. By the autumn of 1983 Philbeach Events had come to realize that the London Fashion Exhibition, its twice-yearly trade show at Olympia, which for the past few years had provided space to groups like the Individual Clothes Show, had run out of steam and would have to be overhauled. Joanne Davis, who ran the LFE for Philbeach, explains, 'There were simply not enough solid exhibitors in the mid-market price range, or high fashion companies or the young designers who were running tiny starter companies, either to create the critical mass needed to guarantee a sufficient and valid buyer base per show, or to use it as a base to build on for future shows, let alone to make a commercial business for Philbeach Events.' While the more mass-market end of the business was to be accommodated at an event called the London Prêt, a new format was needed for the design-led sector and so, says Davis, 'I proposed the strategy of combining the various designer groups and letting them retain their individual brands, adding as many young high-fashion companies and better-end companies, physically getting as many catwalk shows as possible into various rooms at Olympia, re-branding it as the British Designer Show, to take place March and October, slotted between the Italian and French showing dates.'

Coincidentally, for the first time ever, the London Designer Collections found itself without a place in which

In contrast to the hard-edged power-dressing that dominated much of the fashion mainstream in the 1980s, Ghost clothes tended to be soft and relaxed, a sequence of loose flowing separates that could be combined in any number of ways.

'It's a unique product and very feminine,' said Tanya Sarne of her work. Ghost was not tied to any one season. The pieces left and below, for example, date from the label's spring/summer 1993 collection.

to show members' collections. 'The LDC did not have a hotel venue at all for March 1984,' Worsley-Taylor confirms, 'as the French had changed their dates without consultation very late and there was no hotel available.' Joanne Davis now proposed that the group take space in her new event at Olympia and, after it was agreed that the LDC's standards of design and presentation should apply across the entire venue, this is what happened. The first British Designer Show in association with the London Designer Collections took place in mid-March 1984. In addition to the LDC, it featured members of other organizations such as Amalgamated Talent, the Clothes Show Collections, Design Studio, The Exhibitionists and the Individual Clothes Show, as well as many designers who were showing independently. Each group was allotted a specific area within the overall space at Olympia so it could maintain a separate identity: the LDC, for example, took the ground floor at minimal cost and featured some thirty-one designers within its own section, among them Caroline Charles, Edina Ronay, Hardy Amies, Jacques Azagury, Jasper Conran, Jean Muir, Paul Costello, Roland Klein and Wendy Dagworthy.

The outcome was an event far better organized than any of its antecedents and with the further advantage of bringing the best of the country's fashion together in one place, a relief for buyers and journalists who had hitherto been required to crisscross the city if they wanted to see all the collections on offer. No wonder the *International Herald Tribune*'s Hebe Dorsay should write in March 1986 of how the British Designer Show, 'with three hundred exhibitors including the highly polished London Designer Collections, was where the action was. The members of the London Designer Collections alone accounted for £25 million worth of business last season.'

While Davis looked after the main part of the exhibition, the London Designer Collections not only retained independent status and took care of its own designer members, it was also responsible for the visual presentation of the entire space. Olympia hired Annette Worsley-Taylor as visual consultant for the shows, and the British Fashion Council paid her to organize parties and other social events during each London Fashion Week. These included a black tie dinner co-hosted with *Harpers & Queen* at Harvey Nichols in March 1984; a dinner the following year at the Ritz, to mark the tenth anniversary of the London Designer Collections; a supper at the Royal Opera House in October 1985 attended by Norman Lamont; and a dinner for seven hundred at the Reform Club in March 1987 (thrown in association with Harrods).

In addition, the LDC now undertook the challenging task of compiling London's runway show schedule each season. Just like the exhibition scene, until 1984 shows had been held in different venues across London, sometimes in the designer's own premises, more often in whatever place demanded the lowest rental fee. Again this had meant members of the press and retail buyers spent too much valuable time travelling about London, with a detrimental effect on both their tempers and the city's reputation. Circumstances changed in 1984 thanks to an intervention by leading public relations practitioner Lynne Franks.

Although as a fervent supporter of the Labour Party she may not have cared for the description, in many ways Franks embodied Mrs Thatcher's revitalized Britain. The daughter of a north London butcher, she had left school at sixteen and worked as a typist. After a spell with *Petticoat* magazine, at the age of twenty-one she started her own public relations company from her kitchen table; Katharine Hamnett and Wendy Dagworthy were among her earliest clients. She was renowned for her personal idiosyncrasies. During Fashion Week she and her team would regularly start the day with chanting (she was a practising Buddhist). Fashion PR Rosalind Woolfson remembers that on one occasion designer Murray Arbeid complained to her about the strange noises coming from behind his stand – 'which turned out to be Lynne and her staff chanting.' She also had a commitment to wearing clothes by her designer clients whether or not they suited her: 'The puffball skirt came out and I looked terrible.' While some of these foibles would be parodied by Jennifer Saunders for the television comedy *Absolutely Fabulous* (which ironically was first screened in 1992, the year Franks sold her business), there can be no doubt that in the 1980s Lynne Franks was better than anyone else at attracting publicity for her

'You wear them, they don't wear you,' said Wendy Dagworthy (below) of the clothes she designed for her own label, established in 1972. From the start, there was strong demand for Dagworthy's work, distinguished by its use of strong colours and prints and a preference for oversized shapes used for back-buttoning smocks, dirndl skirts, loose-fitting cardigans and cropped jackets. In the early 1980s Dagworthy introduced a menswear collection that shared many of the same features. She closed her business in 1988 and is currently professor of fashion at the Royal College of Art. Right, striped separates from her spring/ summer 1987 collection.

list of clients, which included many fashion designers and, from 1986 onwards, the British Fashion Council itself. 'I always think of the 1980s as colour,' she says, 'whereas the seventies were rather grey and down. Everything seemed to brighten up and everyone had a lot of fun. What made London just explode then was the creativity and the friendship. Most of the designers at the time were also my friends. There was a really loving core of people and that's why we managed to get things happening.'

One of the things Franks managed to get happening was the establishment of a satisfactory runway show venue available to all designers. In 1984, having recognized London's disadvantage in this respect, she took it on herself to discover a suitable location: 'I drove all around to see if I could find a place we could put up a tent.' Having identified the lawn in front of the Commonwealth Institute on Kensington High Street as an ideal site, Franks next had to find the money to pay

A style icon for almost a quarter century until her early death in 1992, Tina Chow was renowned for her discerning eye; she recognized the merits not only of contemporary fashion but also of vintage, at a time when the latter was little appreciated. Following her marriage to fashionable restaurateur Michael Chow in 1972 she spent increasing amounts of time in London. From 1986, this picture by Michael Roberts shows Chow (standing) wearing a jacket by Rifat Ozbek. On her right are shoe designer Manolo Blahnik and designer Ninivah Khomo; in front is actor Rupert Everett.

for the cost of erecting a tent there. This was provided by the Indian-born clothing entrepreneur Mohan Murjani, whose manufacturing business was based in Hong Kong. In the early 1980s, Murjani had achieved phenomenal success with the production of Gloria Vanderbilt jeans, which at the height of their popularity had annual sales of $150 million. The manufacturer was one of Franks' clients and, she says, 'I persuaded him that it would be good PR to put up a tent with his name on it. I was convinced that from a corporate perspective it would be good branding.' A tent called Murjani Fashion Focus was erected in front of the Commonwealth Institute in March 1984 and provided a venue for designers to stage their runway shows.

The Murjani Fashion Focus lasted for three season but then, Franks explains, 'The lawn in front of the Commonwealth Institute started sinking, so we had to look for another space.' This was found at the Duke of York's Headquarters on the King's Road. Thanks to sponsorship from Harrods and Swatch watches, the new venue 'was much bigger and more sophisticated. There were two big tents with room between them for restaurants, etc.' Although more than adequate from the point of view of providing designers with a purpose-built site in which to stage their shows, the trouble with this new arrangement was that it was too far away from the exhibition at Olympia (where some shows were also held in the Pillar Hall and Apex Room); once more members of the press and buyers were having to travel back and forth between the two locations. Writing in the *Guardian* in March 1987, Brenda Polan noted that the allure of the King's Road meant, 'Attendance at Olympia slumped as the visitors succumbed to the charms of the boutiques, antique markets and restaurants in the area. And sales slumped too.' Clearly this was to nobody's advantage (most of the designers who held runway shows at the Duke of York's also took sales stands at Olympia) and accordingly, in October 1986, despite some dissenting voices about showing in a trade fair, the tents were moved to Olympia where, at last, everything was in the one location. In March 1987 Suzy Menkes was able to tell readers of *The Times*, 'British fashion is under one umbrella – and not just in terms of the new line in skirts.'

Lynne Franks, seen here with Jasper Conran and Bruce Oldfield at Fashion Aid, November 1985.

Some of those individual designers also benefited from financial backing provided by a Danish businessman called Peder Bertelsen. One of the most curious characters ever to become involved in British fashion, for many years Bertelsen had been an oil trader, at first in south-east Asia and afterwards in the Middle East. In 1981 he bought a ranch in Colorado which American designer Ralph Lauren later wished to buy. As a sweetener for this arrangement, Bertelsen was offered a stake in Lauren's existing London shop on New Bond Street and the right to open Polo shops throughout Europe. Although the association with Lauren was not a success and only lasted a year, it taught the Danish oilman that designers liked to have their own stores rather than space within a larger retail operation. During the mid-1980s Bertelsen gradually built up a portfolio of fashion outlets in central London. By January 1987 – when the *Evening Standard* named him London's 'most powerful fashion entrepreneur' – his company, called Aguecheek Ltd (after Sir Andrew Aguecheek in Shakespeare's *Twelfth Night*), was running shops for Armani, Ungaro, Valentino, Krizia, Walter Steiger, Luciano Soprani and Comme des Garcons Homme Plus. In addition to the 'name' premises, Aguecheek operated Gallery 28, which sold new designers, co-owned the London branch of Tiffany's and had a discount outlet. For a man who insisted in 1988 that 'When I came into fashion three years ago I knew nothing, nothing at all,' Bertelsen was a remarkably fast learner, as well as someone who both fuelled and profited from the period's retail boom. He was among the first businessmen in Britain to appreciate what was already understood elsewhere: that, provided it received the right promotion and marketing, designer fashion had the potential to generate large sums of money for its backer.

Having established links with a network of key overseas designers, Bertelsen's next step was to develop British labels, beginning with Katharine Hamnett; in 1986 she terminated her retail association with Joseph to move into a Bertelsen-financed flagship store, a former garage redesigned by Norman Foster on the Brompton Road. That same year, Bertelsen agreed to underwrite

Central St Martins College of Art and Design (formerly St Martins School of Art) can claim credit for producing many of Britain's most successful designers over the past four decades. This group photograph features high-profile graduates from the 1970s and 1980s, including Joe Casely-Hayford, Andrea Sargeant, Bruce Oldfield, Ninivah Khomo and Alistair Blair (back row) and John Flett, Nick Coleman, John Galliano and Rifat Ozbek (front row).

Although Alistair Blair had graduated from St Martins in 1978, it wasn't until 1986 that he presented a collection under his own name in London; during the intervening period he worked for a number of couture houses in Paris. Backed by Danish entrepreneur Peder Bertelsen, Blair's British debut caused a huge stir and his clothes soon had an international following, with orders from the likes of Saks Fifth Avenue in New York and Seibu in Tokyo even before Sarah Ferguson, future Duchess of York, ordered her engagement outfit from him. Here he is seen with models wearing his autumn/winter 1988 collection.

a designer, Scots-born Alistair Blair, who, after graduating from St Martins School of Art in 1978, had moved straight to Paris and a job with Dior. After Dior, Blair spent time at Givenchy followed by four years at Chloe working with Karl Lagerfeld. He was then invited to London by Hartnell, which, following the death of its founder in 1979, was trying to rejuvenate the couture house's image. While in England, Blair went to see Peder Bertelsen to ask for advice about the Hartnell proposal and found himself instead being offered the opportunity to start his own business. 'To be given my own label at that time: I'd have been stupid to turn it down. It was a once-in-a-lifetime opportunity. Bertelsen was incredibly generous and it was a wonderful time for me.' Then aged thirty, Blair presented his first collection in March 1986 amid much excitement ('Blair has arrived as quite simply the most stylish designer in London,' declared *Fashion Weekly*) although in *The Times* Suzy Menkes remarked that the designer 'showed all the restraint Karl never had, and none of the master's wit.' Still, she conceded, 'the result was covetable clothes in fitted yet fluid shapes and luxurious fabrics.' The sophisticated maturity of Blair's designs, derived from his couture training in Paris, provided a refreshing antidote to the fun but frequently unwearable clothing produced by younger London-based labels. And the man himself seemed to possess a better business outlook than the majority of his peers, telling the *Dallas Morning News* in December 1987, 'Anyone in their right mind knows that most of the designers do not make their money from their most expensive garments. It's from licences, and that's what I want to break into.' When Sarah Ferguson wore an Alistair Blair outfit for the announcement of her engagement to the Duke of York, the Scottish designer seemed destined for a brilliant future in London.

It was thanks to Blair that Peder Bertelsen went on to back another British designer, albeit one of quite different sensibility: John Galliano. A fellow-graduate of St Martins, Galliano had profited from the publicity he received after his amazing 1983 graduation show, when Joan Burstein had purchased his entire final year collection – called Les Incroyables – and displayed it in the windows of Browns in 1983. Working from a run-down studio in North London and backed by young entrepreneur Johan Brun, Galliano went on to produce a number of other collections which were critically well received but insufficiently commercial to make his new business sustainable, especially after Brun's backing came to an end. As the designer told Colin McDowell in 1997, 'Transferring money and getting it in on time was a problem. I only had a small account at Barclays Bank in Peckham. I was tired of sweating over stinking dye buckets and envying BodyMap their glamour.' It was at this point that Alistair Blair proposed Galliano should meet with Bertelsen and following negotiations, it was agreed that Aguecheek Ltd would underwrite a second designer. The benefits were soon felt by both parties. In September 1987 Kathryn Samuel reported in the *Daily Telegraph*, 'Today, with a third collection under the Aguecheek umbrella, Galliano announces that his turnover is now the largest of Bertelsen's home-grown designers. His clothes sell throughout Europe, Japan and North America and the big-time accolades roll in.'

The accolades rolled in from an increasingly broad demographic: one of the phenomena of the 1980s was the democratization of fashion. A subject that had previously been of interest only to a relatively small, affluent and female section of society now began to have much broader appeal. 'Suddenly London Fashion Week has taken off,' announced *Sunday Times* columnist Stephen Pile in March 1986. 'This is incredible, frankly, because three years ago nobody had ever heard of it. Paris, yes. Milan, of course. London, when? … But what has happened in the past three years is that suddenly people here have twigged that this is a vital part of the national economy.' Actually this trend was by no means exclusive to Britain. 'What's happened', Fred Hughes, president of the Andy Warhol Trust, told Nicholas Coleridge in 1988, 'is that the entire western world – the entire world – is clothes conscious. People are living longer and staying fashion conscious; it's just going to go on and on, getting bigger and bigger and richer and richer.'

Fashion's growing appeal can be measured by the amount of media coverage it received in the 1980s compared to previous decades. New magazines with strong fashion content made their debut: British *Elle* in 1985; British *Marie Claire* three years later. In keeping with the spirit of the times, their message

A page from John Galliano's St Martins graduation sketchbook in 1984; it shows the intense interest in historical research which has characterized his work ever since. Very much reflecting the ethos of the era's New Romantic movement, he was inspired by France's post-revolutionary Directoire period at the close of the eighteenth century, when a group of fashion-conscious men and women – known as 'Les Incroyables' and 'Les Merveilleuses' – dressed in luxurious fabrics and exaggerated styles.

While he was a student at St Martins, John Galliano earned money working as a dresser at London's National Theatre. The drama he saw there has since been reflected in his own shows, beginning with the first he ever staged: his 1984 graduation show, 'Les Incroyables', scenes from which are shown here. Although lasting a mere fifteen minutes, it attracted enormous attention and the entire collection was bought by Joan Burstein of directional store Browns on South Molton Street, where all the clothes were displayed in the windows.

was powerfully consumerist: you are what you wear, and what you wear must constantly change. Existing publications toed the same line. 'Dress designers became household names in the 1980s,' wrote Colin McDowell in *The Designer Scam*, 'because newspapers expanded and, looking for some way to fill their extra pages or hoping to hook into advertising revenue, realized that fashion was a comparatively cheap and easy way to do both. So fashion became news-worthy – or, at least, exploitable.' It could never have become so, of course, had there not been an audience for fashion, an audience with a seemingly insatiable appetite for information on the subject. So, as McDowell noted, whereas coverage of clothes in the print media had until then primarily been confined to key moments in the annual cycle of couture and ready-to-wear collections, 'The 1980s were different because there was no closed season for fashion. It was treated as news seven days a week, all year round: the latest boyfriend of a top model, the new hairstyle of a glamour princess, the island home of a designer, even the flower arrangement preferences of a make-up artist.'

Fashion reached a wider audience thanks to its advent on another medium: television. Jeff Banks played a key role in this development. In addition to his entrepreneurial skills, Banks was a natural communicator, able to convey his enthusiasm for fashion without appearing in any way threatening or elitist; even when discussing dresses he came across as a regular bloke. By the early 1980s he already had a weekly slot on the popular BBC Television chat show *Pebble Mill at One* and when his friend Michael Grade became Controller of BBC One in 1984 Banks sent him a pilot tape for a proposed fashion television programme. This was initially rejected as being 'not of any interest' but two years later, in October 1986, *The Clothes Show* made its debut. 'To be honest,' says Banks, 'the BBC had started doing daytime television and was looking for programmes to fill its afternoon slots.' The first eleven shows, screened once a week, did go out in the afternoon but they attracted enough viewers (more than three million from the second programme onwards) for *The Clothes Show* to be moved to an evening slot where, at its peak, it could claim an audience of more than ten million.

Fashion on television is now so ubiquitous that the novelty of *The Clothes Show* is difficult to imagine. Rosalind Woolfson tells how, 'In the early days, I remember ringing BBC TV News Forward Planning to try and get them to shows, only to be told very patronizingly by the gentleman to whom I spoke that I should realize that in television they used moving pictures! That was pre-*Clothes Show* days.' Featuring reports from runway shows, interviews with designers, exploration of every aspect of the industry and information on how to achieve the current season's look without spending too much money, *The Clothes Show* was initially not welcomed in all quarters. *Fashion Weekly* reported in October 1986, 'Designers have questioned Banks' impartiality as both an active high street retailer/manufacturer and television commentator

Right 'Hats for me are an expression of the spirit,' milliner Stephen Jones has declared. 'They can parallel the whole range of human emotions and may exaggerate them to dramatic effect.' When Jones graduated from St Martins in 1979, hats had entirely fallen out of favour and were rarely worn. His links with the music and club scene of the early 1980s meant examples of Jones's work soon came to public attention and since then he has enjoyed an internationally successful career, designing witty couture pieces for John Galliano and Jean Paul Gaultier as well as his own collections.

Below One of the outstanding fashion commentators of her generation, Kathryn Samuel was deputy fashion editor of the *Daily Mail* before moving to the *Evening Standard*. The author of a number of books on fashion and style, she eventually served as the influential fashion editor of the *Daily Telegraph* from 1985 to 1995. Her career therefore spanned the period during which London's fashion designers moved from periphery to centre stage.

'The English design team Crolla has set its sights on changing the world with its clothing,' *Women's Wear Daily* informed readers in September 1985, going on to quote Scott Crolla, one of the duo behind the label, who explained that after the business had been established at the beginning of the decade, 'The old school people, the stockbrokers and the young royals were the first to find us. We sold to men who had the arrogance and confidence not to give a damn about what people thought.' Not long afterwards the team split up, Crolla going on to work with Callaghan in Milan and his former partner, Georgina Godley, creating her own label. This outfit is from their spring/summer 1984 collection.

on the catwalk shows. Both Katharine Hamnett and Jasper Conran did not want Banks at their shows, and there are fears that in-depth televised presentation of the catwalk shows will make designers' collections even more vulnerable to mass market imitation.' Those fears quickly vanished and it wasn't long before Banks and his co-presenter Selina Scott (and later former co-editor of *i-D* magazine Caryn Franklin) were eagerly welcomed by designers at home and abroad. While the weekly *Style with Elsa Klensch* show had made its debut on CNN in 1980, there was nothing like *The Clothes Show* in Europe. 'Certainly when we started, we were the only television crew on the planet covering fashion,' says Banks. 'The Italians and the French: they didn't have a national programme like *The Clothes Show*. For the first two or three years we were the only kids on the block.' The global standing of the BBC helped to gain access for Banks and his crew. 'Yes, there was the BBC's reputation, and our own production standards. The other thing we had was authority: people knew that the treatment they'd get from us wouldn't be flippant and that we knew our subject.'

The Clothes Show and its spin-offs – from 1989 onwards the annual Clothes Show Live at Birmingham's National Exhibition Centre and later a magazine to accompany the television programme – certainly helped to broaden the market for fashion in Britain and, Banks argues with some justification, also encouraged the print media to give more space to the subject: 'It was only when newspaper editors saw something on television that they started to take it seriously.' Other people involved in the industry also saw the advantages of engaging with as wide an audience as possible. 'We wanted to make fashion names household names,' says Lynne Franks. 'We worked very hard with the television companies to get coverage.'

But *The Clothes Show* was by no means the only method employed to raise the profile of the domestic fashion industry. Just as important was the instigation of an annual British Fashion Awards ceremony, organized by the British Fashion Council, with the first held in 1984. The awards concept originated with Lynne Franks, who was heavily involved in the 1984 show, held at the Grosvenor House Hotel. On that inaugural occasion Katharine Hamnett was the winner of the principal award: British Designer of the Year. Did it make a difference to her career? 'It's hard to tell,' she says. 'I was on a massive roll at the time, with licensing deals in Japan and business booming. But it was certainly a lovely moment; my father had died and I'd decided to make 1984 my year for him.' The rollcall of those who came after her includes Betty Jackson, Jasper Conran, John Galliano and Rifat Ozbek. The last of these remembers how receiving the award 'gave me a sense of courage to carry on. It's a good feeling to be appreciated; it eliminates your self-doubts and is a positive affirmation.' As for the Award's benefit to his business, he agrees, 'It makes your name more known to the customers and makes them more willing to buy your clothes.'

The advantages of public exposure increased in October 1989 when the British Fashion Awards, held in the Royal Albert Hall in front of three thousand guests, were shown on television for the first time and featured the Princess of Wales presenting Workers for Freedom with the Designer of the Year Award. Referring to previous ceremonies, *Vogue* editor Liz Tilberis observed, 'They were rather chic little cocktail parties in the presence of either Mrs Thatcher or the Princess of Wales. And while they were very good, they didn't show the merchandise.' That the British Fashion Awards should be deemed worthy of television broadcast indicates how far fashion had advanced into mainstream culture during the course of the decade.

Another event assisting that process was the charity show Fashion Aid, staged in the Royal Albert Hall in November 1985. Like the multi-venue rock music concert Live Aid, held the previous July and organized by Bob Geldof and Midge Ure, Fashion Aid's purpose was to raise funds for famine relief in Ethiopia. It was the first time members of the fashion industry had come together for such a cause. Fashion Aid's organizing committee included Jasper Conran and Lynne Franks, alongside Geldof, music promoter Harvey Goldsmith, Valerie Blondeau from the Band Aid Trust and Sue Godley, whose husband, Kevin (otherwise one half of Godley and Creme), was to film the show. Eighteen designers featured, half of them British, half from elsewhere. 'All of us thought it should be a global event,' Franks explains. 'We felt it would be more glamorous that way, and would be taken more seriously.' Among the British names featuring in the show were Conran, BodyMap, Wendy Dagworthy, Katharine Hamnett, Bruce Oldfield, Rifat Ozbek,

Jean Muir, Scott Crolla, Zandra Rhodes, Anthony Price and the Emanuels, while overseas designers included Giorgio Armani, Calvin Klein, Yves Saint Laurent and Issey Miyake.

The logistics of the night were frightening (Katharine Hamnett had a band of tribal drummers and the Emanuels a cast of 250, including a 100-strong choir), especially since all participants provided their services for free. 'Everyone was really competitive,' remembers Stevie Stewart of BodyMap. 'It was a question of who'd have the most outlandish clothes. We had Boy George and Michael Clark and Julie Goodyear (otherwise known as Bet Lynch from television's *Coronation Street*). Helen Terry, singer with Culture Club, introduced our show down the catwalk and she'd about seven or eight backing singers who all performed with her.' Wham! sang for Armani, the Eurythmics for Hamnett, Madness for Jasper Conran and Spandau Ballet for Scott Crolla. Jerry Hall emerged from a giant cardboard box at the start of Anthony Price's section, and models dressed in Issey Miyake abseiled down from the roof of the Hall. In his autobiography, Bruce Oldfield recalled that the night 'was great fun because the designers had licence to go wild.' At the same time, they were raising funds for a serious cause. Even before the money from international film rights and merchandising was taken into account, the night generated in the region of £150,000 from ticket sales alone. Events like Fashion Aid could simply not have happened in an earlier era because designers were far less well known than they became in the 1980s. That British names like BodyMap and Hamnett could be shown to an international audience alongside Armani and Saint Laurent is evidence of how far the industry had travelled.

A TIME OF CRISIS

As stock markets opened around the world on Monday, 19 October 1987, each in turn started to go into a steep decline. Word quickly spread, and panic broke out among investors, who frantically tried to offload their holdings. Since the market did not have the liquidity to support such activity, prices plunged even further. At the end of 'Black Monday' the United States' Dow Jones Industrial Average had fallen by 22.6 per cent, the largest one-day drop in stock market history. The consequences were international: by the end of the month, the Hong Kong stock market had fallen by 45.8 per cent; Australia's by 41.8 per cent; Spain's by 31 per cent; and that in Great Britain by 26.4 per cent. A global recession started that would worsen during the early nineties and last almost until the middle of the decade, badly affecting in particular any country whose economy had close links to that of the United States. No sector was immune and the fashion industry was as badly hit as any. In the United States,

Born in Scotland, designer Pam Hogg came to public notice with her first collection, 'Psychedelic Jungle', in 1981. From the start she has moved between the worlds of fashion and music, performing with various bands while designing ranges of clothing, the clothes – like these pieces from her autumn/winter 1982 collection – often distinguished by a blend of club and punk. Although she gave up running her own label in the early 1990s, Hogg has never abandoned fashion, designing for performers including Kylie Minogue and Siouxie Sioux. In October 2008, Browns was the first store to carry her new Hogg-Couture collection.

for example, clothing sales had three successive years of falling figures, with a 4.4 per cent drop in 1993 compared to the previous year, the sharpest such decline since 1952. The situation was similar elsewhere. In 1992 Germany's leading fashion house, Escada, lost US$70 million, while Italy's Gruppo GFT, until then the world's leading producer of designer wear, had losses exceeding $60 million, forcing its owners, the Rivetti family, to make a deal the following year in which they sold control of the company.

Inevitably the British fashion industry, which for years had focused on developing the American market, suffered. Many London-based companies found themselves in serious trouble. In retrospect, some of those hardest hit wondered whether it had been a good idea to devote so much attention to a market that turned out to be fickle. When the going got tough, buyers for American stores understandably preferred to support their own fashion industry. 'The American market's totally protectionist,' says designer Caroline Charles. 'It's always been fantastically against imports. Tell me one British designer who's made a serious impact on America; we're just the icing on the cake.' Her sentiments are echoed by many other designers. 'The American dream doesn't exist,' contends Bruce Oldfield, whose career began with a season working in New York for the Henri Bendel department store and who consequently knows first-hand how capricious the US market can be. 'We were just window dressing, we never, ever did much business in America because of the currency differential, because of protectionism and because Americans buy American.' Similarly Jasper Conran, who trained in New York, recalls, 'We were always told to break into the United States but we were a novelty act there. That really dawned on me in 1987; having built up these American businesses, suddenly there's Black Monday and I think nearly every one of my American accounts took Chapter 11. I got nothing but responsibilities and debts.'

Accustomed to a more laissez-faire approach at home, the ruthlessness of American retail took British designers by surprise. In 1986 Betty Jackson travelled across the United States meeting store owners and presenting her collection to their customers in what are known as trunk shows. 'By the time I got to San Francisco, the clothes I'd shown three weeks earlier in New York had already been marked down there … I don't think Americans have any loyalty in this respect. They'll cut back without any wavering.' She also remembers visiting one department store where her clothes were sold: 'I was in the buying office and there was a dress hanging up with a copy of one of my prints. That happened all the time, although it wouldn't now because of

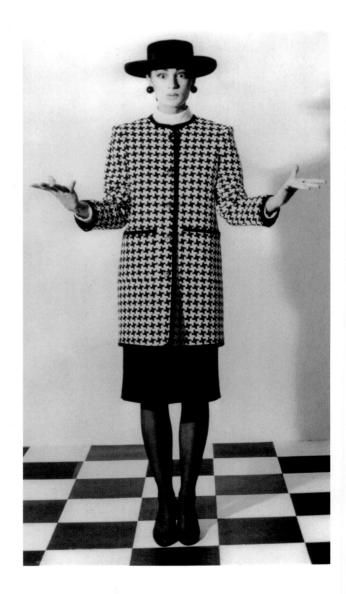

An outfit from Caroline Charles's autumn/winter 1986 collection. Thanks to the classically wearable character of her clothes – as well her sound business sense – Charles has remained at the forefront of British fashion for more than four decades.

'From 1983,' Wendy Dagworthy recalled in the *Independent* in 2006, 'the Americans became fascinated by Britain in a big way.' She recalled how, 'Saks Fifth Avenue flew us over just to do a promotion in their store. It was a huge party all the time.' Betty Jackson told the *Sunday Times* that in 1986 she was exporting some 40 per cent of everything she produced to the United States. But when a global recession began the following year, the American market forsook British designers, with unfortunate consequences for many of them.

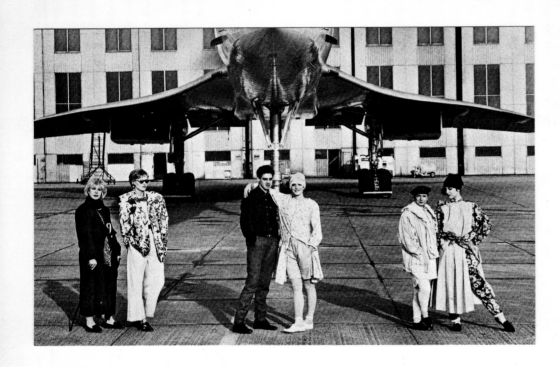

611 Fifth Avenue
New York, N.Y. 10022

FIRST CLASS
U.S. POSTAGE
PAID
Saks Fifth Avenue

Saks Fifth Avenue invites you to "A Changing of the Avant-Garde!" Join us for a British revolution of runaway fashions by London's design innovators Betty Jackson, Wendy Dagworthy, Reubeen Tariq! Thursday, April 4th at 5:30 pm on the Fifth Floor. Saks Fifth Avenue, New York. It's an evening that will rock your senses!

better copyright laws.' Jackson describes British designers of the time, including herself, as 'naive' in believing that they had some kind of special relationship with the American market. Securing payment for goods posed a major challenge to small British businesses with restricted credit facilities. In her 1996 autobiography, Helen Storey describes the problems she faced getting paid by an American chain of stores called The Limited, which had placed an order with her company eight years before: 'Pursuing an invoice from The Limited, you felt you were pestering a sleeping giant ... In the end, we lost £5,000 to the markets when the funds finally cleared.' And even an order that seemed large in terms of the British market could look insignificant when it crossed the Atlantic. 'You'd go to New York,' remembers fashion writer Liz Smith, 'and you'd see the British designers hanging in the shops, but there'd only be a few little bits. Nobody bought in depth or in quantity. They came here for the ideas but they didn't buy that much.'

In fact, American stores had an entirely pragmatic approach to their business, recognizing that the only way they could stay afloat during the bad years was by meeting the precise demands of local consumers. In matters of fashion, the American market has always been noted for its conservatism and this trait becomes even more apparent during times of recession. British designers who were in any way adventurous tended to find themselves quickly out of favour. Speaking of American store representatives, BodyMap's Stevie Stewart told Nicholas Coleridge in 1988, 'We find them more conservative than the European buyers, especially on colours. They'll only buy colours they think aren't too far out of line for that particular season.' As Robert Forrest observed around the same time, the great majority of Americans 'are deep down very conservative, they don't want to be that different from the next man. Kids in England as soon as they're eighteen they want to look different, until they're twenty-five when they settle down and become suburban again. In America it doesn't happen that way.'

The focus among British designers on the United States meant another potential overseas market was frequently ignored. In 1982 Paul Smith was invited by a fashion talent scout to visit Japan, with the possibility of entering into licence agreements with manufacturers. 'I went with my girlfriend, now my wife, Pauline,' he remembers. 'It was a sixteen-hour economy flight via Anchorage but I was really excited and humbled to be invited there. I thought if I only went once it would be enough.' Two years later, Smith entered into his first licensing arrangement with the Japanese. 'What was great about it was the fact that although the amount was quite small, a fee of about £15,000 per annum, it gave me a bit of stability; I knew the money was coming in and it was a safety net.' Over the next few years, Smith paid a lot of attention to developing his market in Japan, repeatedly returning to the country and working closely to develop a good relationship with his licensees; he still travels to Japan annually and keeps a permanent office in Tokyo. 'I was willing to take the trouble whereas a lot of other designers are so arrogant – they just take the royalty cheque.' (Taking the trouble has paid off: in 2008, between shops in department stores and free-standing premises there were 208 Paul Smith outlets in Japan, many more than he had in Great Britain and the United States combined, while annual retail sales of £230 million in Japan accounted for two-thirds of his worldwide business.)

The Japanese had long been avid consumers of traditional British brands such as Burberry and Aquascutum, the appeal of which was precisely their traditions and heritage. In this respect, Paul Smith – with his 'classic with a twist' style – fitted into an existing pattern; it was the familiar made new. For Betty Jackson Japan also provided a lifeline during an otherwise difficult period. She had a licensing agreement with Seibu, a Japanese chain that offered distribution of

Left Sir Paul Smith and his wife, Pauline, in 1997. Unlike many of his fellow British designers, Smith did not depend on the American market but instead from 1982 onwards focused on growing his business in Japan.

Below Betty Jackson has said that she admires strong women, 'bold and casual like Lauren Bacall', and her own strength of character was severely tested during the economic recession that struck down so many other British fashion companies at the end of the eighties. But, as she told *Vogue* in September 1991, 'I started in a recession, and now I'm in one again. I'm used to it.' Her resilience has ensured that she continues to be a force in the national industry to the present day.

international labels from the 1960s onwards, and 'When the dollar went, our market shifted to Japan and that carried us through the bad years.' Bruce Oldfield wasn't so lucky: he and his business partner flew to Tokyo to meet a potential licensee on Black Monday and the deal never went through.

But only a handful of designers established ties with Japan. The majority concentrated on the United States, with unfortunate results. 'America doesn't need the rest of the world,' remarks John Wilson of the British Clothing Industry Association. 'In the eighties they weren't long-term bedfellows for British fashion. And as soon as the currency shifted, they ditched you.' Currency differentials have bedevilled efforts to sell British clothing to the United States for a long time. During the first half of the 1980s the dollar had been a strong currency, peaking in early 1985 when it almost achieved parity with the pound. Thereafter its value steadily dropped to a point in September 1992 when the pound was worth two dollars. Obviously this had the effect of making British goods much more expensive and much less attractive to American consumers, especially when coupled with high import taxes imposed by the American government to encourage the sale of local goods. Sterling's strength also discouraged transatlantic travel, meaning fewer buyers and journalists could afford to come to London to see what designers there had to offer. In October 1988 the Paris shows, which usually followed immediately after those in London, were put back a week. In consequence, *Women's Wear Daily* reported, 'Many American buyers have delayed their visits [to London] until later in the week, or aren't coming at all.' The following March the same publication noted how, 'The poor retail climate in the US means London more than ever is an item market – for accessories, knitwear, strong evening looks and the occasional new design discovery. As a result there are fewer executives from the big stores.' American buyers might bypass London but they never missed Paris and so, as *Women's Wear Daily* also observed in March 1989, 'A number of British designers – including Betty Jackson, Workers for Freedom and Rifat Ozbek – are being forced to show in Paris as well.' It was the beginning of a trend that over the next few years would have unfortunate consequences for London's status as a global fashion capital.

If British goods were now expensive to export to the United States, a weak dollar made their American equivalent relatively cheap to import. In fact, between 1985 and 1990, American imports to Britain more than doubled in value, from $11 billion to $23.5 billion. Among the goods shipped across the Atlantic in ever-greater quantities was clothing; the late 1980s was an era that saw the international rise of American fashion.

While the United States had always had a strong clothing industry, until the

The British Fashion Council has called Betty Jackson a 'directional classicist'. This outfit from the late 1980s exemplifies her style – never extreme but always striking.

last quarter of the twentieth century it focused almost exclusively on the domestic market, which until then was regarded as big enough to satisfy the appetites of manufacturers and designers. But in addition Americans traditionally had felt somewhat inferior when it came to fashion, believing that Europe – and particularly Paris – was the centre of good design (American store buyers visited Paris every season to purchase couture clothing that could then be copied for their own customers). The Council of Fashion Designers of America had been established in 1962. A not-for-profit trade association, its brief was to promote the status of fashion design as a branch of American art and culture both within the United States and overseas. But the attitude of Americans towards their own designers only decisively changed after a fashion show held at the Château de Versailles on 28 November 1973. This joint Franco-American event, devised in large part by tireless New York fashion publicist Eleanor Lambert and staged to raise funds for the historic palace's restoration, featured five designers from each country. The host nation was represented by Hubert de Givenchy, Marc Bohan at Christian Dior, Yves Saint Laurent, Pierre Cardin and Emanuel Ungaro, while the visiting team featured Halston, Bill Blass, Anne Klein, Stephen Burrows and Oscar de la Renta. The former were expected to trounce the latter, but in fact the opposite happened. Whereas the Paris designers all showed couture, with its elitist and old-fashioned connotations, the Americans showed fresh, modern ready-to-wear. The French conceded defeat on the spot, the Duchess de la Rochefoucauld sadly admitting, 'The French were good, but the Americans were sensational. *C'était formidable.'*

By the time of the Versailles show, two of the industry's key players – Ralph Lauren and Calvin Klein – had started their own companies (both of them in 1968) and were on the way to global success. Right from the start these designers and others who followed, like Donna Karan and Tommy Hilfiger, viewed what they were doing as a commercial business (tellingly, Lauren studied not fashion but business management). Like their equivalents in Italy, they were able to call on generous financial support for their ventures; at the beginning of his solo career, Lauren received $50,000 from Manhattan clothing manufacturer Norman Hilton, while the young Calvin Klein's enterprise benefited from a $10,000 loan from his business partner, Barry Schwartz. Few British designers could hope to find that kind of funding at home. Again like the Italians, American fashion designers tended to gain experience with an established company before branching out on their own: Calvin Klein, for example, worked for various suit and coat manufacturers between 1964 and 1968, and Donna Karan spent a decade as head designer at Anne Klein prior to creating a label under her own name in 1984.

Naomi Campbell photographed in Rifat Ozbek in 1988, when he was declared British Designer of the Year. Born in Turkey, Ozbek first studied architecture before switching to fashion at St Martins. He is rightly much admired for his ability to mix different motifs and shapes drawn from an eclectic range of global cultures, not least those of his own country.

As for the American designers' clothes, while well made they were often not especially interesting or innovative; but that satisfied the conservative domestic market. And what Lauren, Klein et al also identified and encouraged was the growing trend towards a more casual dress code. Popular American designers at their best produced ranges of informal, comfortable and relatively inexpensive clothing that not only won approval from domestic consumers but also travelled well around the world.

Lauren and Klein were the first of their generation to export American fashion overseas; in the early 1980s, they both arrived in London and opened premises in partnership with Browns. Donna Karan would follow in 1986. Their casual style proved wildly popular, especially in the second half of the decade when the weakening dollar made American clothing less expensive. Transatlantic informality received a further boost in 1987 when the first Gap store opened in London. Twenty-one years later, Emma Soames recalled in the *Daily Telegraph* the excitement generated by the American chain: 'It was a "yes" moment,' she wrote. 'Retail *wünderkind* Mickey Drexler, the chief executive of Gap, had realized what we wanted: work shirts, basic tees and jeans that didn't go baggy round the bottom on the second wash; clothes that were slightly fashion conscious, entirely un-class conscious – and fabulously cheap.' (Gap, in other words, provided the British consumer with an American version of the high street. No wonder it was welcomed with open arms.)

Particularly during a period of economic recession, when consumers were less inclined to take risks, the plain no-nonsense fare offered by American designers was sure to do well at points of sale. Writing in the *New York Times* in March 1990, Anne-Marie Schiro quoted Bruce Binder, vice- president for fashion direction at Macy's Northeast, as remarking that one of London's principal department stores, Harvey Nichols, 'looks like an American store, the way they buy and the way they show American designers.' Harvey Nichols' director of fashion buying, Amanda Verdan, told Schiro,

'The Americans produce a sophisticated pared-down look that people seem to want at the moment. Calvin Klein's colour palette, his minimum tailoring and the washed silks – they don't stay in stock very long.'

British fashion, on the other hand, with its frequently quirky character, posed more of a challenge, especially in the international marketplace. Monica Kindler, an Italian buyer, told Chris Scott-Gray of *Fashion Weekly* in October 1990, 'English design is good, but it is not easy to sell. It is very fashion-based and only two of our customers understand the clothes. For example, English designers were offering high-waisted pants four years ago, but the rest were only doing so last season. The English are too early.' Nicholas Coleridge, managing director of Condé Nast in Britain and a former British Fashion Council chairman, remarks that 'The very successful designers in the world have tended to do rather conventional, conservative clothes – and I mean that in a good way – it's true of plenty of the Italians and all the Americans. It's not so much the case with the British.' As a rule, clothing of a conventional and conservative cut appeals to the broadest segment of the market, which is one of the reasons why, as the 1980s drew to a close, the Italian and American fashion industries, backed by well-funded marketing campaigns, grew in global popularity.

So too did French fashion, which only a decade earlier had seemed on the point of expiry. There were a number of reasons for this, one of which was the unexpected revival of interest in haute couture during the boom years of the early-to-mid 1980s; this was helped by heavy spending across the Middle East and among a group of high-profile and competitive American women who were eager to publicize their association with what had appeared to be an increasingly arcane art. In addition, the French fashion establishment had by now accepted that haute couture, while invaluable as a showcase for the country's unique creativity, was no longer enough: the significance of prêt-à-porter also had to be acknowledged. Didier Grumbach's Créateurs et Industriels of 1971 had been a private initiative, similar to that taken in Britain four years later with the establishment of the London Designer Collections. If the Chambre syndicale de la haute couture were not to become entirely irrelevant, it needed to take note of altered circumstances and change its own character. This it did in 1973 when, in order to recognize the important position of ready-to-wear clothing in the fashion world, the Chambre syndicale was reformulated as the Fédération française de la couture, du prêt-à-porter des couturiers et des créateurs de mode. Representing the interests of members (and in this respect, acting much like its predecessor), the new body assumed responsibility for setting the dates and location of Paris's fashion weeks, those of both couture and prêt-à-porter, and for establishing industry-wide standards of quality. It provided French ready-to-wear designers with the support of a central organization which would not only assist individual businesses but also promote their collective cause at home and abroad. Over the next few years, a new generation of Parisian ready-to-wear designers – among them Thierry Mugler (1973), Claude Montana (1977) and Jean-Paul Gaultier (1977) – established their own labels and this helped Paris to regain the interest of international buyers and journalists.

The restoration of Paris's reputation as a centre of innovation in fashion was further helped at the start of the 1980s by the arrival in the city of two Tokyo-based designers, Yohji Yamamoto and Rei Kawakubo of Comme des Garçons; Yamamoto would later explain that he had left Tokyo because it was 'dominated by the common sense of a boring bourgeoisie'. Their fellow countryman Kenzo Takada, customarily known as Kenzo, had moved to Paris in the mid-1960s and opened his first outlet there, called Jungle Jap, in 1970. Likewise Issey Miyake had been intermittently living and showing in Paris from 1965 onwards (as well as spending time in New York, where he worked with Geoffrey Beene for two years). But these two Japanese designers had adopted an essentially western sensibility and could be absorbed into the mainstream. The same could not be said for Yamamoto or Kawakubo: when their work was shown for the first time in Paris in 1981 it was uncompromisingly different from anything that had been seen before. The predominantly black palette, distressed fabrics and unfitted form of their collections led to the clothes being branded by critics as 'post-atomic' and 'Hiroshima chic'. 'Completely new cuts, totally different standards of workmanship, absolutely new shapes', wrote Colin McDowell in 1994, 'electrified the fashion world and petrified most other designers.' The initially negative response left the Japanese untroubled – Kawakubo has said that 'A fundamental element of my career was the fact of living it as a means of being exposed to the reaction of the public' – and before long their persistence paid off: layers of loose black clothing became the very epitome of chic, especially among fashion professionals. The Japanese New Wave would be one of the most notable features of 1980s fashion and since its leading figures had chosen to associate themselves with

A latter-day Charles James, Anthony Price has never received either the acclaim or the commercial success he merits. He has, however, always been greatly admired by fashion cognoscenti and his clothes have been worn by many musicians, including the Rolling Stones and Roxy Music. He also created dresses to accompany milliner Philip Treacy's shows. In 1983 he sold tickets to a 'Fashion Spectacular' at London's Camden Palace and two years later he announced, 'I'm not a fashion designer . . . I'm in the theatrical business.' Modelled by Yasmin Le Bon, this dress dates from 1989.

Paris (and were perforce members of the Fédération), they added lustre to the city's reputation.

So too in the later 1980s did the arrival of a generation of Belgian designers, all of them graduates of Antwerp's Fine Art Academy. The first to appear in Paris was Martin Margiela, who for three years from 1984 worked as design assistant to Gaultier. He was followed in the late 1980s by a group of six avant-garde young designers from Antwerp, including Dries Van Noten, Ann Demeulemeester and Walter Van Beirendonck. This group arrived in London in March 1987 and showed their work collectively at the Olympia exhibition both that season and the one following. In March 1988 the Belgian Six applied to the British Fashion Council to stage a runway show as part of London Fashion Week's official calendar – and were refused. They went ahead anyway and held their event at an off-site venue; it was a success and attracted many buyers but, disappointed by the response they had received from London Fashion Week, the Belgians decamped to Paris, where they were given a warmer welcome and where they have chosen to show ever since. A member of the adjudicating panel that turned down the Belgian request for a runway show, Annette Worsley-Taylor admits that in retrospect the decision was ill-advised: 'I felt strongly, but wrongly, at the time that this was a British event and I couldn't see the international picture.' London's loss would be Paris's gain.

Indeed, as the 1980s progressed, the French capital's fashion reputation once more grew in prestige. In 1983 Karl Lagerfeld, who for almost twenty years had been working as a freelance designer for a number of labels including Chloe, Krizia and Fendi, was appointed design director of Chanel, which had been languishing ever since the death of its founder in 1971. Lagerfeld skilfully managed to update the brand without changing its distinctive character, and made Chanel once more an internationally renowned, and extremely profitable, fashion house. It is worth comparing the French label's history with that of the nearest English equivalent: Hartnell. Even before Norman Hartnell's death in 1979, this too had entered a period of decline. However in the mid-1980s a group of investors led by entrepreneur Jim Cassidy sought to restore the house's reputation by bringing in new blood. Their fundamental mistake was to divide responsibility for the Hartnell collection between three men – Victor Edelstein, Sheridan Barnett and Allan McRae – all fine designers but with quite different stylistic sensibilities. This suggested a want of confidence on the part of manage-ment, and the outcome was predictable. In *The Times* in March 1986 Suzy Menkes was unenthusiastic about the trio's first presentation: 'I do not see the point of refurbishing Hartnell's faded grandeur, without taking his own work as a frame of reference. Karl Lagerfeld has revitalized Chanel by steeping himself in Mademoiselle's own work and moving on from there. Of the three at Hartnell, two sank to the occasion. Only Edelstein might be able to produce something worthy of the master's memory.' It was not to be. In June 1987 the *Daily Telegraph* reported that the house of Hartnell had been declared insolvent after clothes ordered by stores had 'failed to be made or delivered on time. Bad management was blamed.' It limped on for another few years under the chairmanship of Manny Silverman. Marc Bohan, formerly of Dior, was brought in as head designer in June 1990. But not even his extensive experience was enough to save the business, and Hartnell closed for good in the autumn of 1992.

While the attempt to revive England's best-known couture name failed, what Karl Lagerfeld had achieved at Chanel would be much emulated by other labels in France and elsewhere. In 1985 a businessman called Bernard Arnault acquired the bankrupt French textile company Boussac which had backed Christian Dior in the 1940s and still owned the label, along with a number of other assets including Paris's oldest department store, Le Bon Marché. He also underwrote Christian Lacroix when the designer opened his own couture house in 1987. Like Peder Bertelsen in England, Arnault had no previous experience in fashion; after graduation from the École polytechnique he helped to manage his family's construction business before emigrating in 1981 to the United States where he worked in property development. Nevertheless he was acutely attuned to the fashion world's sensibility and also in possession of a sound commercial instinct. Thanks to this he foresaw the worldwide growth in demand for designer clothing and accessories that would become such a feature of the 1990s and beyond. His takeover of Boussac was only the beginning of the development of a fashion and luxury goods empire which, after its acquisition in 1989, was based around the publicly quoted company Louis Vuitton Moët Hennessy (LVMH) group. Through the course of his career, Arnault has shown himself to be tenacious, ruthless and prepared to wait for his investment to show a return. In a profile written for *Vogue* in October 1989, Sarah Mower described him as 'the Rupert Murdoch of French fashion, a Parisian Donald Trump, a wolf in cashmere clothing', before going on to quote Suzy Menkes explaining, 'We're in a different world now. If Arnault seems brutal, it's because he's facing up to reality – and because he's brought business realities out in the open, he's taken a lot of stick.' In 1989 those business realities included removing Marc Bohan as head designer at Dior and replacing him with the Italian Gianfranco Ferré (who would, in turn, be supplanted at Arnault's instigation by British designer John Galliano eight years later). Since acquiring control of LVMH, Bernard Arnault has built the business into one of

The author of a frank and perceptive memoir about working in British fashion, designer Helen Storey spent several years in Italy before returning in 1984 to London, where she joined forces with Amalgamated Talent, the agency run by Caroline Coates. 'One of the reasons that I am here and a lot of my contemporaries aren't,' she said by way of explanation for her success, 'is because I sit on the knife edge between good and bad taste, fashion and theatre, business and imagination.' Those qualities are evident in this gold corset and striped skirt/trousers dating from spring/summer 1992.

the world's leading fashion companies: in addition to Louis Vuitton and Dior, it owns many other labels including Kenzo, Céline, Givenchy and Loewe. By 2005 the company had assets worth 14.3 billion euro and Bernard Arnault was the richest man in France. His only rival in this area emerged in the late 1990s when a company called Pinault-Printemps-Redoute run by François Pinault, a billionaire who made his initial fortune from a business specializing in the import and distribution of timber, outmanoeuvred LVMH for control of the Gucci Group, which also owned Yves Saint Laurent. PPR has since gone on to acquire several other high-profile fashion brands including Balenciaga, Bottega Veneta and Sergio Rossi shoes, as well as underwriting the start-up of new labels for two British designers, Alexander McQueen and Stella McCartney.

One of the strengths of men like Pinault and Arnault is that they have been able to identify and promote the marketing power of a fashion brand name while at the same time preserving its aura of exclusivity. This was also a talent demonstrated by a number of Italian fashion houses in the 1980s, notably Armani but also Versace and Dolce & Gabbana. The populist nature of American fashion meant designers based in the United States were less likely to emphasize exclusivity (although Ralph Lauren has successfully done so with his more expensive lines), but they also spent much time and money in the 1980s developing a strong brand identity, not least because this allowed them to produce goods other than clothing that carried their name and reached the broadest possible consumer audience right around the world. One way to achieve maximum market penetration has been to enter into licensing agreements whereby a designer hands over responsibility for the manufacture of products to a third party in return for a share of the profits, typically 4 per cent on sales of perfume, 8 per cent for ready-to-wear and 10 per cent for accessories. The generation of Milan designers who emerged in the 1970s made just such arrangements with Italian fabric and clothing manufacturers, to the advantage of both parties. Key French designers did likewise, and so too did their American equivalents. A survey of the global fashion industry published by *W* magazine in June 1993 noted, 'The profit margins of top designers are typically greater than those of apparel manufacturers, as they earn huge cheques from royalties without the costs of running factories.' During that year alone Pierre Cardin made US$70 million from his licensing agreements, the house of Dior $68 million, Armani $65 million and Yves Saint Laurent $62 million. The list of worldwide wholesale volume of all products bearing an individual designer's name was headed by Saint Laurent ($1.45 billion) and also included Dior ($1.13 billion), Chanel ($800 million) and Cardin ($750 million). British names are notably absent from these lists.

In 1987 Amanda Wakeley, who had been living in the United States, returned to London and with a partner started making clothes for private clients. Self-taught and inspired by a desire to create beautiful, wearable pieces, she achieved sufficient success to launch a label under her own name in 1990; since then she has won three British Fashion Awards for Glamour.

By the end of the 1980s, four cities had emerged as the world's principal fashion capitals, the same quartet that has dominated the international circuit ever since: Paris, Milan, New York and London. In terms of scale of operations, the last of these was also the smallest. This was a matter of growing concern, especially as 1992 approached; that year saw the advent of the Single European Market, allowing the free movement of goods, capital, services and people between member states of the European Union. From 1992 onwards there would be no tariff barriers to inhibit access of European clothing to the British market (and, of course, vice versa). The 1991/92 annual report of the British Clothing Industry Association gloomily predicted, 'Although completion of the Single European Market at the end of the year will bring few direct advantages to the UK apparel industry, it is bound to have a great psychological impact on companies, not least our Continental competitors, who will be seeking to increase their share of the UK market.' Strong marketing heavily bankrolled by manufacturers had already led to an increase in British consumer demand for French and Italian fashion (and also German: in September 1992 Norma Major, wife of the then Prime Minister John Major, caused something of an outcry when it emerged that instead of buying a local brand she had paid in the region of £550 for an Escada suit). As has been seen, during the same period American imports were also rising sharply. Overall, imports of clothing climbed from representing 38 per cent of sales in Britain in 1987 to 50 per cent in 1991. In October 1990, Sir Ralph Halpern, who had recently succeeded Sir Edward Rayne as Chairman of the British Fashion Council, told the *Daily Telegraph*, 'If you put all the turnover of the British fashion designers together, it wouldn't amount to one Calvin Klein or Ralph Lauren.' That same month and in the same newspaper, Hilary Alexander observed, 'The business some designers do in twelve months represents a third of what Italian fashion giants consider the start-up cost of launching a designer label.' She quoted David Cohen, husband and business partner of Betty Jackson, who remarked, 'Compared to the Italians, we are peanuts. . . .What Donna Karan has been able to do in New York, no one has been able to do in England. It needs big money, more back-up, better manufacturing.' Similarly Jean Muir pointed out, 'Our collections are scrutinized the same way as Valentino, Armani or Saint Laurent. We have to work six times as hard as any comparable designer.'

London remained the fashion world's undisputed capital of creativity, but the city had yet to turn this situation to its advantage. Licensing of the kind commonplace elsewhere, for instance, was almost unknown in Britain, with just a handful of designers entering into profitable partnerships with manufacturers. Caroline Charles had licences with, among others, Aristoc Hosiery,

Having worked in advertising and on film scripts, in 1981 Arabella Pollen established her own fashion label, even though she had received no formal design training. Producing a range of clothes based on the hunting styles of the early 1900s, she showed the collection to wealthy publisher Naim Attallah, who was sufficiently impressed to provide financial backing for Pollen's business. Her style was relaxed but smart: as she told the *Sunday Telegraph* magazine in June 1983, 'I try to do clothes that you can more or less slum around in, but that look elegant at the same time.'

Left Few London-based designers have displayed the kind of pragmatism exhibited throughout his career by Frenchman Roland Klein. His stylish but commercial approach to design is evident in this all-white ensemble from his spring/summer 1993 collection.

Below 'I think modern women are tired of being dictated to by faddish whimsy,' Arabella Pollen once informed *Vogue*. 'Fashion should be alive, expressing, not swamping, personality.' This pinstripe sleeveless dress from her spring/summer 1993 collection typifies her approach.

and Mappin and Webb (for jewellery and scarves). Sir Hardy Amies, the Queen's dressmaker and a skilful player in the industry, had built up a stable of more than forty licences – including ten in Europe, three in the United States and sixteen in Japan – which generated annual sales of £50.8 million. And among the younger generation, in July 1990 Arabella Pollen sold a minority share in her business to Courtaulds Textiles in return for an injection of cash. (An arrangement much envied by Pollen's peers at the time, it ended badly in May 1993 when Courtaulds, which had subsequently acquired a bigger stake, pulled out of the deal and the designer was forced to close her business.) But these were the exceptions rather than the general rule: the majority of British designers were not able to secure licensing agreements in their own country. When Vivienne Westwood won the British Fashion Designer of the Year award in 1990, she let it be known that she would like to produce an inexpensive line for the Topshop chain. However, it would be another decade before any designer came to such an arrangement with one of the country's leading high street brands.

In the meantime, Westwood, like many British designers, had more immediate preoccupations, not least the challenge of staying in business. In *Chic Savages*, his 1989 survey of the global fashion industry, John Fairchild the owner of *Women's Wear Daily*, compiled a list of the world's most influential designers that included only one Briton: Vivienne Westwood. She was, he wrote, 'the designer's designer, watched by intellectual and far-out designers ... copied by the avant-garde French and Italian designers.' Yet, Fairchild noted, 'Copied as she is, Westwood struggles in her World's End shop in London, living from hand to mouth.' After Westwood had again been awarded

Vivienne Westwood's remarkable career has seen her move from being sited far outside the British fashion establishment to becoming acknowledged as its *grande dame*. Over the course of some thirty-five years, her devotion to national tradition has grown increasingly evident, as can be seen in the use of Harris tweed for this range of tailored suits from the designer's autumn/winter 1988 collection.

the title of British Designer of the Year in 1991, she announced her intention not to hold a runway show the following season, since, 'My priority now is to concentrate on finding a backer.' Liz Tilberis, then editor of *Vogue*, was quoted by Roger Tredre in the *Independent* in October 1990 declaring of Westwood, 'It is disgraceful that no one has had the courage to back her. She has been at the forefront of British fashion for twenty years and her name must be worth a fortune.'

If that were the case, it had gone largely unnoticed in Britain. Nor was Westwood's predicament exclusive to her. Kurt Salmon Associates, in their survey of the national fashion designer industry undertaken in 1989, interviewed more than 170 individuals and businesses. In 1991 they reported that that while sales of British designer clothing had grown by 60 per cent between 1987 and 1989 to being worth £185 million (with 65 per cent of this growth being in exports), less than 20 per cent of the companies involved had annual sales of more than £1 million – and 60 per cent had sales of less than £500,000 per annum. (At the same time, in a testament to the abiding power of the British high street, Jigsaw had an annual turnover of £18 million and, with just twenty-seven outlets, it was not even one of the country's bigger chains.) A handful of designers bucked this trend: Katharine Hamnett, by then manufacturing entirely in Italy, ran a business generating sales of £25–30 million worldwide, while Paul Smith's turnover was in the region of £40 million. But despite their contribution, the British designer industry came nowhere near matching that of its competitors: the French equivalent was five times larger; the Italians' eight times larger; and the Americans' thirteen times. In Britain, 19 per cent of the fashion companies represented 80 per cent of the industry's value. Furthermore, the widespread lack of licensing partnership arrangements in Britain meant 60 per cent of indigenous companies were entirely owned by the designer involved, who would usually have poorly developed business skills, if any at all.

The 1991 report was important because it made plain that while designer fashion in Britain had grown despite the absence of support, it was likely to remain a cottage industry within the international context unless help was forthcoming from some source. And yet, even in the face of such clear evidence, designers were by and large left to muddle along as best they could during the course of an economic recession. At the start of the 1990s, industrial production was in decline and inflation on the rise, along with unemployment and

Vivienne Westwood has never lost her ability to surprise or to play the joker and this has kept her work consistently fresh when so many others of her generation have faded into gentility. This Harlequin and Columbine duo was part of her autumn/winter 1989 collection.

By 1987, when Wendy Dagworthy produced this collection for spring/summer, she was one of the best-known names in British fashion, with a seemingly inviolable business. But a year later she had to close down her company owing to the bugbear of the industry: financial problems.

interest rates (this hit 15 per cent that year). All of which was bad for any small business dependent on consumer spending. And it transpired that the initiatives of the Thatcher years intended to encourage the growth of entrepreneurship had often been decidedly flawed. In 1988 a report from the National Audit Office demonstrated that government programmes provided funding largely for those who would have become self-employed anyway and that one in six entrepreneurs assisted by the Enterprise Allowance Scheme went out of business within a year. Furthermore, most of the new small companies never created enough jobs, because too many of them were one-person shows (this was certainly true of the fashion sector).

It was a tough time, as plenty of designers can attest. In 1990, for example, Bruce Oldfield was obliged to shut his ready-to-wear operation and concentrate on the core custom-made business. But at least he stayed afloat. After fifteen years in operation, Wendy Dagworthy closed down completely in 1988. What went wrong? 'Money problems,' she summarizes. 'Because we'd always been self-financed. We'd a series of bad debts – shop owners defaulted on payments. Also there were production nightmares. Our cloth came from Italian mills and they'd look after their big clients first, so there was late delivery of our collections and then cancelled orders. It came to a point where I thought: hang on, this just isn't worth it. We did try to find a backer and thought we had one – in Jersey – but then they pulled out at the last minute and that was it. We'd never had a business manager and that was our mistake; we couldn't do everything ourselves. We put the company into liquidation and had to remortgage the house.' In 1990 Sheilagh Brown was also forced to close the company carrying her name: 'We just didn't make enough profit, it was as simple as that – and not having the right business advice.' Jasper Conran almost went the same way. 'We'd been doing really well,' he remembers, 'but essentially we had no back-up so it all fell on my shoulders.' When his American business went into decline in the late 1980s he was suddenly left with a company that threatened to lose money. 'It was just horrifying, whatever I'd made I had poured back into the business to help it grow. At the same time there was rampant inflation; the rent on my studio went up by five times and I was locked into a

twenty-year lease. I had to buy my way out of that by selling my house. Almost everything you could imagine rained down on me, and on a lot of other people too.'

Nevertheless, it would be wrong to suggest all British designers suffered during this period. Some, in fact, thrived. In 1989, after more than twenty years' experience of working for manufacturing companies, Roland Klein decided to establish his own label. 'I underwrote it myself and it was entirely my own business. It was kind of easy because I knew my clients. To be honest, I knew I was a commercial designer and not a particularly creative one. I was always quite happy to have people turn their noses up at me, because I was doing a fantastic job. When I started, Kathryn Samuel gave me a full page in the *Daily Telegraph* and I had an amazing response. I could hardly keep up with the orders.' Tanya Sarne's Ghost also performed well in the late 1980s/early 1990s. 'Women will always buy clothes they can wear to the supermarket or out to dinner,' she explains. 'What I made could be worn anywhere, they were flattering and easy to wear. There was very little on offer at our point of the middle market; everything was either very expensive or it was high street. What we offered was something different.'

The kind of commercial pragmatism displayed by Klein and Sarne, more frequently found among American and Italian than British designers, went a long way to ensuring that their businesses remained buoyant while others sank. The same was also true of Joseph Ettedgui. 'I remember in the 1970s when things were very grey,' he says, 'seeing in Michael Chow's restaurant this huge bunch of roses that must have cost a fortune. When I asked him about them, he told me, "During a recession I need the flowers; when it's busy, people don't see them." Luckily, in the late eighties I was in a situation where I could afford to do things like that. It helped us to run our business efficiently.' Anya Hindmarch, who only started her handbag business in 1987, tells a similar story. 'Three years in is when you have to put down good foundations,' she says. 'That was the most turbulent time of growth and very hard. But I cut out a lot of dead wood, I worked from home and kept my over-heads incredibly low. It was quite stressful and I had to be tough – I remember sitting in a store and saying I wasn't leaving until I'd been paid. You become a bit of an alley cat, and that means you have to be fit and lean.' Likewise, in 1987 Amanda Wakeley returned from the United States and started to make clothes for private clients. By 1990 she had enough capital, and confidence, to set up on her own. The gamble paid off; in 1992 alone her wholesale turnover tripled.

Regrettably, the sort of assurance displayed by Hindmarch and Wakeley was not shown in some quarters where it might have been expected. In July 1988 Peder Bertelsen's Aguecheek ended its backing of Alistair Blair, and not long afterwards that of John Galliano. The association with Katharine Hamnett had already come to an acrimonious close the previous month. Though the Danish businessman had been generous with his support, this was solely financial – it had not been accompanied by the creation of management structures of the kind

In September 1987 the *Daily Telegraph*'s Kathryn Samuel could report, 'Today, with a third collection under the Aguecheek umbrella, Galliano announces that his turnover is now the largest of Bertelsen's home-grown designers', producing clothes such as these from the following year's spring/summer collection. But by the end of 1988 Bertelsen had withdrawn his support and Galliano began looking to Paris.

Bernard Arnault installed when he became involved with companies like Dior. Money, although welcome, was not enough on its own: designers had to be given other assistance if they were to achieve lasting success in the market-place. At the time Blair was gracious about the termination, describing it as 'amicable' and explaining to Andrew Collier of *Women's Wear Daily* that he 'needed a little bit more promotion and marketing than Aguecheek would offer.' Now he admits, 'I was very keen to continue but it became clear Peder was not happy to carry on. I wanted to get into licences, but he couldn't grasp the licensing concept. He probably thought he had gone as far as he could go; fashion for him was still a bit fluffy.' In 1997 Galliano told Colin McDowell that while Bertelsen himself had been sympathetic and supportive, other people in Aguecheek 'were working to assumptions and formulas which I'm sure were right for them – but not for me. Our ideas were so different that even though I explained where I was going and what I was doing, and even though they listened, it all fell on deaf ears. It ended abruptly, with everything being chucked into skips.'

Both Blair and Galliano subsequently moved to Paris. Their departure came at a particularly bad moment for the British fashion industry, already bruised by the news in 1989 that Katharine Hamnett had decided to leave London and to present her collections in the French capital. Hamnett's move to Paris, often described at the time as a 'defection', attracted a lot of publicity, little of which reflected well on the state of London as a fashion capital. Writing in the *Sunday Telegraph* in June 1989, Kathryn Samuel sagely commented, 'Hamnett matters. She is one of a band of four or five British names who have status with international buyers. If she decamped to Paris, where the French are determinedly and rather successfully bidding for the position of European fashion capital, who might follow her?' In the following month's edition of *Vogue*, Sarah Mower was concerned that, 'If British designers lose their toehold in the international fashion market, it has a knock-on effect on the reputation of London, even as a place to look at as a source of interesting merchandise.' Hamnett was unrepentant. 'The UK has nothing any more,' she informed James Fallon of *Women's Wear Daily* in October 1989, days before her first Parisian runway show in the Cirque d'Hiver. 'They don't know how to treat designers here. That is the tragedy of England . . . . They deal with designers so much better in Italy. They really bend over backwards to work with you. They understand designers there.' Hamnett was personally familiar with the merits of the Italian fashion industry because she had moved all her manufacturing to that country after signing a licensing agreement with clothing manufacturer Zamasport, which had already worked

with Walter Albini, Gianni Versace and Romeo Gigli and would go on to produce and distribute lines for Gucci. Zamasport assumed responsibility for her main womens- and menswear collections, while a second Italian company manufactured her Hamnett II lines, with the result, Fallon reported, that the designer 'expected to increase her annual sales of £20 million by as much as 30 per cent this year.'

Increasingly it became necessary for British designers to move their entire production and distribution operations to Italy. Experience had shown that trying to have some garments made there without entering into a proper licensing agreement with a manufacturer just did not work; bigger names were given preference and the British designer was pushed to the end of the line. Anna Orsini, who has promoted London fashion on the international market since the early 1990s, remembers, 'Made in England: it's badly made. Made in Italy: it comes late. That was the reputation British designers had then.' The only way to ensure punctual deliveries of well-made clothing from Italy was by joining forces with one of that country's big producers. This is what Rifat Ozbek did. Not long after Katharine Hamnett had signed her agreement with Zamasport, he entered into a similar arrangement with Aeffe, which already produced lines for Alberta Ferretti, Moschino and Pollini. 'My business had built up successfully in London,' he explains, 'but there were production problems and I couldn't get everything made here – our sales were outgrowing production facilities. Once this rack of jackets arrived from some outworkers and all the sleeves had been stitched back to front.' Having moved his production to Italy, it made sense for Ozbek to show his collections in Milan, which he finally did from March 1992 onwards. 'Aeffe said it was much better for me to show there, they thought of the business end of things.' From that time on, while Ozbek continued to live in London and work from a design studio in the city, all his seasonal collections' production, fittings, publicity and clothing distribution were done in Italy.

More and more designers would follow the same course. Vivienne Westwood moved production of her main line to Italy in 1993. 'For years I struggled to manufacture in England,' she told the *Guardian*'s Susannah Frankel in February 1997, 'and the breakthrough came for me when I finally started to produce in Italy, because before that I could never really overcome the problem of production quantities .... The gap between cottage industry, which is where I started ... and the kind of people who produce for Marks & Spencer, is an unbridgeable chasm. There isn't the infrastructure or the mentality to help anybody manufacture from a creative point in England.'

In fact by that time the British clothing industry had entered the closing stages of its long, sad decline. Whereas clothing production in Britain was traditionally based around large factories, by the late 1980s/early 1990s most of the big manufacturers had gone out of business and what production there was had shifted to pocket units that, on average, employed no more than ten people or relied on outworkers. The Kurt Salmon Associates report of 1991 noted, 'The United Kingdom industry is composed of smaller organizations than USA or Europe … [and] contains more owners/designers/managers.' British designers who wanted to produce at home usually had to rely on several small factories, rather than working with one large one as was the case in Italy. This posed its own challenges at a time when there were more than enough other troubles to face.

The essence of the problem remained the same as it had ever been: British manufacturers' failure to modernize and to recognize that the market was changing. Towards the end of the 1980s Bruce Oldfield worked with a number of British knitwear firms but found, 'They would be reluctant, at the outset of new business at least, to invest in machinery to produce more contemporary products. They were competing with modern styling and techniques that were coming out of the Far East, but they chose, or perhaps were constrained, to continue making old-fashioned-looking knitwear on old-fashioned machines.' Writing in the *Sunday Times* in March 1993, Brenda Polan railed against 'an astonishing post-war lethargy in the industry, which did not invest in plant and technology and watched its workforce evaporate into more modern-minded, better-paying manufacturing industries, into service industries and offices. In Yorkshire, the wool-worsted industry, for instance, bloody-minded in its refusal to update, reinvest or modernize its product, dwindled to a hand-ful of mills, all rapidly outclassed by the re-gearing Italians, Germans and Japanese.' Trying to deal with British manufacturers, says Anya Hindmarch, 'was really sad to be honest, and very frustrating. I worked with very small units who were hand-to-mouth and a lot of trouble. But I wasn't really big enough then to be any real use to them …. It was the most incredible piece of education for me to see that happening, and absolutely tragic.'

There seemed to be an almost wilful determination on the part of manu-facturers not to recognize what was going on. Paul Smith remembers as a relatively young designer participating in a television discussion with a factory owner and a trade union representative to consider the decline of the Yorkshire fabric mill industry. 'I said that I thought one of the problems at the time was that the mills weren't innovative enough and were dominated by producing large quantities for the big chains. The guy from the mill was shouting me down, saying "Bloody rubbish" and that the problem was cheap imports. To be honest, he was wrong because the Italians were busy rein-venting themselves and there was no flexibility here.' Accustomed to receiving big orders from the high street stores, British manufacturers had grown complacent, but they were forced to face up to harsh reality when hitherto-reliable customers, seeing production costs were cheaper elsewhere, took

Head of the British Fashion Council's international department, in charge of international press and buyer relations and overseas guest programmes, Anna Orsini first began her association with London Fashion Week in the mid-1980s.

their business abroad. Factories in Asia, with lower labour costs, greater versatility and quicker turnaround times, began to produce more and more clothing for the British market and the country's old factories were left looking at empty order books.

In a Canute-like effort to stem this decline, in April 1987 the Department of Trade and Industry held a reception at Lancaster House as part of a Better Made in Britain campaign, chaired by businessman Sir Basil Feldman. Sir Basil (later Lord Feldman) had organized the first Better Made in Britain exhibition for the clothing, knitwear and footwear sectors in 1983. The event was sufficiently successful for a Better Made in Britain organization to be formed; this was chaired by Sir Basil from 1984 to 1995. Following discussions with some of the country's fashion designers, Annette Worsley-Taylor approached him about establishing a complementary, and perhaps more relevant, promotion called Better Designed in Britain. The idea behind this was to link designers with high street manufacturers, a scheme from which both parties might have benefited, the former by gaining access to a wider consumer base, the latter by improving the quality of the goods they sold. Although Worsley-Taylor worked on this project with Feldman for nine months (and during that time spoke to many key players, including Sir Christopher Hogg of Courtaulds, Sir Terence Conran, Sir Ralph Halpern of the Burton group and Next's George Davies), the scheme did not come to fruition because, she says, none of the high street retailers were prepared to become involved in a campaign that also featured their competitors. Short-sighted thinking once again triumphed over long-term national goals.

In any case, by that date, it was already too late for Britain's clothing manufacturers to respond with any degree of success to the new world order. Any business wishing to survive could only hope to do so by moving production out of Britain. This is what happened with Courtaulds, once Europe's largest textile company and a substantial employer in Britain. By the end of the 1980s, unable to compete with competition from Asia, Courtaulds had shut most of its British factories; its textile wing, now part of Sara Lee Courtaulds, continues to manufacture clothing for the British market but predominantly overseas and through a series of joint ventures. Between 1995 and 2000, 1,300 British clothing firms and 400 textile firms went out of business. The number of jobs in these two industries halved between 1981 and 1999, from 600,000 to 300,000; in just one year, from September 1998 to September 1999, some 36,000 textile and clothing workers were made redundant, representing an average of 650 job losses per week. Meanwhile, the value of imports of cheap clothing more than trebled, from £2.3 billion in 1986 to £7.5 billion by the millennium. During the 1990s imports from

Internationally renowned handbag designer Anya Hindmarch set up her own company just before the onset of recession in 1987 after borrowing money from her father, 'which I had to pay back, with interest'.

Hong Kong trebled, those from Turkey increased 14 times, those from China 20 times, and even those from major European countries by 350 per cent. (And by 2005 – the year in which long-standing World Trade Organization quota agreements on the movement between countries of textiles and clothing were abolished – more than £1.6 billion worth of clothing, 65 per cent of all imports in this area, came from China.) Although some 11,000 clothing and textile companies were still in operation in Britain in 2001, the majority of them employed fewer than a hundred workers. The days of the big British clothing factory were firmly over.

In the early 1990s the likelihood of British designers remaining in their own country also looked dubious, especially after the departure of Katharine Hamnett, John Galliano and Rifat Ozbek. Vivienne Westwood, who had shown in Paris from 1982 but returned to London in 1987, moved back to Paris in 1991, followed two years later by John Richmond, at the time one of the most highly regarded of the younger generation of British designers (he subsequently moved on to show in Milan). In January 1993 the French trade *Journal du Textile* was writing of a haemorrhaging of talent from the London shows to those in Milan and Paris, which, it claimed, were 'more prestigious and offering a more interesting output'. Obviously, the more high-profile designers deserted London, the harder it became to persuade international buyers and members of the press that the city was worth visiting during the twice-yearly show circuit. 'In the three-horse race for the title of European capital of fashion,' wrote the *Independent*'s Roger Tredre in October 1990, 'the broad consensus was that London was running a very poor third.'

In the autumn of 1989, a young French entrepreneur called Jean-Pierre Fain, who had noted the success of the British Designer Show, decided to stage a similar exhibition during the Paris shows. The majority of exhibitors at this highly successful event, Paris sur Mode, were British designers – whose stands were subsidized by the Department of Trade and Industry – making it even less likely that international buyers would feel under an obligation to visit London.

By the time Paris sur Mode started, it had become apparent that Olympia, the venue for the British Designer Show combining London's main selling exhibition with the majority of the season's runway shows, was no longer satisfactory. Many designers were not prepared to stay there any longer; one of Katharine Hamnett's stated reasons for moving her presentation to Paris was because she would no longer tolerate staging the event 'in a tent in a car park'. In March 1990, in an effort to placate the designers, the runway shows were relocated to Westway Studios in Shepherd's Bush, a venue more used to

accommodating film and television productions. Functional but bleak, it proved equally unsatisfactory, not just because of the dreary surroundings but also because, once more, the shows were separated from the selling exhibition and the latter therefore suffered a decline in attendance. 'This year's London venue has neither adequate facilities nor an easy-to-reach location,' wrote *Today*'s Claire Roberts. One American buyer complained to the *Daily Telegraph* that the Westway Studios were 'in a pretty run-down area and once there getting a cab back is hopeless.' Meanwhile, over at Olympia the ongoing economic recession meant many fashion companies could no longer afford to take a stand and in order to fill the hall and cover costs Philbeach Events began to let space to a broader range of exhibitors, thereby lowering the overall standard and leading to further complaints. In the *Daily Telegraph* Maurice Weaver wrote that Olympia had grown 'down-at-heel and shabby . . . Elegant is not the word to describe this venue. For the exhibitors, the fact that London can offer nothing better is a permanent source of irritation.'

What London Fashion Week needed was an independent organizing body to take care of all logistical arrangements, and a permanent venue in which both the runway shows and a designer fashion exhibition could be staged. The challenge was to find just such a venue. Around this time former *Vogue* editor Beatrix Miller and her two friends Jean Muir and Lady Henderson – the same triumvirate who had played such a key role in getting the British Fashion Council properly established some years before – came up with an ambitious and exciting plan to build a New Crystal Palace within Hyde Park in the area of the Serpentine Gallery. This would be an updated version of Joseph Paxton's 1851 structure. Like the original, it could be used as an exhibition space to promote the best of British design, 'a celebration in itself', as the draft document suggested, using 'modern technology to make a quantum leap into the future, and an enduring source of national pride'. Its objective was to create in central London for the first time since the mid-nineteenth century 'a focal point of the arts, design and creative thinking'. In addition to offering facilities for many other events, the New Crystal Palace would have had sufficient space to house both a fashion trade exhibition and runway shows during the spring and autumn fashion weeks. Sadly the project was still-born, a lost opportunity that received token approbation from various government departments but never developed any further. Meanwhile in Paris work was proceeding on the creation of just such a permanent, well-run venue for the French fashion industry, the Carrousel du Louvre, which made its debut in March 1994.

Since the New Crystal Palace concept was not going to come to fruition, alternative action had to be taken to distance London Fashion Week from the increasingly downmarket event at Olympia. In the autumn of 1990, the London Designer Collections organized a meeting of designers at the English Speaking Union's Dartmouth House in Mayfair where attendees agreed to support an independent, designer-controlled Fashion Week held at a new venue. The British Clothing Industry Association's chief executive, John Wilson, offered to underwrite the cost of this venture, while the London Designer Collections contributed its savings of £60,000. This gave the LDC a majority shareholding in European Designer Collections Ltd, the new company formed to organize the London Designer Show. There were three directors: the LDC's Annette Worsley-Taylor; John Wilson from the BCIA; and Dick Polak, husband and business partner of Edina Ronay. In mid-October *Women's Wear Daily* reported that the British Fashion Council had just announced, 'that beginning next season the London runway shows will be held at the Duke of York's Headquarters on the King's Road in conjunction with an exhibition for about 130 companies.' It went on to note the BCIA's financial support, pointing out that 'It would be the first time the London shows have received funding from Britain's clothing manufacturers.' Not long afterwards, writing in the *Financial Times*, Alice Rawsthorne commented, 'These developments have come at a critical time. London's designers have struggled for years with fragile finances, inexperienced management, inadequate government support and a poor rapport with the mainstream fashion industry. Those problems have intensified in recent years as other international centres have become larger and more powerful.'

The London Designer Show was held for the first time at the Duke of York's Headquarters in March 1991. Shortly before the show opened, the *Evening Standard*'s Lowri Turner explained that the venture was 'a deliberate effort to rid London of its chaotic image. The 130 stands will not only ... showcase the best of British fashion, but also act as a slick shop window for the whole of the industry.' Since the whole event had to be organized in just five months, additional resources were required to help existing personnel. Exhibition organizer Tim Etchells, who had just put on a restaurant show in tents at the Duke of York's Headquarters, acted as consultant, while designer Jasper Jacob, who had transformed Olympia for the British Designer Show, took care of how the venue would look. The result: a series of interlinked tents offered visitors a selling exhibition featuring work by some 120 designers, plus spaces for runway shows, a press office, photographers' lounge, bars and a variety of other facilities. This would come to serve as a model for how London Fashion Week has since presented itself.

However, the surrounding circumstances were such that the first London Designer Show almost didn't take place. Britain's ongoing recession meant many retail outlets across London had closed down, making sponsors and advertisers hard to find. In addition, the British Designer Show's organizers had advised international buyers and press that their event was ending, and this led to some confusion, with many people erroneously assuming that London Fashion Week itself had been cancelled. January 1991 saw the outbreak of the first Gulf War, with the launch of Operation Desert Storm. 'It is difficult to distinguish between the effects of global recession and the immediate effects of the Gulf,' declared an editorial in *Drapers Record*. 'All companies which do business in the US have been hit by the dollar exchange rate and heavy import taxes, aimed at encouraging US consumers to buy US-made products.' Then in February the IRA launched a mortar bomb attack on Downing Street, which, as James Fallon of *Women's Wear Daily* commented, 'On top of general fears of terrorism and the recession, will mean even fewer buyers than usual will come to the London Designer Show in March.' As if there weren't enough problems, because the Duke of York's Headquarters was owned by the military, all visitors to the shows and exhibitions had to be checked in by numbered pass.

No wonder, therefore, 'We lost £70,000,' says Worsley-Taylor, 'but our insurance covered the loss because officially the country was at war.' Considering the difficult circumstances in which it had taken place and despite an estimated drop of 30 per cent in the number of international buyers when compared with previous years, the first London Designer Show was deemed a success and a considerable improvement on its predecessors. In the *Daily Telegraph*, Kathryn Samuel applauded, 'The British have finally got their act together. But it is going to take a steady nerve and more than one season to communicate this fact to the world's buyers, who were, as predicted, thin on the ground.' That steady nerve allowed the London Designer Show to be presented in the same location and format until October 1992 – and then it faltered. The reason was simple: money. It was agreed the show was superior to anything seen before: in October 1992 *Vogue* noted that during the previous season, 'Attention to detail – the availability of fax machines, phones, typewriters, food and loos – and the proximity of the exhibition tent containing 125 quality stands were applauded

by everyone', before going on to quote Saks Fifth Avenue buyer Helen O'Hagan, who enthused, 'It was so simple nipping from the runway to the exhibition to examine the clothes after a show, and good to come across new names too.' But there weren't enough of those names, since recession-hit designers increasingly found it hard to come up with the money to present their collections at the London Designer Show.

The event's organizers were also having trouble finding the necessary funds to keep going. Costing in the region of £600,000 per season, the show was being run not by a commercial organization but by a private company set up by and for members of the fashion industry, who were expected to come up with sufficient funds to run it. Although officially held under the auspices of the British Fashion Council, the London Designer Show received no monetary aid from that organization – because it had none to give. While designers, through the London Designer Collections, contributed as much as they could afford, a key part of the show's backing was provided by the British Clothing Industry Association, whose initial investment in European Designer Collections Ltd of £60,000 in September 1990 was followed by £50,000 the following year and a further £30,000 in September 1992, as well as a great deal of assistance in kind.

In October 1992 James Fallon of *Women's Wear Daily* quoted the BCIA's chief executive, John Wilson, arguing, with justification, 'It is ludicrous for us, a non-profit trade association, to have sole responsibility for the funding of London Fashion Week.' In any case, this funding was not enough to cover the costs of the London Designer Show and so in October 1992 it was decided to charge buyers an admission fee of £12. This led to ill-feeling among both buyers and designers. It was time for either the government or a commercial sponsor to underwrite the event, but neither showed any willingness to take on the role. In 1992, at the request of the Department of Trade and Industry, Annette Worsley-Taylor drafted a document setting out a three-year strategy. Her proposal was that the British designer fashion industry should have its own centre which would co-ordinate members' activities, improve business efficiency (especially among young designers) and encourage links between industry and fashion. Again, this proposal was not acted upon.

The situation became increasingly fraught. In March 1993 the Duke of York's Headquarters had to be relinquished as the venue for London Fashion Week: there just wasn't the money to pay for it. Instead, the London Designer Collections organized a four-day selling exhibition at the Ritz, returning to the place where the original New Wave show had been held nineteen years before. Sixty designers took space in suites spread over three floors, and thirteen of them held runway shows in various venues near the hotel. In order to encourage young talent and at the suggestion of Patrick Gottelier of knitwear company Artwork, the British Fashion Council subsidized six new designers to show as part of the LDC show at the Ritz. This scheme was the start of New Generation and the first half-dozen designers it supported were Paul Frith, Copperwheat

Previous pages A shot taken during the London Designer Show, spring 1991. Among the audience: Sir Ralph Halpern, then chairman of the BFC, writer Hamish Bowles, and Amanda Verdan of Harvey Nichols.

Below Annette Worsley-Taylor in early 1991, working on the organization of the London Designer Show from the LDC's small office in London's Beauchamp Place.

Below As chief executive of the British Fashion Council John Wilson dextrously managed London Fashion Week during the first twelve years the fledgling organization had sole charge of this event. It was in large part due to his skill and tenacity that LFW remained a successful international event during a difficult period.

Blundell, Sonnentag Mulligan, Abe Hamilton, Lisa Johnson and Alexander McQueen. The Department of Trade and Industry provided £30,000 for the event, the first time it had ever contributed any money to the promotion of British fashion. Trade Secretary Michael Heseltine also hosted a reception for five hundred guests at Lancaster House. When asked whether his department would continue to provide financial aid Mr Heseltine refused to commit himself, instead declaring that it was time to learn how 'to mobilize the remarkable design talent we produce out of the fashion colleges'. Funding was evidently not to be part of that mobilization process. In the *Daily Telegraph*, Hilary Alexander rightly contrasted the Department of Trade and Industry's reluctant and modest support with what the Italian government was providing to its own fashion industry. Writing from Milan she noted an announcement by the minister for overseas trade, Claudio Vitalone, that 'the Italian fashion industry would benefit from a £17 million promotion.'

If things looked bad for the future of London Fashion Week in March 1993, they grew a lot worse before the following October when, for the first time in two decades, there would be no central designer exhibition at all. In the months leading up to Fashion Week the mood within the industry became steadily more disconsolate, particularly after the Department of Trade and Industry, asked to give financial assistance once again, declined to do so: its grant that spring was not to be repeated. There was even talk of moving London Fashion Week to Paris, where British designers could be assured of finding buyers and press. Twelve months earlier, Betty Jackson had told *Vogue*'s Rosie Martin, 'I suggested to the British Fashion Council three years ago that they take the London Designer Show to Paris, but nothing came of it.' In October 1992, the British Fashion Council's chairman, Sir Ralph Halpern, bluntly told Suzy Menkes of the *International Herald Tribune*, 'If I had a blank cheque I would take the London Designer Show and move it to Paris, where the buyers are.'

Now this became a real possibility, the rationale being that since key members of the international media and retail business could not be persuaded to come to London, then it was better to go to them. 'My recollection is that it was something discussed as opposed to actually planned,' says Alexandra Shulman, who in 1992 had become editor of *Vogue* and also a member of the British Fashion Council. 'I remember a big meeting to discuss the state of British fashion and one of the things that came up was that if we couldn't get Mohammed to the mountain, then why not bring the mountain to him. The idea was to take a slot or chunk in Paris Fashion Week and show designers there.' The logic of this argument was probably flawed: Paris was already a heavily crowded marketplace where French designers received top billing and, as a number of British *émigrés* had discovered, it was hard to get much attention. But the fact that discussions of this nature should have taken place indicates just how precarious the situation had become. As October 1993 approached, it seemed increasingly possible that London Fashion Week might not survive into the next year.

In 1992 Alexandra Shulman was appointed editor of British *Vogue* and not long after she also became a member of the British Fashion Council.

COOL BRITANNIA

In a 1990 interview with American *Vogue*, Linda Evangelista said of herself and Christy Turlington, 'We have this expression, Christy and I: we don't wake up for less than $10,000 a day.' The two women were part of an elite group which over the preceding couple of years had come to be known as the supermodels; as well as Evangelista and Turlington, their number included Claudia Schiffer, Cindy Crawford, Naomi Campbell and Kate Moss. Memorably, the January 1990 cover of British *Vogue* featured four of the above (Turlington, Campbell, Evangelista and Crawford) plus the marginally less famous Tatjana Patitz. Individually and collectively supermodels were able to command higher fees for fashion shoots and runway shows than had any of their predecessors. In 1991, for example, Turlington signed a contract with cosmetics company Maybelline by which she was paid $800,000 annually for just twelve days' work. Four years later, Claudia Schiffer reportedly earned $12 million from her various modelling assignments. Supermodels became celebrities, their social and personal lives covered by the media in a way that had never been the case before. Any designer who hired them was obliged to pay a lot of money; in *Model*, his 1995 study of the industry, American writer Michael Gross estimated that for a single show that year Gianni Versace had spent more than $100,000 on his models. Gross quoted a Milanese model agent arguing that fashion houses employing supermodels saw a proportionate increase in their business: 'It's like buying a Gucci bag. You show the world you have the money. Especially for an unknown company, they show the world that small as they are, they have the twenty thousand dollars.'

The supermodel phenomenon was both a blessing and a curse for the international fashion industry. On the one hand, it brought even more notice to a business that has always thrived on public attention. On the other, too much of that notice was focused on the models themselves rather than on

Naomi Campbell and Kate Moss at the 1993 British Fashion Awards, staged at the Natural History Museum in London.

the clothes they were wearing; designers could easily find whatever publicity their shows attracted went to a handful of women who had already exacted a steep price for their presence. Perhaps as a consequence of this, the super fell from favour almost as quickly as she had risen. Curiously the only two members of the group from that period who remain in the spotlight to this day are both Londoners: Naomi Campbell and Kate Moss. Campbell started working as a model in 1986 at the age of fifteen (she appeared on the cover of *Elle* during her first twelve months in the business), while Moss was only fourteen when in 1988 she caught the attention of Sarah Doukas, founder of Storm Model Management, and was signed to the agency.

While both Moss and Campbell regularly appeared on runways as part of London Fashion Week, the same was not true of the other supers: British designers simply could not afford their phenomenal fees. This situation might be seen as confirming London's bottom place in the quartet of world fashion centres, but it also meant that visitors to the city during Fashion Week concentrated on the collections and not a roster of expensive models assembled for the occasion. In any case, even before the supermodel moment had run its course, two new categories within the profession had surfaced in Britain: on the one hand what might be called the thoroughbreds, such as Stella Tennant, Honor Fraser and Iris Palmer, all of whom combined outstanding good looks with aristocratic backgrounds; and on the other the idiosyncratics like Karen Elsen and Erin O'Connor, who offered an alternative to the classical ideal of beauty.

However, a number of the supermodels did turn up in London in October 1993 for the first runway show staged by milliner Philip Treacy. Originally from the small Irish town of Ahascragh, in 1988 Treacy won a scholarship to London's Royal College of Art and he stayed in London after graduating three years later. Even as a student he had been making hats for shows staged by other designers, including John Galliano and Rifat Ozbek, and he went on to establish professional relationships with Karl Lagerfeld at Chanel, Gianni Versace and Valentino; through them he had come to know many of the supermodels. But he had never put on a show of his own because, he felt, hats in themselves were not enough to hold an audience's attention. This view changed after Treacy received a phone call from Amanda Verdan, director of fashion buying at Harvey Nichols. 'She said the store was going to have a show during Fashion Week and she wanted me to put on a show "and bring all your supermodel friends here for it." Well, Amanda Verdan was the fashion business goddess of London so fear of her made me obey! I rang up Christy Turlington and asked would she come to London and she said yes, and then she got Naomi and Kate to come too.'

Singer Grace Jones in a Philip Treacy hat at his glitzy Asprey's presentation during London Fashion Week in February 1999.

Model Honor Fraser wears a hat in the shape
of a fully rigged eighteenth-century galleon,
at Philip Treacy's March 1995 show.

The Treacy show was actually one of a number staged by Harvey Nichols during this period in association with American Express in order to provide a platform for the New Generation – the designer group who had been sponsored at the Ritz. Over the previous few years, Amanda Verdan, together with creative director Mary Portas, had made Harvey Nichols the destination venue in London for anyone interested in innovative fashion ('Harvey Nicks' was regularly name-checked in *Absolutely Fabulous*, first televised in 1992). The two women had a vested interest in maintaining the store's reputation, which is why it agreed in October 1993 to host and underwrite two New Generation shows, the first featuring six young designers, the second devoted to Philip Treacy alone. The latter event, which had an inscrutable Valentino sitting in the front row, caused a sensation. 'Treacy's was certainly the stand-out show in London,' wrote Marion Hume in the *Independent*.

But it was not just Philip Treacy who received applause: the October 1993 London Fashion Week itself was judged to be a great success. Given the events of the previous couple of years this turnaround came as something of a surprise. In the months and weeks leading up to October, there had been fears that Fashion Week – actually shrunken to the duration of a mere weekend – would be a disaster and only add weight to the argument that London should be abandoned for an official British presence in Paris. Perhaps the fear this might actually happen provided the necessary catalyst for all concerned because somehow, far from being a calamity, London Fashion Week that October was an outstanding achievement, one of the best of its kind. 'The Brits are back,' announced James Fallon in *Women's Wear Daily*. 'London is abuzz again in a way not seen since the early eighties.' In addition to the Harvey Nichols shows, the cosmetics store Space NK sponsored a fashion show for newcomer Sophia Malig, and elsewhere around the city, designers determinedly staged their own runway presentations as best they could within the constraints of severely limited budgets. Annette Worsley-Taylor found a new venue for the shows – the lawns of the Natural History Museum in Knightsbridge – and, thanks to money raised from the sale of tables at that year's Fashion Awards, which were sponsored by Lloyds Bank, the British Fashion Council was able to pay for a tent. 'Far from demolishing the future of London,' wrote Kathryn Samuel, 'these shows have given new hope for its survival. There was a buzz as the fashion pack hurtled back and forth across London from a tent outside the Natural History Museum to shows held in jam-packed showrooms or restaurants ... the designers have proven that the British give their best when their backs are to the wall.' Samuel also noted

that over the weekend, 'There has been a better turn-out of international buyers and press than in previous seasons, including representatives from American magazines *Vogue*, *Elle*, *Harper's Bazaar* and the *New York Times*. Leading the international buying contingent is Ellin Saltzman, the influential fashion director of New York store Bergdorf Goodman. She is making her first appearance at London Fashion Week in four years.' To make up for the lack of official support, reported Hilary Alexander in the *Sunday Telegraph*, 'Fashion's underground was buzzing too. Marks & Spencer's design department stumped up more than three hundred bottles of champagne for the 'Britain Bites Back' party given by the trade journal *Fashion Weekly* at the Embargo Club. Here students from St Martins filmed a hard-hitting video demanding more government recognition of the industry, which was dispatched to the Department of Trade and Industry.'

The October 1993 season marked a turning point in the fortunes of London Fashion Week and indeed of British fashion as a whole. The fashion world is cyclical in character and if London had suffered from being out of favour for some years, it now regained its rightful status on the international circuit, not least because fashion itself underwent a fundamental change. For much of the late 1980s and early 1990s, the womenswear market had been dominated by conformist business suiting of the kind that was the specialty of Italian and American designers like Giorgio Armani, Calvin Klein and Ralph Lauren. But 1993 was the year of grunge, which, although a short-lived trend, helped to initiate a shift in the way women dressed and to encourage greater distinctiveness in fashion. Since the era of punk London had developed a reputation for idiosyncrasy and as this had returned to favour, so too did London. In October 1993 the editor of British *Elle*, Nicola Jeal, observed, 'There has been a major change in fashion over the past year from corporate style to individualism. Fashion is

going London's way right now, it is a new mood, a new spirit and its heart belongs to London.' Around the same time, Suzy Menkes – since 1988 fashion editor of the *International Herald Tribune* – declared, 'I'm always interested in London: small people at the cutting edge is where fashion starts.'

Over the years ahead there would be hiccups and hang-ups to resolve, disagreements and disappointments to overcome, but circumstances were never again as bad as they had been at the start of the 1990s. Though problems still lay ahead, prospects would only grow brighter for a national fashion design industry which had suffered far too many setbacks for far too long. Of course, in October 1993 none of this was apparent and, other than leaving participants with an agreeable afterglow, that season's Fashion Week had not solved any of the fundamental difficulties faced by London. In December 1993 the *Evening Standard*'s Lowri Turner dramatically warned, 'London Fashion Week is now teetering on the brink of extinction.' Not only did many of the city's biggest names already prefer to show abroad, she noted, but there was the possibility that those designers who had remained would still be expected to present their work outside London, if not in Paris, then in Birmingham where a prominent trade event called Premier Collections had already welcomed some of

Below Graphic designer Nathan Church was responsible for producing exciting images for London Fashion Week from the late 1990s onwards, including collage, a neon installation and six-foot high polystyrene letters. This logo, which made its debut in February 2003, helped to rebrand the event as LFW.

i AM LFW

Left To mark London Fashion Week in February 1995 *Vogue* commissioned this photograph of some of the younger generation of designers, including Paul Frith, Pamela Blundell, Barbara Sonnentag, Abe Hamilton, Hussein Chalayan, Lee Copperwheat, Owen Gaster and Tracy Mulligan.

Below A total original, Italian fashion writer Anna Piaggi has been the muse of many British and international designers, including Karl Lagerfeld and milliner Stephen Jones. Manolo Blahnik describes her as 'The world's last great authority on frocks'. According to a 2006 exhibition held at the Victoria and Albert Museum, Piaggi has a clothes collection that includes 2,865 dresses and 265 pairs of shoes.

their number the previous spring. While the runway shows in October had done much to redeem London's international reputation, the city's want of a proper centralized exhibition space remained to be solved.

By this date the London Designer Collections was being wound down and Annette Worsley-Taylor, while retaining a role as creative and marketing director of Fashion Week, prepared to pass overall responsibility for the event to the British Fashion Council. But in the absence of any other organization assuming liability for the spring 1994 season, that February the LDC made arrangements for a tent to be erected outside the Natural History Museum, and this provided space for designers' shows. Harvey Nichols once more featured two New Generation shows and department store Liberty, together with the shopping district St Christopher's Place, hosted selling exhibitions of young, emerging designers. While the young designers did not excite quite as much interest as they had the previous season, nevertheless they proved a popular draw: in the *New York Times*, Amy Spindler reported, 'Saks Fifth Avenue has never believed the cries of "couture is dead," and this season they ignored reports that London was too, and showed up in force to see the collections. As if to reward their faith, they are returning to New York having bought the work of not one, but two young couturiers just starting their ready-to-wear collections.' These two were Deborah Milner and Nicholas Knightly.

If newcomers to the scene were delighted to take help from wherever it was offered, many of Britain's established designers were still not confident that the British Fashion Council was the best body to represent their interests. 'When I became chairman of the BFC,' says Clinton Silver, 'one of the first things I found out was that the Council was utterly despised by many designers, who felt it didn't understand what they were up to.' The BFC, which proclaimed itself to be 'the central co-ordinating body for the UK fashion exhibitions' (1989/90 annual report), which hosted the British Fashion Awards and co-ordinated London Fashion Week, should have been the first port of call for any designer seeking support and practical assistance. However, the Council's very limited financial resources meant that this perfectly understandable expectation could not be realized, and this had led to disappointment and frustration among designers. They often found it difficult to understand the BFC's *raison d'être* and frequently grumbled about this to the press, which, in turn, was inclined to present the Council in a negative light. 'Designers got on to the press,' confirms Claudia Crow, who started looking after the British Fashion Council's public relations at this time, 'and the press would write that the BFC was not doing its job.' The situation was only made worse by certain

Vidal Sassoon with his wife, Ronnie, Jerry Hall and Edina Ronay, in 1995.

sections of the national media, which seemed almost to relish finding fault with every aspect of the domestic fashion industry, forever comparing it to better-funded counterparts in Milan and Paris.

Still not prepared to put their faith in the British Fashion Council, towards the close of 1993 a number of designers including Amanda Wakeley, Bella Freud, Roger Saul and Helen Storey, had taken part in discussions with Worsley-Taylor about the possibility of establishing a new organization to replace the London Designer Collections. Provisionally named the Federation of British Fashion Designers, its broad aims, outlined in a document distributed by Patrick Gottelier, were 'to look after the sole interests of British designers, give them a mouthpiece with which to communicate with the government and trade associations, and oversee our best interests in all promotional and marketing activities' – echoing the original paper from the British Designer Executive outlining the aims of the BFC.

In the end, the Federation never came into being (and the London Designer Collections did come to an end), because during 1994 the fortunes of both London Fashion Week and the British Fashion Council started to improve and everyone, including designers, enjoyed the benefits of this. One of the biggest and most consistent problems faced by the organizers of Fashion Week over the previous two decades had been a chronic shortage of money, making it well nigh impossible for London to compete with better-funded European coun- terparts. Although the influential 1960s London hairdresser Vidal Sassoon had moved to the United States in the early 1980s, he retained an interest in his native city and regularly returned there. On one such occasion, hearing from his wife, Ronnie, that Fashion Week was in trouble, he persuaded Procter & Gamble (which had owned the Sassoon brand since 1985) to provide necessary sponsorship. For the first time ever London Fashion Week received something approaching adequate commercial funding: £250,000 over three years. The arrangement proved so satisfactory for both parties that it continued until 2002, after which sponsorship came from another division of Procter & Gamble. (In 2006 this role was assumed by Canon, who reconfirmed in February 2009 for a further three years.) With Vidal Sassoon committed, other commercial businesses began to look at funding London Fashion Week and by the end of the century the event's total sponsorship had trebled in value. In October 2007 London Fashion Week received over £1 million in sponsorship each season and had a larger number of sponsors than any of its international equivalents.

In addition to the financial assistance provided by Vidal Sassoon, Fashion Week (and the national fashion industry as a whole) profited from the appointment in January 1994 of Clinton Silver as chairman of the British Fashion Council. Until this point Silver had spent his entire professional life with Marks & Spencer, retiring as the company's managing director of buying and its deputy chairman (he was also, as was pointed out in a February 1997 profile in the *Independent*, the man responsible for the invention of the chicken tikka sandwich). In part because of his association with Britain's best-known high street label, his arrival at the BFC was not altogether welcomed in some quarters. Of himself he says that, at the beginning, 'I had very little familiarity with what was going on. I went into it like Parsifal, the Holy Fool slowly growing wiser.'

In fact Clinton Silver was the first of a series of proactive British Fashion Council chairmen who appreciated that positive intervention was demanded if the organization was to fulfil its mission and truly represent the best interests of Britain's fashion industry. 'He was the right man at the right time,' comments Claudia Crow. 'He had enough gravitas, and the great thing about him was that he was incredibly well respected and respectful of designers and their position. He spoke to them all and tried where and when he could to help them.' Indeed, that help sometimes involved direct intervention: when Sonja Nuttall returned to showing a collection in February 1997 after a two-year hiatus, she was able to do so in part thanks to a personal donation from Silver himself. In the meantime, he had done much to ensure the Council was financially stronger than had hitherto been the case. Silver's business connections helped here, and he was not shy about approaching the high street for help. Among those asked for a contribution to the British Fashion Council was John Hoerner, chief executive of the Burton Group (and later Silver's successor as the Council's chairman). 'I'd given him my pitch,' Silver remembers, 'and then he asked to come and see me, and I explained my plans further. Afterwards he said to me, "I like what you're saying, so I'll give you £10,000, and another £10,000 for the past five years when we should have been involved." That way I raised a lot of money.'

Then-chairman of the British Fashion Council Clinton Silver with Zandra Rhodes in 1995, when the BFC presented her with a Hall of Fame award.

Silver also persuaded the government to support the British Fashion Council's efforts once again; it helped that the head of the Department of Trade and Industry, Michael Heseltine, was also his local MP. Having come from a similar retail background, John Hoerner would be equally pragmatic in approach when his turn came to chair the Council. 'He invited people who paid money to become members of the BFC and sit on the monthly council meetings,' says Claudia Crow. 'It was a really sensible move because it meant those people who were paying for the place had a say in what the Council was doing.'

One of the other initiatives achieved during Silver's time was the British Fashion Council's assumption of full responsibility for the New Generation fashion shows and exhibition stands at the London Designers' Exhibition, which by now had been established at the Natural History Museum. There was a feeling that the Council should be more directly responsible for encouraging young British designers, and should be seen to be doing so rather than leaving the task to a commercial business like Harvey Nichols. Furthermore, it was agreed that beneficiaries of New Generation support ought to show their work in the BFC's tents rather than off-site. This could only happen if the costs involved were underwritten by a commercial sponsor. Silver's links with Marks & Spencer put him in a powerful position to ask that company for assistance, and it did indeed take on this role. From 1994 to 2001, M&S annually spent more than £120,000 on funding runway shows in the BFC tent for some designers and stands at the adjacent exhibition for others; Matthew Williamson, Antonio Berardi, Julien Macdonald and Alexander McQueen were among those who enjoyed this backing over the years. Under the authority of the BFC, a panel of established designers, senior buyers and fashion journalists and the exhibition vetting committee would select each season's recipients. (When Marks & Spencer was obliged to withdraw from the scheme, the sponsorship opportunity was quickly snapped up by another well-known high street name: Topshop.)

Assistance of this kind was essential for young designers, whose numbers continued to increase with every passing year. In 1998, for example, just over 1,500 students were given places on one of Britain's fashion courses; by 2002 that figure had climbed to over 4,000. It was only in the 1990s that fashion graduates started to receive any kind of practical help to ease their transition from the theory of college to the reality of the commercial world. One useful development was the establishment of Graduate Fashion Week, which made its debut in 1991 and is now a feature of London's annual fashion calendar. Vanessa Denza, who, with Jeff Banks, was then an external examiner at

Stella McCartney studied fashion design at Central St Martins and her graduation collection in 1995 (shown here) was modelled by friends including Naomi Campbell, Kate Moss and Yasmin Le Bon. The event received international media coverage and the entire collection was bought by London store Tokio, while McCartney's designs were sold to Browns and Joseph as well as to Bergdorf Goodman and Neiman Marcus in the United States. In March 1997 she was appointed chief designer at French fashion house Chloe, but left four years later to establish her own label.

Harrow College, describes how Graduate Fashion Week started: 'In those days colleges had their own shows all over the country and you couldn't get to see most of them, so we decided there was an advantage in pulling everything together in the one place.' Banks, at the time still presenting *The Clothes Show* on television, was involved with a big fashion show due to take place at the Islington Design Centre and sponsored by Smirnoff vodka; he persuaded Smirnoff to underwrite a runway show for British graduates in the same venue. Banks and Denza joined forces with show producer John Wolford to organize the first Graduate Fashion Week. 'In a rather haphazard way, we pulled it together,' Denza recalls. 'It wasn't badly organized, but we didn't have the money they do now. Our very first winner was Christopher Bailey: we couldn't give him money but he got a scholarship to the Royal College of Art.' (After leaving the Royal College, Bailey went on to work first with Donna Karan in New York and then with Tom Ford at Gucci in Milan before joining Burberry as creative director in May 2001.) Other familiar names who have since participated in Graduate Fashion Week include Stella McCartney and Antonio Berardi. The event not only showcases new talent but also allows participants and undergraduates to look at the work of their peers from other institutions. 'That has made a considerable difference to the working relationship that exists between different institutions,' Professor Maureen Wayman of Manchester Metropolitan University told the *Independent*'s Lucy Hodges in June 2005. 'Of course we are competing, but at the same time we are also collaborating.' Furthermore, it was not long before Graduate Fashion Week became a magnet for talent scouts and recruitment agencies looking to offer jobs to the best of Britain's new designers. As Alice Smith, of consultants Smith and Pye, explained to Lucy Hodges, 'It makes it much easier because you all go to the same place.' The reputation enjoyed by British fashion colleges of producing graduates of a higher calibre than those found anywhere else in the world has helped

Born in London's East End, the son of a taxi driver – but from a family that had produced generations of tailors – Alexander McQueen left school at the age of sixteen and served an apprenticeship with Savile Row tailors Anderson and Shepherd and costumiers Bermans and Nathans before going to Italy to work for Romeo Gigli. On returning to London, he enrolled for an MA at Central St Martins and presented his first bravura runway show in October 1993. For the rest of the decade McQueen, with his hard-edged and wildly creative designs and spectacularly theatrical presentations, could be relied upon to electrify audiences. This feral headpiece is from his autumn/winter 1997 collection; the laser-cut metal skirt is from spring/summer 1999.

to make the week of international interest. In May 2008 Alice Fisher of the *Observer* quoted Ricardo Alvar, vice-president of American recruitment agency 24Seven, saying, 'British students have creativity and knowledge of technical foundations, and these things are not always present in American schools. There's a global demand for talent from London because the quality is amazing.'

The truly amazing quality of London's fashion talent became evident from 1993 onwards when new designers appeared one after the other in a remarkable display of synchronicity. Among the first, both chronologically and in terms of ability, was Central St Martins graduate Alexander McQueen. Considering the attention-grabbing character of his runway shows in the second half of the decade, it is remarkable how quiet a debut McQueen made, as one of the first six New Generation designers who showed their collections in the Ritz in March 1993. Annette Worsley-Taylor remembers a young man wheeling a rack of clothes into one of the hotel suites and then leaving. When it was suggested he might meet buyers, he responded, 'I'm not interested in selling my collection: I want to become an international designer.' Although his clothes drew some notice, he was not necessarily considered the most remarkable of the six; in *The European*,

The Turkish-Cypriot Hussein Chalayan was one of the most high-profile graduates of Central St Martins in the 1990s. Much of his work has a distinctly architectural quality, evident in the tiered wooden table/skirt dating from autumn/winter 2000 and also in the upper section of a yellow dress from the previous season. 'Watching a Chalayan show is like listening to Mozart,' one commentator has observed. 'It is moving and magical, always with a hidden meaning, which to detractors sounds pretentious.'

Jane Mulvagh declared that, 'The most outstanding is Abe Hamilton', and one well-known fashion writer erroneously referred to him in her report as 'Alistair McQueen'.

The young designer attracted a lot more attention the following October with his first, uncompromisingly belligerent runway show. This was the time when punk, albeit in the diluted and prettified form of grunge, had come back into vogue, and buyers and journalists were hoping London would deliver a 'new punk' experience capable of attracting as much press attention as had the old one. They found it at McQueen. After his first show Marion Hume of the *Independent* wrote that she had 'felt an unease I don't remember experiencing since the first girl in my form to get her nose pierced walked into school assembly ... The shock of the new has to be just that: shocking.' In the *New York Times*, Amy Spindler also took note, observing, 'The last show of the season gave editors the aggressive British attitude they had been expecting. A little of it, of course, goes a long way, and Alexander McQueen provided a lot.' Thereafter for the rest of the decade, McQueen played the part of British fashion's bad boy and, with his unexpurgated language and hard-edged designs (not least his much-emulated, low-slung bumster trousers), could be relied upon to titillate the audience at each of his stunningly theatrical runway shows, which came with titles like 'The Highland Rape' and 'The Hunger'. Of course, thanks to his earlier Savile Row training, he also offered impeccable cutting technique and craftsmanship of the highest order.

While McQueen might have been best at grabbing front page press coverage, he was certainly not the only British designer of note to surface in the mid-1990s. Among the most impressive was Hussein Chalayan, an aloof character who brought new intellectual rigour to British fashion. Chalayan's entire 1993 Central St Martins College graduation collection was bought by Browns and displayed in the windows of their South Molton Street shop, just as John Galliano's 'Incroyables' had been a decade before. Unlike McQueen Chalayan did not set out to shock, but he did wish to challenge preconceptions of fashion and clothing. In this respect, his sensibility was closer to the Japanese new wave of the 1980s than to that of his own compatriots.

In 1998, the Curator of the Costume Institute in New York's Metropolitan Museum of Art, Richard Martin, commented that, 'More than any other fashion designer with the possible exception of Rei Kawakubo, Chalayan uses clothing as an art to reinterpret and reform the human body in a continuous *tour de force* of body/identity conceptualism and dressmaking.'

If Hussein Chalayan was cerebral and Alexander McQueen visceral, then the work of yet another Central St Martins graduate, Antonio Berardi, could best be described as sensual. Perhaps thanks to the influence of his Sicilian parentage, his clothes were glamorous, sexy, provocative. And although quite different in character from Chalayan and McQueen, like them Berardi attracted attention at a very early stage in his career, attention he encouraged because, as he says, 'It was a very competitive era, you had to make sure you were noticed.' With so many exceptional designers entering the marketplace at the same time, the importance of being able to stand out from the crowd was never greater. So, for his 1994 graduation collection (which was bought by both Liberty and the independent Knightsbridge store A la Mode), Berardi commissioned shoes from Manolo Blahnik and left a vial of his own perfume on each of the front-row seats, a gesture which was, he says, 'deliberately done tongue in cheek' but which helped to ensure he was remembered by buyers and press attending the event. A year later, he presented his first commercial collection which, in addition to Blahnik shoes, featured hats by Philip Treacy and bags by Anya Hindmarch. It received

New fashion talent flourished to an extraordinary degree in 1990s London. Among the most important designers to emerge at the time were Antonio Berardi (above left, at the end of his show in 1998), Clements Ribeiro (below left, in 1997) and Bella Freud (below, in 1997). Berardi, Clements and Ribeiro were graduates of Central St Martins, while Freud worked with Vivienne Westwood as well as studying in Rome.

universally enthusiastic reviews: 'Here at last was a happening,' wrote Alison Veness in the *Evening Standard*. 'There were tantrums, tears and not everyone got in. Antonio Berardi was the hot ticket of London Fashion Week.'

But there was a phenomenally large number of hot tickets at this time: Sonja Nuttall; Fabio Piras; Anthony Symonds; Robert Cary-Williams; Nicholas Knightly; Owen Gaster; and Bella Freud, among many others. A brilliant future career was predicted for each of them (although this did not always come to fruition). For some reason, a lot of the new designers preferred to work in pairs – Copperwheat Blundell, Sonnentag Mulligan, Clements Ribeiro, Pierce Fionda, Flyte Ostell, Antoni & Alison. (And towards the end of the decade, other partnerships established labels like Preen, Blaak, and Boudicca.)

The sheer diversity of fashion coming out of London in the 1990s was astonishing. Whereas during the previous decade London fashion could be broadly divided into two categories – the Classicists and the Streetwise – now there was a seemingly endless multiplicity. The Classicists continued to add to their number, thanks to the arrival of designers such as Tomasz Starzewski (yet another Central St Martins former student) and so too did the Streetwise. But neither of these classifications could be applied with complete conviction to McQueen, Chalayan or Berardi, just as they could not to Bella Freud, Clements Ribeiro or Pierce Fionda. While all of them demonstrated an awareness of London's classical heritage (not least through their strong tailoring) and also its ever-changing street trends, they were never in thrall to either. The most thrilling aspect of fashion during this period was the eclecticism of what was offered, the consistent unpredictability of what any particular season might turn up. Though there are probably many reasons why this came about, surely one of them was that designers based in London no longer tended to come from the same background; they had personal histories as different as the clothes they created. McQueen grew up in London's East End, Berardi's parents were Italian emigrants, Hussein Chalayan had been born in Cyprus and lived there until the age of eight (likewise the Gibraltese Galliano moved to London when he was six). And so it would go on to the end of the decade, with Frenchman Roland Mouret presenting his first collection in 1998 and the Greek Sophia Kokosolaki making her post-Central St Martins debut at the start of the new millennium. This lack of homogeneity distinguished London from other, more conformist global fashion capitals, a sense that difference was welcomed, a feeling that cultural miscellany was celebrated. Stylistic standardization was not expected in London and nor was it admired there.

The new millennium saw the emergence of new fashion names, among them Sophia Kokosolaki (left, spring/summer 2003), Roland Mouret (centre, spring/summer 2002) and Boudicca (right, autumn/winter 2001). Athens-born Kokosolaki and Frenchman Mouret are just two examples of young international designers who were drawn to London because it offered them a platform where creativity was valued beyond commercial success. 'Freedom of clothing and of expression is the basic assumption of their style,' wrote one observer of the designers behind the Boudicca label; the same could be said of many designers working in London today.

But if British designers of the 1990s came from a wide variety of back-grounds and viewed fashion from many different perspectives, one trait they often shared was a far better understanding of business than their predecessors. This was a more commercially savvy generation, perhaps because they had seen what disasters could befall even as talented a designer as Galliano unless the right corporate structures were put in place. In any case, unlike designers of the 1970s and 1980s, those starting out in the 1990s did not have to learn every lesson the hard way: help and advice was on hand. In 1997 at the request of the Department of Trade and Industry and the British Fashion Council, Helen Storey's business partner, Caroline Coates, was commissioned to write the still-relevant *Designer Fact File*, an invaluable document that drew on the experience of established businesses to provide information for those just beginning. It offered young designers practical guidance on everything from setting up a company to export insurance and pricing for profitability. Many of the designers quoted by Coates in her document demonstrate an awareness of the need for their work to be grounded in good business practices. 'You can only find finance when you have a viable business plan,' noted Ben de Lisi, while the Copperwheat Blundell duo advised, 'Designing is the easy bit; we quickly found we were running the company during the day and designing in our spare time and at night.'

Coates' *Designer Fact File* contained the first statistical analysis of the fashion industry in Britain since the publication of the Kurt Salmon Associates report in 1991. The new document reported that the designer sector comprised some 210 companies with aggregate sales of £600 million (estimated to be up from £185 million in 1989). Over 80 per cent of all designer companies were based in London and, as ever, exports remained important, with over 60 per cent of all companies engaging in export. But even allowing for the sector's growth over the previous few years it remained relatively small, directly employing only around 1,500 people. And almost 60 per cent of investigated companies had annual sales of less than £400,000. On the other hand, by 1997 five per cent of British designer companies had annual sales of £10 million or more, whereas the Kurt Salmon report had found that only five per cent of the companies it surveyed had an annual turnover greater than than £5 million. Not long after Coates' work appeared, British publishers Emap (which was respon-sible for producing *Drapers Record,* among other titles) began to issue an annual *UK Fashion Handbook* which, while not directly aimed at helping

Trained at Central St Martins, Robert Cary-Williams established his own label in 1998 and won the British Fashion Council's New Generation Award the following year. He has become noted for creating clothes that are experimental and often employ distressed fabrics yet still remain highly wearable. For his spring/summer 2002 collection, Cary-Williams drew on historical influences and reinterpreted these in a contemporary fashion, evident in this jacket and skirt that feature crushed silk and chiffon, antique lace and sequins, 'spiked by enough natural and fretted leather to give characteristic edge'.

young designers, was replete with information of use to them, since it provided an overview of the industry and facts on subjects such as consumer behaviour, fashion retail and distribution, and company profiles of key players in the market.

The importance of being well informed and well financed was a lesson young designers of the 1990s seemed to have learned, together with the realization that without these attributes their work, no matter how exceptional in character, was unlikely to reach a sufficiently wide market. For this reason more and more of them followed the example of the British Fashion Council and sought out commercial sponsorship. Alexander McQueen, for example, joined forces with American Express and when the company launched a gold card in 1997, he created a dazzling gold suit. (On the other hand, McQueen wanted to call the show featuring his suit – and also models coming down a Plexiglass runway in torrential rain – 'The Golden Shower'. This proposal was firmly vetoed by the sponsor.) 'What you're tapping into with McQueen is someone who's very creative,' a director of American Express told the *Independent*'s Susannah Frankel in September 1999, 'and it did present some challenges. In the end, though, he's a sound businessman as well. That's why we're interested in him.' Describing a British fashion designer as a sound businessman would hitherto have been deemed an oxymoron, but not any more (and particularly not when McQueen's runway shows were estimated to cost in the region of £150,000 to stage). When Helen Storey sought commercial sponsorship for her shows in the late 1980s, it was considered unusual and perilously close to selling out; within ten years, it had come to be seen as making sound sense.

The sensual designs of Antonio Berardi attracted attention from his very first runway show, staged a year after he had graduated from Central St Martins in 1994.

So too had the matter of working with a reliable manufacturer, whether in Britain or, more likely given the near-total collapse of British clothes production, overseas. While the *Designer Fact File* found that in 1997 over 90 per cent of companies surveyed still manufactured at least to some extent in Britain, it remained the case that 'Designers have had great difficulty sourcing British factories that are appropriate to their needs.' As Paul Frith remarked, 'It's a nightmare, it's totally word of mouth, one factory tells you about another.' Frith further observed of those factories with which he had worked, 'Typical problems are they cut corners, they don't respect the cloth – you have to be very specific.' Understandably, some younger designers trying to grow a healthy business looked elsewhere. With his Italian roots, Antonio Berardi found it relatively easy to establish connections in his parents' home country and in December 1996 he signed a contract with Rimini-based manufacturers Givuesse, which agreed to take care of the production side of his label. 'An Italian fashion talent scout came to see me in London,' he explains, 'and then he took me to see various companies. Once we'd agreed the deal with Givuesse, he sold the collection through his showrooms.' By the end of the first year after signing with his Italian manufacturer, he had over a hundred stockists worldwide.

One quality Berardi shared with many designers of the period was his appreciation of publicity. At a time when a lot of young talents were competing for the spotlight, the best way to gain maximum notice for a collection was to present it in a style and setting quite different from that used by anyone else. Although the British Fashion Council now had well-organized runway tents available outside the Natural History Museum, as a rule these were spurned by younger designers as being too sterile and insufficiently in tune with their own sensibilities. Instead they preferred to seek out quirky venues all around London. Nicholas Coleridge, chairman of the British Fashion Council for four years from 2000 onwards, says of his term, 'I've never been to so many abattoirs, skating rinks, waxwork museums, horticultural halls ...' It seemed almost a matter of pride for designers to seek out the most obscure or far-flung spot in which to stage their shows. Helen Storey presented her final collection in a London Underground tunnel, Hussein Chalayan had a fondness for showing in the East End, Alexander McQueen once used the aisle of Hawksmoor's splendid Christchurch, Spitalfields, as a runway for his collection. During the course of a day buyers and journalists could travel from one end of the city to the other, from the Royal Opera House to a disused warehouse. They grumbled less than they used to because the effort was usually (although not invariably) worthwhile.

London fashion shows during the 1990s increasingly became pieces of theatre, fifteen-minute stage productions, one-act dramas with a script devised not by the designer alone but with the assistance of a stylist. 'At some point over the last few years,' wrote the *New York Times*' Amy Spindler in April 1994, 'fashion stylists, with soothing smiles on their faces but whitened knuckles, began wresting creative control from fashion designers.' The familiar, but increasingly rare, format of the fashion show was for models to appear one after another on the catwalk, process its length and then retire. Many London designers found this style of presentation insipid, and certainly not powerful enough to convey the concept behind their collection. The rise of the fashion show as spectacle owes not a little to John Galliano who, from the time of his graduation with Les Incroyables always wanted to show his clothes within the context of a narrative. In this process, he was aided for twelve years by Amanda Harlech (until she moved to work with Karl Lagerfeld at Chanel). Harlech was often described as the designer's muse, but in truth she was more his dramaturge, simultaneously a source of inspiration and a sounding board. As she told the *Observer*'s Lynn Barber in August 2007, when she met Galliano, he was 'the visual response to everything I could have imagined

Below Since opening Browns on South Molton Street in the late sixties, Joan Burstein has become one of the most respected women in fashion, admired for her ability to recognize emerging designers. A Browns window is the ultimate accolade for any new fashion graduate.

Described by fashion writer Colin McDowell as 'the last woman in the world whom I can imagine wearing jeans and sneakers', the late Isabella Blow, stylist and fashion editor, was uncompromisingly chic and turned heads wherever she went. She actively promoted and supported young designers such as Alexander McQueen and Philip Treacy. She is seen here with Treacy outside London's Design Museum at the opening of the 2002 exhibition 'When Philip Met Issie'.

– he did shows which were stories and adventures – so I went with him.' Within a few years, the relationship between Harlech and Galliano was mirrored by that between another patrician woman, Isabella Blow, and a young designer – in her case first Philip Treacy (who lived in the basement of Blow's London home while starting his career) and then Alexander McQueen. Treacy was quoted in an obituary of Blow carried by the *Independent* in May 2007 as saying, 'She was a great champion of young people. She came from the Establishment but was a punk at heart. Her love was talent, rather than money. Her ethos was beauty and elegance. And her encouragement was rare.'

So too was her flair as a stylist, although, as with designers, around the mid-1990s all at once there seemed to be a lot of outstanding people working in exactly this field in London. Many of them – like Lucinda Chambers, who would later become creative director of the Italian label Marni – began their professional lives working at *Vogue*. Other significant British stylists to emerge during this period included Alistair Mackie (who has worked with Sophia Kokosolaki, Marc Jacobs and Martine Sitbon), Katy England (Alexander McQueen), Katie Grand (Prada, Giles Deacon, Luella Bartley), Sophia Neophitou (Roland Mouret) and Charlotte Stockdale (Paul Smith, Dolce & Gabbana and Patrick Cox). Stylists didn't just work on runway shows; as Tamsin Blanchard explained in the *Observer* in November 2002, they 'are the people who decide not so much what we are going to wear, but what we are going to buy. They choose the clothes on the pages of the magazines; they decide that Jennifer Lopez looks great in that Versace dress; they are the ones who select the clothes that will make it on to the runway and into the buyers' order books.' But their influence was most visible at the time of the twice-yearly Fashion Week when designers came to rely on stylists for advice on how best to introduce a new collection to ever-more critical and jaded buyers and journalists. Speaking to Blanchard of his work with Kokosolaki, Alistair Mackie explained, 'We meet up and look at funny references together and I'll bring fabrics and she'll take them sometimes and reinvent them. We'll talk about the vibe of the show. We don't always agree, but by now we totally understand each other.' In an era when the straightforward runway presentation fell out of favour, the contribution of a stylist became of crucial importance in determining whether or not a designer enjoyed success. 'Stylists help designers complete ideas, and they're very good at helping you with things you don't always have time to think about,' Hussein Chalayan told Constance White of the *New York Times* in September 1998. 'They also see a lot of clothes. And they become like a sounding board.' Four years earlier, the same newspaper's Amy Spindler had observed that the stylists 'are the great fixers, the ones who come in at the last minute before a show and direct a designer with 120 pieces and nowhere to go. It is not uncommon, after a bad show by a good designer, for editors to inquire suspiciously who the stylist was, or after an abnormally brilliant show from a mediocre designer, to congratulate the stylist ... One downside to the rise of the fashion stylist is that designers sometimes substitute good styling for good design.' This baleful influence was sometimes even apparent in London, Suzy Menkes remarking in the *International Herald Tribune* after the September 1997 Fashion Week that many of its shows had been 'over-styled and way too long'.

But overall it can be said that the drama of London's runway presentations added greatly to their appeal and helped to renew international interest in British fashion after a period of unjust neglect; overseas visitors understood that what they were going to see would be stimulating and quite different from anything found elsewhere on the global fashion circuit. 'If there was one topic of conversation that dominated this season's collections,' *Vogue* informed readers in February 1997, 'it was British cool. Fashion editors, photographers and stylists were captivated by the fashion which has emerged in London.' Hence the revival of interest from American stores in the 1990s when the United States, together with Japan, once more became the most important export market for British designers. London's fashion 'went down very well with American buyers,' says Gail Sackloff who by now was employed by Saks to find new and interesting labels for the

Former merchandising manager Graham Fraser and designer Richard Nott (below) launched their label Workers for Freedom in 1985. From the start their work caused a stir and attracted international sales, and Workers for Freedom was declared British Designer of the Year in October 1989. A key feature of the company's designs was its lack of interest in passing trends; Workers for Freedom adopted an evolutionary style that transcended seasons. The label favoured natural fabrics and a monochrome palette in which black, white, ivory and indigo blue predominated. Nott once characterized the company's clothing as 'very gentle': an apposite description of this sleeveless shift from the spring/summer 1997 collection (left).

store to carry. 'Americans had moved on by now. I think the customers were reading more about Britain, the fashion and the music, and it was our time again. They were coming into the store having heard about these British designers and wanting to buy them. They're very celebrity-conscious in the United States.'

They were also a lot less conservative than they had been when Susanne Bartsch had tried to introduce new British fashion to an American public in the early 1980s. By August 1998 the chairman of Saks Fifth Avenue could tell Anne-Marie Schiro of the *New York Times*, 'We were going to the London markets and saw a lot of newness and vitality that we hadn't seen in recent years. We wanted to be the first store in America to present in a cogent, intelligent way a host of British designers, artists and people ... It's a celebration of their creativity, as complete a statement as has been made anywhere about contemporary England.' The following month, the Manhattan department store – by then annually turning over more than $25 million in sales of British fashion – hosted a ten-day event called 'British Invasion, Part II' ('Part I' being the wave of British fashion that had crossed the Atlantic, along with the Beatles, in the mid-1960s). McQueen, Chalayan, Berardi, Macdonald, Rocha and Treacy were among the designers featured, with window displays given over to re-creating their runway shows, an ideal means of conveying to the average American consumer just how stirring British fashion had become of late. 'It's really not about trends,' Saks' fashion director told *Women's Wear Daily*. 'It's about individualism. These designers are all so sincere in their sense of ethic, and so different. It's really striking to see all this talent ...' The American love affair with British fashion would continue long after Saks' promotion had ended, helped by the fact that in the new millennium a number of London designers – among them Matthew Williamson, Luella Bartley and Roland Mouret – would opt to show their new collections in New York, where the indigenous industry's generally conformist and commercial attitude meant their work looked even more striking than it did at home. 'It's an unbreakable cycle in London,' Williamson told Charlie Porter of the *Guardian* in September 2003, by way of explanation for his departure from the city some time before. 'London is a great platform when you're new and just out of college, but it doesn't embrace growth.' However not all designers had to move across the Atlantic in order to win an American audience: Manolo Blahnik's shoe business in the United States experienced growth thanks to the exposure he received on the HBO television series *Sex and the City* from 1998 onwards. (In one episode, when the heroine, Carrie Bradshaw, played by Sarah Jessica Parker, was confronted by a mugger, she pleaded, 'Please sir, you can take my Fendi baguette, you can take my ring and my watch, but don't take my Manolos.')

If the United States was better informed about British fashion and better prepared to embrace its sensibility, this may in part be because during the 1990s there was something of an invasion of the American fashion media by British journalists and editors. The presence of London writers in New York (and the dismay this caused in some quarters) was nothing new, as had been demonstrated by the presence of washed-up British hack Peter Fallow in Tom Wolfe's 1987 satiric novel *Bonfire of the Vanities*. But most of the British journalists and editors who rose to prominence in the American media were rather more disciplined than Fallow (although not all, as shown by Toby Young's 2002 memoir *How to Lose Friends and Alienate People*). Most were also women, Tina Brown being the original of the species. A former editor of *Tatler* in London who moved to New York in 1984 to edit *Vanity Fair*, which she transformed from a near-moribund publication into a must-read monthly, in 1992 Brown moved to the *New Yorker* (where her fortunes were mixed) and thence in 1999 to start *Talk* magazine (which was a failure). While none of her American editorships were of a fashion magazine, under her direction most came to have a strong fashion content. London-born Anna Wintour has made a more significant contribution to this sector, since her appointment as editor-in-chief of American *Vogue* in 1988 – the same year another English woman, Suzy Menkes, became fashion editor of the *International Herald Tribune*.

Opposite Born and raised in Wales, Julien Macdonald was taught knitting by his mother and it was as a knitwear designer that he first made his name, creating pieces for Karl Lagerfeld at Chanel as well as for Alexander McQueen; he launched his own label in 1997. Three years later he was appointed successor to McQueen as chief designer at the Paris house of Givenchy (a position he held until 2004) and in 2001 he was named British Designer of the Year. He was one of the first to appreciate the usefulness of celebrity links, and here (left) he is photographed with former Spice Girl Mel B at his 1999 show.

Suzy Menkes (centre), ex-fashion editor of *The Times*, was appointed fashion editor of the *International Herald Tribune* in 1988, the same year that Anna Wintour (right) became editor of American *Vogue*. Liz Tilberis (below, with Alexander McQueen) was editor of British *Vogue* until she became editor of *Harper's Bazaar* in New York in 1992, a position she held until her untimely death in 1999.

Left Born in Santa Cruz in the Canary Islands, shoe designer Manolo Blahnik opened his first shop in London in 1973. Long admired by fashion cognoscenti, it was when his work appeared repeatedly in the American HBO television series *Sex and the City* that he achieved global recognition.

Wintour's position made her the most important individual in fashion publishing in the world. Her sensibility is widely acknowledged to be more American than British, but that has not stopped her espousing some British designers, notably John Galliano, whom she heavily promoted in the early 1990s. She has also employed a number of fellow Britons at *Vogue*, among them creative director Grace Coddington and writers Plum Sykes and Hamish Bowles. In 1992 another British editor, Liz Tilberis (who four years before had succeeded Wintour at the helm of British *Vogue*) assumed responsibility for the principal rival to American *Vogue*'s hegemony: *Harper's Bazaar*. Under Tilberis' leadership, this magazine was radically overhauled to give it a character more in sympathy with the *Harper's Bazaar* of forty years before, when Carmel Snow had been in charge. Four years after the arrival of Tilberis, yet another Briton was appointed to the editorship of an American fashion monthly. Glenda Bailey had previously launched British *Marie Claire* and now took over responsibility for its transatlantic sibling; in 2001, two years after Tilberis' death from ovarian cancer, Bailey became editor of American *Harper's Bazaar*.

There is no evidence this influx of British writers and editors into the American fashion media led directly to the latter devoting more space to London and its designers. In any case, the approach taken by fashion magazines on either side of the Atlantic was, and remains, quite different. As Wintour explained at a seminar in London in May 1997, 'The British fashion journalist often sees herself as an artist or craftsman. Her work is very hands-on, she cares a lot about originality and less about readers or advertisers ... the New York editor, on the other hand ... works in a tightly coordinated and organized system which leaves less scope for her individuality.' In other words, what might work within a British context would not necessarily travel well across an ocean. But the fact that so many of the country's best editors were poached by the United States is a testament to the influence of London as a global fashion capital. And even publications without a British editor were prepared to acknowledge the significance of the English capital:

'Forget Paris and Milan,' proclaimed *W* magazine in September 1996. 'Merry old London is the only place to be for the hip and happening.' As if to prove this point, the same month American designer Tommy Hilfiger chose to debut his womenswear collection during London Fashion Week. (In the *New York Times*, Amy Spindler reported Grace Coddington drily commenting 'Nice styling', as Hilfiger's models trooped down the catwalk.) Just a couple of days later, Donna Karan threw a memorable party to celebrate the opening of her new shop on Bond Street and on the same night Naomi Campbell, Claudia Schiffer and Christy Turlington, keen to capitalize on any remaining interest in the supermodel phenomenon, opened their Fashion Café in London's Leicester Square (it would close just three years later).

New York wasn't the only city wishing to benefit from an injection of London's fashion wizardry during this period. The mid-1990s saw a wave of British designers being invited to assume responsibility for some of Paris's most renowned houses. This movement began in July 1995 with the appointment of John Galliano as head designer at Givenchy, following the retirement of its eponymous founder. Galliano had enjoyed mixed fortunes since basing himself and his label in Paris in 1989 and it was only after Anna Wintour took up his cause in 1994 that he began to experience some kind of financial stability; prior to that, as Colin McDowell noted in 1997, the designer 'slept on friends' floors and he borrowed money for the Métro.' Givenchy was by now part of Bernard Arnault's ever-expanding LVMH empire and it was he who invited Galliano to take the position. A year later Arnault asked Galliano to become head designer at Dior, a job hitherto held by Gianfranco Ferré. The British designer received acclaim for his very first Dior collection, the *New York Times*' Amy Spindler writing, 'Mr Galliano's show was a credit to himself, to M. Dior, whose name is on the door, and to the future of the art, which is always in question.' His departure to Dior had once more created a vacancy at Givenchy, and Arnault filled it with another British designer, Alexander McQueen. The choice was considered odd, the fit between the man and the label uncomfortable – and so it proved to be. McQueen's outlook was not particularly in sympathy with the tradition of French couture, or its clientele. 'There is a place for the work Mr McQueen is capable of producing for Givenchy,' Spindler argued after the designer's initial collection for the house had been shown, 'a customer who, like him, wants to provoke people's thoughts instead of boring them with beauty. His first show was many things, but boring it was not.' Nor were those that followed. McQueen remained with Givenchy until 2001, when 51 per cent of his eponymous own

From the *London Fashion Week Report*, a sketch by illustrator Gladys Perint Palmer of front row guests at London Fashion Week's shows in February 1998, featuring (top): Isabella Blow and Alexander McQueen at Philip Treacy; (middle) Suzy Menkes, Nicky Haslam and Hilary Alexander at Philip Treacy; (bottom left) Constance White and Ronnie Cook Newhouse at Lainey Keogh; (bottom centre) Princess Michael of Kent, Michael Roberts and Ronnie Sassoon at Philip Treacy; (bottom right) Richard Branson at John Rocha.

label was acquired by LVMH's rival the Gucci Group, and his place at the head of the French company was taken by another British designer, Julien Macdonald, who some years before had already spent time working with Karl Lagerfeld at Chanel.

Meanwhile, in 1997 Lagerfeld's old domain Chloe acquired a British design head, twenty-six-year old Stella McCartney. Another graduate of Central St Martins, she was also the daughter of Beatle Paul McCartney and this connection led to suggestions in some quarters that her appointment owed more to her famous father than to inherent ability. However, her first collection for Chloe, presented in Paris in October 1997, confounded the naysayers, with Suzy Menkes in the *International Herald Tribune* writing that the show, 'was a mix of the sleekly cut 1970s tailored pantsuits with a young aesthetic … McCartney wisely sent out a simple, unpretentious show literally filled with little nothings: dresses as light as a scarf; wispy printed blouses with floaty flower-child sleeves; slithery negligée dresses, always with the dressmaking details.' Later McCartney told fashion writer Andrew Tucker, 'I didn't design it with a theme in mind; it's about my friends, and what I get up to when I'm in London.'

It was precisely this London spirit that Paris wanted – and has continued to want ever since. Following McCartney's departure from Chloe in 2001 (like McQueen's, her own label became part of the Gucci Group), the house appointed her assistant, friend and fellow Londoner Phoebe Philo as head designer. In March 2008 the same job went to yet another British designer, Hannah McGibbon; Philo was subsequently appointed creative director of Celine by Bernard Arnault. Other labels would follow the same path. Vionnet, for example, appointed Sophia Kokosalaki as its head designer in 2006 (but then lost her after barely a year when she decided to concentrate on her own company). And in October 2005 Matthew Williamson took over as creative director of the Italian label Pucci.

No wonder that during the second half of the 1990s London could reclaim its former title as the world's most fashionable city. That status was confirmed in March 1997 when *Vanity Fair* ran a story decreeing 'London Swings! Again!', the magazine's cover showing Oasis singer Liam Gallagher and actress Patsy Kensit lying sprawled on a Union Jack bedspread. A sub-heading to David Kemp's story on London explained, 'As it was in the mid-60s, the British capital is a cultural trailblazer, teeming with new and youthful icons of art, pop music, fashion, food, and film. Even its politicians are cool. Or, well, coolish.' That last point referred to the revamped Labour party, which, with Tony Blair at its head, would soon win the British General Election of May 1997. The Conservative party had run the country since 1979 and though the national economy had since recovered from recession and was well on the way to a fresh boom, the outgoing Prime Minister, John Major – represented on television satire *Spitting Image* as a grey-faced man in grey clothing who ate grey peas off a grey plate – symbolized a tired

Prior to establishing his own label in 1997, Matthew Williamson spent two years designing for the high street chain Monsoon, and he spent much of this time in India. The effect has been seen in his work ever since, notably in a fondness for beading and embroidery and a fearless approach to colour. Here Naomi Campbell wears a white fringed and embroidered dress from Williamson's spring/summer 2000 collection.

regime that had long since run its course. 'Great Britain is the first of the major European Union countries to emerge fully from the recession of the early nineties,' wrote Kemp in *Vanity Fair*, 'its growth rate being the EU's highest, its unemployment rate among the lowest. But what truly speeds the city along is a confluence of random, mutually beneficial circumstances that have simultaneously transformed London into the seat of a thriving indigenous film industry, the nerve center of pop music's most cohesive scene since the Pacific Northwest grunge explosion of 1991, and a center of gastronomy and fashion that outclasses Paris.'

One aspect of London's creativity during the period that *Vanity Fair* overlooked, presumably because it had no desire to publicize potential rivals, was the rash of new style magazines coming out of London at the time, among them *Dazed & Confused*, *Don't Tell It* and *SleazeNation*. Above all there was *Wallpaper**, which first appeared on newsstands in September 1996. The brainchild of Canadian journalist and longtime London resident Tyler Brûlé, *Wallpaper** was quite unlike any magazine that had been seen before, seamlessly blending travel, interior design and architecture, fashion and entertainment. As the *New York Times* explained a year later to anyone still unfamiliar with the publication, *Wallpaper** had gone far 'beyond traditional shelter publications by photographing fictitious living rooms inhabited by terminally hip models, wearing the latest fashions and dining on stylish but birdlike meals. For the magazine's newly arrived readers, every item, down to the wine in the glasses and the ambient-style music on the DVD player, is listed, with prices and store information.' After producing just four issues, Brûlé was able to sell his creation to Time Inc (although he was obliged to remain as editor for some time afterwards).

Wallpaper*'s assured blend of different elements of contemporary culture was in keeping with the mood of the moment. After all, *Vanity Fair*'s account of Swinging London Mark II did not feature fashion as standing alone or apart from other disciplines. On the contrary, in 'Cool Britannia' designers mixed with artists and musicians and writers in a swirl of collective creativity. Or at least that was how the magazine portrayed London, juxtaposing Damon Albarn of Blur with Alexander McQueen, Damien Hirst with Stella McCartney.

Certainly it is true that by this time fashion itself had become generally fashionable. A democratization process begun in the 1980s had now reached the point where fashion was a subject with broad appeal and received as much media coverage as visual art or music. This was particularly so in Britain,

Reflecting the increasingly close links between fashion and art, in May 2000 *Vogue* invited a number of well-known artists, including Marc Quinn, Tracey Emin, Gary Hume, Sam Taylor-Wood, the Chapman brothers and Sarah Morris, to represent model Kate Moss 'in any way they choose'. A digital illustration of Moss by Morris that appeared on *Vogue*'s cover was adapted for the cover of the *London Fashion Week Advance* magazine in September 2000 and used by designer Nathan Church as the image for Fashion Week.

where the rise of a new generation of designers had been paralleled by the emergence of what came to be known as Young British Artists or YBAs. This loosely affiliated group included not just Damien Hirst but also Tracey Emin, Jake and Dinos Chapman, Sarah Lucas, Mark Wallinger and Rachel Whiteread. Like their counterparts in the field of fashion, the majority of whom had studied at Central St Martins, many of these artists had graduated from the same London college (in their case, Goldsmiths) and they displayed similar marketing and self-promotional skills. In her 2008 book *Seven Days in the Art World*, Sarah Thornton quotes a Sotheby's representative commenting that, 'a lot of artists today are succeeding on sound business principles,' just as were a lot of young fashion designers. The YBAs knew the value of establishing good connections, not least with collector Charles Saatchi, who, in his active engagement with the market, might be considered BritArt's equivalent of Bernard Arnault. During the first half of the decade, Saatchi organized a series of exhibitions in his St John's Wood private gallery before contributing work from his personal collection to 'Sensation', a show of new British art that opened at London's Royal Academy of Art in mid-September 1997 – and duly caused a sensation. The parallels between fashion and art were noted before the end of the month by the *International Herald Tribune*'s Suzy Menkes in her review of London Fashion Week: 'With a rasp of cotton wadding, the dress was torn open – and out from the model's latex-encased body flew a cloud of bugs. Shock! Horror! Make that "Sensation" – the name of the Brit/Art show currently packing them in at the Royal Academy, where Damien Hirst's bugs circle a decaying cow's head. The bug dress was shown in a buzzy London Fashion Week, in which the cutting-edge designers mirror avant-garde art in their obsession with sex, death, leather, rubber, metal – and publicity. Alexander McQueen is on the cover of *Time Out* and Hirst graces *Dazed and Confused*. But the real sensation of London Fashion Week was not how shocking designers could be – but how fast and far the event has grown since the city was the lame duck of fashion capitals in the early 1990s.'

Over the next few years, it would not seem unusual for Tracey Emin to write in *Vogue* of her enthusiasm for Vivienne Westwood (April 2004), or for the same magazine to devote increasing amounts of space to coverage of contemporary art. In July 1999 Bethan Cole wrote in *Vogue* of the links between the two disciplines, noting that, 'Once, fashion was fashion and art was art. Separate concepts, individual disciplines, sharply defined boundaries.' Increasingly, however, the lines were blurred, as 'collaborations between artists and designers have never been hipper.' In spring 2000, for example, Sarah Morris's image of Kate Moss was used in the publicity for London

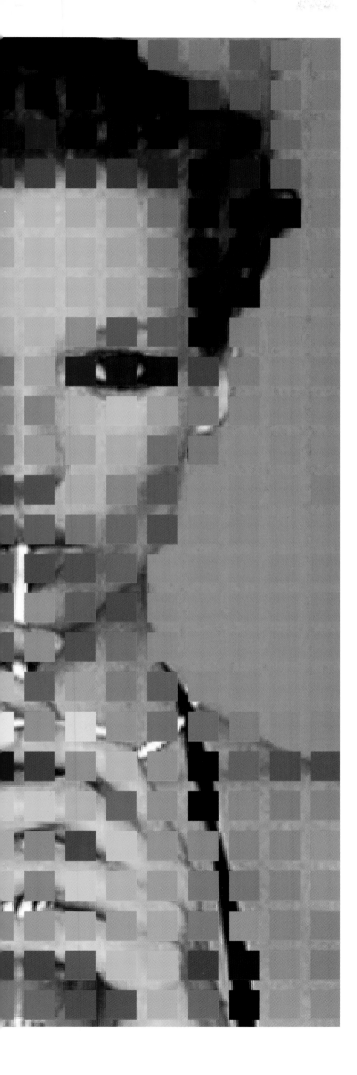

Fashion Week, while in 2005 Tracey Emin created a site-specific pink neon artwork for the entrance to the London Fashion Week tents and in September 2008, the fashion label Mulberry invited east London art space Fred Gallery to open in its Bond Street store during the annual Frieze art fair.

In 1998 London's Hayward Gallery examined the matter with an exhibition called 'Addressing the Century: 100 Years of Art and Fashion'. As the show's title indicated, there had, of course, been alliances between the two disciplines before, notably during the interwar years and involving a handful of French designers like Chanel and Schiaparelli and artists who were living and working in Paris at the time. But there were two crucial differences between the fashion/art links of that period and those forged in the late 1990s. The first of these was that some designers saw connections of this kind as a means of raising the status of their own work, not least by having it shown in the context of a gallery (most famously the Giorgio Armani retrospective held at New York's Guggenheim Museum in 2000, which was subsequently shown at the Royal Academy of Art in London). But for other designers the motives were more straightforwardly commercial: contemporary art and contemporary fashion had both become so modish that it made sense to look for collaborations, such as Marc Jacobs' invitation in 2000 to Japanese artist Takashi Murakami to re-envisage the Louis Vuitton signature monogram pattern; the result was profitable for everyone involved. Should fashion be considered art or not? Did it matter so long as positive publicity – and sales – were generated? Tellingly, in 2008 Darya Zhukova, partner of Russian plutocrat Roman Abramovich, owned both a fashion label and a contemporary art gallery.

In the closing years of the 1990s, British designers had not only to be aware of these cultural trends but also to pursue the right contacts, because competition between them was growing ever more intense. Each season seemed to produce another outstanding designer – or several – who threatened to draw the spotlight away from everybody else. Under these circumstances, getting noticed grew harder and harder. Matthew Williamson made a memorable debut in September 1997 with a collection called 'Electric Angels'. Unlike the usual jumble of ideas presented by a debutant, his show had a coherent character and featured just eleven outfits, each of them distinctive because of the designer's juxtaposition of liquorice-allsort colours, feminine shapes and handcrafted details. Williamson, wrote Suzy Menkes in the *International Herald Tribune*, 'had a real hit with a tightly edited collection. His pretty, unpretentious clothes in delicious colors, with subtle dragonfly or peacock-feather embroidery, made a very fine impression.' That fine impression was created not only by the quality of the clothes but also by the fact that

For 'Electric Angels', Matthew Williamson's debut catwalk show in September 1997, he presented just eleven outfits, all of them shown on high-profile friends – including Jade Jagger, Helena Christensen and Kate Moss – who waived their modelling fees in return for being allowed to keep the clothes.

they were being modelled by high-profile friends of the designer such as Jade Jagger, Helena Christensen and Kate Moss – thereby ensuring that he received plenty of press attention right from the start. Williamson, like so many of his peers, realized that in addition to ability, knowing the right people could make all the difference to his prospects. After graduating from Central St Martins, he initially worked for the Italian label Marni and then spent two years with the high street chain Monsoon before starting his own label. At which point, as he told Mark Tungate in 2005, 'I wanted to get some publicity, so I opened a copy of British *Vogue* and scanned the editorial page. I thought going straight for the editor might be a bit over-ambitious, so I chose a writer called Plum Sykes, because I liked her name.' In fact, Sykes was an extremely well-connected journalist and she responded with gusto to a letter from Williamson, not least because it came accompanied by one of his very pretty scarves. She told him that if he produced some clothes and sold these to a shop, *Vogue* would run a full-page story on him; Williamson promptly visited A La Mode in Knightsbridge, which placed an order for several dozen dresses, and his career as an independent designer had begun. (He also got his page in *Vogue*.)

Success was surely going to come to Matthew Williamson whether or not he had been able to persuade famous friends to model in his first show. But their presence bears witness to yet another feature of this period: the growing links between fashion and celebrity. As fashion was found to be fashionable and as it reached an ever-broader demographic, so it became of interest to figures in the public arena – to musicians and actors, to television presenters and that inexplicable band, the famous-for-being-famous – all of them eager for association with whichever domain was known to have the widest popular appeal. And in return fashion could not but see the merits of a connection with celebrity. For the two groups to join forces was a mutually beneficial arrangement; this now seems self-evident, and yet it was all very new at the time. The connection was made manifest by the increasing use of celebrities on the cover of fashion magazines, traditionally a territory reserved for models. The drive for readership in an increasingly crowded market led editors to recognize that celebrity could help to sell a publication. This was the case even for such august titles as *Vogue*: as early as February 1989 it had given a cover to Madonna (and seven months later to actress Isabella Rossellini) and by 2002 it was carrying a *Vogue Celebrity Style* supplement ('Get to know your favourite celebrity with *Vogue*'s guide, which takes you on a tour behind the scenes of fame'). Two years before, James Sherwood in the *International Herald Tribune* had warned of 'celebrity saturation' and quoted writer and editor Sarah Mower arguing, 'I think people are bored to death with celebrity and particularly with the same naff, overexposed soap and pop stars currently dominating British fashion magazine covers.' But the demise of celebrity as a tool to sell magazines has been greatly exaggerated. In November 2002 *Vogue*'s editor, Alexandra Shulman, told Susannah Frankel of the *Independent*, 'Models come and go so quickly these days that they have no recognition factor … We are not a boutique magazine aiming to sell 35,000 issues. When you want to sell as many magazines as we do, it's very important.'

The association between fashion and the famous also extended to other areas of the industry. Until the mid-1980s, the audience at a runway show had been of interest to nobody other than those present. Front row seats were occupied by the most powerful editors and buyers and those behind them were filled by other members of the same professions. That all changed once celebrities started to attend shows. 'Pop stars are the new status symbol at the shows,' observed Terry Keane of Ireland's *Sunday Independent* in October 1988, writing of the just-concluded London Fashion Week. 'Simon Le Bon and Duran Duran at Anthony Price and Boy George at Katharine Hamnett caused a flurry of excitement and neck craning and flash bulbs popping …' The year before, the *Daily Telegraph*'s Hilary Alexander –

Left Gleaming metallic reflectives from Michiko Koshino's autumn/winter 2001 collection.

Below Glam-rock Swarovski crystal chains over a black body suit, from Julien Macdonald, autumn/winter 2001.

always quick to spot an emerging trend – had listed some of the well-known names at Alistair Blair's latest show, among them Simon Le Bon (a regular at these events, as his wife, Yasmin, was a model), actress Fiona Fullerton, photographer and former girlfriend of Prince Andrew Koo Stark, Viscount Linley and 'Elton John's wife, Renata'. As the 1990s progressed and fashion became part of mainstream popular culture, designers who thrived on publicity found it beneficial to have a quotient of celebrities occupying front row seats at their shows (in Milan, Gianni Versace's press office would fax fashion editors and journalists a pre-show release providing no information on the clothes but listing the famous names expected to attend). With the mass market media taking an ever-greater interest in fashion, celebrity endorsement provided an obvious means for designers to become better known among the general public, although this approach did have its drawbacks: as had been the case with the supermodels, the focus could shift away from what ought to have been the main interest – the clothes. In March 1998, Julien Macdonald paid an ironic tribute to the celebrity fad when he planted a Michael Jackson lookalike in the audience at his show. The trouble was, Suzy Menkes noted in the *International Herald Tribune*, that the doppelganger 'hamming it up in the front row distracted attention from the quiet elegance of simple black outfits in lacy stitches.' As Susannah Frankel wrote in the *Independent* in November 2002, 'What designers gain in publicity they stand to lose in credibility ... High fashion should, by its very nature, be inaccessible – a closed world committed to scaling imaginative and innovative heights. Appeal to the masses and you might just as well sell your proud-to-be-elitist soul.'

Far left Clements Ribeiro is the husband-and-wife team of Brazilian Inacio Ribeiro and English-born Suzanne Clements, who both studied fashion at Central St Martins. They launched their label with a collection for spring/summer 1994. This military-style jacket and dress is from the autumn/winter 2001 collection.

Left Antoni & Alison (Antoni Burakowski and Alison Roberts) was established in 1987 as a business creating T-shirts that bore ironic or surreal slogans and sometimes social commentary. The range proved wildly successful and since then the company has expanded into womenswear, such as these separates from autumn/winter 2001.

Below Paul Smith made his reputation as a designer of menswear and only after this business was firmly established did he even consider moving into the area of women's fashion, with a first foray in 1998. In many ways this follows the same principles that had already made him so successful in menswear. The clothes are not avant-garde but are based on traditional models. Nevertheless, there is often some element of quirkiness that distinguishes a Paul Smith item from other designers' work. This autumn/winter 2003 double-breasted coat, for example, has a classic shape but unexpected colouring.

Some designers went a stage further and invited celebrities to move from the audience to the catwalk. Kylie Minogue appeared on the runway at Antonio Berardi's very first show in September 1995. 'I used to make stage clothes for her when I was at St Martins,' he explains. 'So when I told her about my show and said she was welcome to come along, she asked "Can I be in it?"' Once more this rage for celebrity models quickly ran its course. In February 2000 Victoria Beckham made her catwalk debut for Maria Grachvogel, with mixed results for the latter. Susannah Frankel remarked in the *Independent*, 'Grachvogel is a competent designer but has little credence outside the British domestic market. Yet her show, opened and closed by Victoria Beckham, gained more publicity in Britain than any other outfit, from any other show, in any other fashion capital this season.' The backlash began within days when Hussein Chalayan, accepting his award as British Designer of the Year, commented, 'I'd like to take this opportunity to say how disappointing it was this week that all the press were still so impressed by celebrities appearing on designers' catwalks. It was especially disappointing because that space could have been given to all the designers who bust their gut in the last week or so. … it's Fashion Week, not Celebrity Week.'

Chalayan was by no means the only designer less than enamoured of the ever-closer ties between fashion and celebrity. Six months earlier, Victoria Beckham's office had telephoned Alexander McQueen to request a front row seat at his forthcoming show: the request was declined. A spokesperson for McQueen subsequently commented that Beckham's presence would be 'inappropriate' and might detract from the clothes. (In April 2008, after opening a new shop in Los Angeles, McQueen declared that were Paris Hilton to pass the premises, 'Hopefully she'll just keep walking. … I can't get sucked into that celebrity thing because I think it's just crass.')

Eight years later, in September 2008, Victoria Beckham launched her own line of clothing during New York Fashion Week, showing that once a brand name had become sufficiently well known, it could be attached to almost any product (in June 2003 *Time* ran a feature on the former singer and her footballer

husband, David, entitled 'Brand it like Beckham'). By that time, many other celebrities had entered the fashion arena, either producing clothing ranges under their own names (P Diddy, Beyoncé Knowles) or else working with a well-known chain of stores (Madonna with H&M, Kate Moss at Topshop). Branding was an exercise in which American and Italian designers like Ralph Lauren and Giorgio Armani had long shown themselves adept, with the result that by the 1990s their names had achieved global recognition. Unfortunately, the same could not be said about British designers other than Paul Smith and, to a lesser extent, Vivienne Westwood and John Galliano.

Even those British fashion names known around the world did not achieve sales figures to match the scale of their renown; they were more admired than bought. This was particularly the case with old-established clothing businesses, of which Britain had a great many, including Burberry, DAKS, Aquascutum, Austin Reed and Jaeger. While they were all highly respected heritage names, these companies had failed to update their product and were in danger of being swamped by more sophisticated competitors with a better understanding of the market. That scenario changed in the early 1990s, when these companies began to recognize that they must modernize or suffer the consequences. In October 1992 the chief executive of Jaeger, Fiona Harrison, told Lisa Armstrong of the *Independent* that the old stratifications of fashion had gone for good: 'Age, and to an extent even price, is no longer the great issue ... What counts is attitude and that's what we're trying to capture.'

Psychological adjustment took another few years, but a major breakthrough came with the appointment of former Saks Inc president Rose Marie Bravo as chief executive of Burberry in 1997. At the time, the 142-year old company best known for its waterproof raincoats was profitable but looking tired, and it was hampered by an ageing customer base. New Yorker Bravo applied the lessons she had learnt from American fashion to the British label: she cleared away redundant licences (and closed down two factories in Britain) and returned the focus to the core brand image, specifically the Burberry check. At the same time, Bravo hired Italian designer Roberto Menichetti (who had launched the Jil Sander menswear label) to produce a new contemporary clothing range, named Prorsum, which was launched in September 1998. Art director Fabien Baron revamped the brand logo and Mario Testino photographed the advertising campaign material using model Stella Tennant to convey the sense of a clothing line that was simultaneously traditional and modern. 'There are three natural ingredients at work,' Bravo told the *Daily Telegraph*'s Hilary Alexander in August 2000. 'First, the brand was already there with its history and heritage. Then, I have had a very special team who understand the core values of

Previous pages John Galliano had enjoyed critical acclaim but little commercial success while he was based in London during the 1980s. When he moved to Paris in 1988 his clothes began to attract the clientele they deserved. In 1996 he became chief designer at the house of Givenchy but just a year later he moved to Dior, where he has remained ever since. Here Galliano is seen with models Stella Tennant and Kristen McMenamy in the autumn/winter 1997 ready-to-wear collection he produced for Dior.

Right A talent to create a stir can evidently pass down the generations. The exotic and erotic lingerie company Agent Provocateur was started in 1994 by Serena Rees and Joseph Corré, son of Vivienne Westwood and Malcolm McLaren. Their provocative ads starring celebrities and supermodels including Kylie Minogue, Kate Moss and Naomi Campbell (seen here) have kept their profile high and enabled a global spread of Agent Provocateur shops.

what we are doing. Finally, there is the support of the board of directors, who believe in the vision of a British luxury brand.' The results of her handiwork were immediately hailed as a triumph by the press ('The trench coats, the plaid, the innovative fabrics – they're all there, but reinvented for a new age,' wrote Anne-Marie Schiro in the *New York Times*) and, more importantly, by store buyers throughout the world.

Britain was no more immune to the appeal of Burberry than anywhere else. In 2001 the *Economist* claimed the country was 'in the grip of Burberry mania. Two years ago, the label was shunned by all but Asian tourists for its naff plaid-lined raincoats that not even dead men would be caught wearing. Today, everyone from Posh Spice to Cherie Blair, who wore Burberry to the state opening of Parliament, is sporting its signature camel, black and red plaid design.' By the time Burberry was launched on the stock market in 2002, annual revenue stood at almost £500 million – up 16 per cent on the previous year.

Though Bravo finished her term as chief executive in early 2006 (and Roberto Menichetti had been replaced by British designer Christopher Bailey five years earlier), Burberry continues to serve as a role model for how best to revitalize a fashion label. 'Doing a Burberry' became shorthand for overhauling an old business and transforming it into a profitable global brand. Other companies followed suit, such as Mulberry which in 2001 established a partnership with Singapore-based entrepreneur Christina Ong and installed Scott Henshall as its new designer (in 2005 Henshall was succeeded by Stuart Vevers; when Vevers later went on to be creative director of the Spanish fashion house Loewe, his position at Mulberry was taken by Emma Hill). Aquascutum also underwent an overhaul in the same year, while Jaeger, which was acquired by Harold Tillman in 2004, has since been revitalized thanks to the appointment of Belinda Earl as the company's chief executive and Karen Boyd as its in-house designer. In a feature in *The Times* in October 2008, Tillman specifically referred to Burberry, noting how, like Burberry, 'Jaeger had a Britishness to it. I felt it had the potential to become a complete lifestyle brand.'

But could the same be true of individual British designers? Could they also achieve the same kind of widespread branding success as a long-established business like Burberry or Jaeger? A formidable barrier to realizing this ambition was cost: designer clothes were too expensive for the mass market and this inhibited growth beyond a certain affluent sector. Even if customers knew a designer's name, they could not necessarily afford the goods. Other design labels around the world had overcome this problem by producing less expensive diffusion lines, thereby making their product accessible to a much greater number of consumers. Ironically, however, creating an inexpensive secondary

Left New Yorker Rose Marie Bravo, as chief executive, together with Italian designer Roberto Menichetti and later Christopher Bailey, revitalized the traditional Burberry brand by updating its existing product and producing a new contemporary clothing range, Prorsum. By the time this leather skirt and wool jacket were produced in autumn/ winter 2002, Burberry had become one of the world's most sought-after labels.

Right The Jasper Conran label achieved a resurgence in the late 1990s, thanks in part to his association with high street chain Debenhams, which brought his name – and work – to a wider customer base. Many of his peers, he says, disapproved: 'But I didn't see it like that.' And Conran still continued with his main line, such as this suit from autumn/winter 2001.

line was beyond the means of most designers, who struggled even to produce their existing ranges. Again, in Italy and the United States this hurdle had been overcome thanks to licensing agreements with manufacturers who were prepared to carry much of the cost involved in return for a share of the profits. In Britain, first hostility from domestic manufacturers and then the decline of that sector made such arrangements impossible.

Impossible, that is, until the high street, hitherto perceived as British designers' greatest threat, chose to become their ally. As has been seen, for most of the twentieth century British chain stores had demonstrated little or no interest in quality design. This situation had begun to change from the 1970s onwards with the emergence of new high street names like Jigsaw, Warehouse and, above all, Next. But while these companies employed in-house design teams, the designers' names were unknown. Designer anonymity was also preserved at Marks & Spencer. Although from the late 1980s onwards designers such as Betty Jackson and Paul Smith were invited to act as consultants, the link was never publicized. Jackson remembers attending a meeting with Sir Richard Greenbury (chairman of Marks & Spencer from 1988 to 1999), 'And he said, "St Michael: Betty Jackson. I think our name is the bigger one."' Clinton Silver confirms that, at Marks & Spencer, 'We had arrangements with designers to work with the company, but their names were nowhere on the labels; there was mutual disdain at the idea.'

But as designer names continued to grow ever bigger, it became progressively more difficult for the high street to ignore the significance of this trend within the fashion industry, especially given the evidence from Italy and the United States of just how commercially viable diffusion lines could be. The situation finally started to change in 1993, when department store chain Debenhams, then part of the Burton Group, asked milliner Philip Treacy to produce a range of affordable hats for its nationwide outlets. Priced at between £85 and £120, these proved so successful that the following year Debenhams joined forces with designer Ben de Lisi to create an eveningwear range exclusive to its store. Much of the credit for this innovation in British fashion belongs to Terry Green, who had been appointed chief executive of Debenhams in 1991 and remained in that position for the next nine years. 'I would say this,' he remarks, 'that there was always a disconnect between the fashion you saw on the catwalk and what was available on the high street. Designers had a suspicion we were trying to knock them off so I thought maybe the answer was to get them to do diffusion lines for us.'

'Today, people take it for granted,' Debenhams' design director Stephanie Chen told the *Daily Telegraph*'s Hilary Alexander in December 2003, 'But it was difficult in the early stages and it was a tremendous leap of faith for the designers, who had never done anything like this before … the important thing is that we understand how to make things easier for the designers to be creative. We put the resources behind their brands, we handle the production, but they do the design work. We do protect the integrity of their names. We don't just bung someone's name on.' The real breakthrough came in 1996, when Jasper Conran, one of the best-known names in British fashion, agreed to design a line of womenswear – simply called J – for Debenhams. Initially, he says, many of his peers were aghast at the idea: 'There was a lot of looking down, a lot of shock and horror. But I didn't see it like that. Everyone in America and Italy was doing second lines that sold a lot more. What added up for me in working with Debenhams was that I had a 100-store business and manufacturing behind me – everything I'd never had before. It was a relationship I could have had with any British manufacturer, but by then they'd all gone.' With Conran on board, Terry Green realized that the next move was to devote an area inside every store to his new designer acquisitions, but first he had to persuade his board of the logic behind this development. 'I needed to get to £50 million sales – the same as we already had for childrenswear – before I could have divisional status for the designers.' Sales of Conran's clothing helped to realize this target and before long Green had a section within each outlet called 'Designers at Debenhams' and featuring more than thirty of the best-known names in British fashion.

As a way of encouraging participants to engage fully with the process, Debenhams paid relatively modest design fees but offered designers a percentage on all sales. 'The more they sold at full price, the more they earned,' Green explains. 'And at certain reduced prices they earned nothing.' Along with Conran, one of the biggest earners from the scheme has been designer John Rocha, who in 2000 launched four diffusion lines in Debenhams covering women's, men's and childrenswear as well as homeware – the first time all departments had been simultaneously covered. 'It's not like in France or Italy,' he explains. 'In Britain we don't have a very strong home base for designer fashion, so to be successful you have to have a retail presence on the high street to maximize your potential. Now that's an acceptable thing. Although at the time people said I'd sold out, from my point of view it made sense.' As Hilary Alexander commented in the *Daily Telegraph* in January 2001, 'Such ventures will not make millionaires of the British fashion pack, but they do bring their designs to a wider audience, something that might not otherwise happen. More importantly, because of the high street stores' manufacturing and distribution expertise, the designs are made available in a much broader range of sizes than would have been possible under the designer's name alone.'

John Rocha taking his catwalk bow in 1994, when he was named British Designer of the Year. Rocha grew up in Hong Kong of Chinese and Portuguese parentage, studied fashion in England and has been based in Ireland for more than three decades. Like Jasper Conran, he has established a highly successful association with Debenhams. 'Having a licence with Debenhams', he says, 'allowed me to generate capital to do the other things that I'm good at', such as the white coat on the right, from his autumn/winter 2001 principal line.

In fact, the arrangement could be financially advantageous: Rocha makes the point that the designers who most profited from the association with a high street chain were those who most actively engaged with the process from start to finish. 'The thing about licences', he says, 'is that you get what you put into them. A lot of designers like the idea of extra income but don't realize it's a two-way partnership.'

The Debenhams model proved such a winning formula that by the end of the decade it had become ubiquitous through British retailing and would even attract the participation of renowned non-national designers such as Karl Lagerfeld, Roberto Cavalli and Rei Kawakubo of Comme des Garçons, all of whom produced ranges for H&M (in 2004, 2007 and 2008 respectively). The Topshop chain proved especially adept at offering consumers 'designer' fashion at high street prices. As Caroline Evans has written in *The London Look* (2005), 'Topshop successfully tapped into a desire to mix high street, vintage and designer in one look, rather than looking too obviously "designer". The look, combining high style and mass market, is identifiably "British" yet shows how much of what is considered to be British style is often London-oriented and London-led. Topshop arguably revolutionized women's fashion more than the individual designers, whose eclectic boutiques also characterized the city's fashion culture in the late nineties.'

The arrival of good design at reasonable prices was acknowledged in the media, not least by *Vogue*, which in April 1996 for the first time ever devoted an issue to high street fashion. 'And that's not just because the past few years have made many of us more conscious about what we're getting for our money,' explained an editorial in the magazine, 'but because chain stores in general have perked up dramatically … Style, as anyone who has it will tell you, is as much a question of knowing where to shop as anything else.' Thanks to an injection of designer flair, the local high street was *the* place to shop for clothes. From now on it was a matter of pride among discerning consumers to mix cheap diffusion pieces with items from a designer's more expensive primary range; barriers between one side and the other had broken down. The pages of that April 1996 *Vogue* – and many subsequent issues – were filled with clothes that had come from outlets such as Next, Principles, Warehouse, Miss Selfridge, Topshop and Oasis. Two months later, again for the first time, a model appeared on the cover of *Vogue* wearing an item from a high street name: Amber Valetta was photographed in a £21 Marks & Spencer blue shantung shirt. Before long, high street had become main street. In May 2004, for example, *Vogue* carried a supplement, called the *Cheap Chic Guide*, entirely devoted to chain store clothing.

Though catching up somewhat later than other chain stores, even the dominant presence in British retail could not ignore the rise of designer diffusion clothing. After closing her own business, Sheilagh Brown had been appointed head of womenswear design at Marks & Spencer in 1990, and she embarked on a struggle to persuade the company's management that stocking well-designed clothes made commercial sense. It took some time but eventually, as Brenda Polan wrote in the *Evening Standard* in November 2000, Marks & Spencer 'dared to trust designers to design.' The previous March Britain's leading high street company had unveiled its new Autograph label, a series of collections designed by the likes of Betty Jackson, Matthew Williamson, Julien Macdonald, Hussein Chalayan and Katharine Hamnett.

As might have been predicted, this met with immediate approval from the consumer, so much so that while the rest of Marks & Spencer's business was stagnant, sales of womenswear were the one section showing improvement. In the *Independent*, Julia Stuart reported from a branch of the store in central London on the day Autograph made its debut, noting 'By 10.30 a.m. on Saturday there was already a disgruntled queue of women waiting to get into one of the boutique's four changing rooms. "We can't stack the shelves fast enough," said sales consultant Susan Coleman, bringing out yet more bright pink tops by Macdonald. "Katharine Hamnett wanted the minimalist look on her section, with only three items on each rail, but that's impossible with the amount of people in here. We've sold out of two of the Betty Jackson and Julien Macdonald ranges already." ' Conquering the hitherto impenetrable edifice of Marks & Spencer, as the new millennium arrived British designers had decisively moved from the periphery of the nation's fashion industry to its very centre.

Nicole Farhi was born in Nice and studied in Paris before moving in the early 1970s to London, where she and entrepreneur Stephen Marks created the French Connection label. In 1983 the Nicole Fahri label was born; it has since established a loyal following thanks to its understated but stylish clothing. 'My collections over the years have become more and more feminine,' she once said, adding that the work was 'altogether softer, using layers of colour and texture. I think a woman should express her sexuality ... not in a blatant way, but subtly – perhaps just by using fabric that is pleasing to the touch' – as in this dress from Farhi's spring/summer 2004 collection.

Postscript:

THE NEW MILLENNIUM

I n mid-October 2003, London's Royal Albert Hall was taken over by some of the world's most famous musicians and clothing designers, who for one night combined forces for Fashion Rocks. The charity event, which benefited the Prince's Trust, was the brainchild of Nicholas Coleridge, managing director of Condé Nast and at the time also Chairman of the British Fashion Council. His initial idea had been to stage a fashion show for the Trust, but the committee he assembled to help with the project quickly realized that something more would be needed if a large sum of money were to be raised from one night. 'So we came up with the idea of rock meets fashion,' says Claudia Crow, who played a pivotal role in bringing the show to fruition. 'It had to be the best of the best, otherwise why would an audience pay lots of money to be there?'

Fashion Rocks lasted three hours and featured the combined efforts of 17 international designers and an equal number of musicians, plus 150 models, 72 hairdressers, 84 make-up artists, 108 dressers and an uncounted quantity of bodyguards. Each designer – ranging from Giorgio Armani and Ralph Lauren to Julien Macdonald and Alexander McQueen – teamed up with a live performer. Among the latter were Robbie Williams (for Versace), Beyoncé Knowles (Armani), Duran Duran (Donna Karan) and Bryan Ferry (Yves Saint Laurent couture). Afterwards Coleridge told the *Daily Telegraph* that the musicians had been easier to deal with than their fashion counterparts: 'We had box office envy, dressing-room envy, model envy, billing envy, rock-star envy. Some of the designers and the people that surround them were hyperventilating with the sheer number of potential problems they could foresee.' In fact, none of the imagined problems arose and Fashion Rocks took place without a glitch.

In the new millennium London retained its reputation as the place to find cutting-edge creativity, with new designers such as Gareth Pugh, who is yet another graduate of Central St Martins. A debut show at the club Kashpoint's Alternative Fashion Week won Pugh Fashion East sponsorship in 2005.

This ballooned dress is from his summer 2006 collection. The following season he staged his first show during London Fashion Week. *Vogue* described Pugh's collection as 'an incredible, unmissable show' and wrote that 'his genius is undeniable.'

'I think the event is sensational,' designer Tom Ford told Godfrey Deeny of *Fashion Wire Daily*. 'The staging is excellent and the Albert Hall is really rocking.' Some £750,000 was raised for the Prince's Trust.

Fashion Rocks proved many things, not least that designers who were rivals in the global business community could temporarily lay competition aside for the sake of charity. But above all the night demonstrated that London was still the fashion world's leading centre for innovation within the international fashion industry. 'It is particularly a London event,' Coleridge told the *International Herald Tribune*'s Suzy Menkes a week beforehand. 'This is the only city where it would work, because of its cosmopolitan character.' As had been the case with another fund-raising occasion, Fashion Aid, held in the same venue almost exactly eighteen years earlier, Fashion Rocks showcased the extraordinary vitality and diversity of fashion in London. Other cities might be more commercially oriented but none could come near to matching London's dynamism.

Since the start of the new millennium that dynamism has been more in evidence than ever, not least thanks to London's ongoing ability to deliver new talent season after season. Jonathan Saunders, Basso & Brooke, Gareth Pugh, Christopher Kane, Giles Deacon and Marios Schwab are just some of the better-known designers who have begun their careers in London post-2000 and every year Britain's colleges seem to produce a fresh crop of outstanding graduates. The multiplicity of cultural backgrounds from which London's designers are drawn, already evident in the 1990s, has since become more apparent. A feature on new British fashion names carried in the May 2006 issue of *Vogue* observed, 'Their roots are as far afield as Afghanistan and Australia, but they've got two things in common: their home city – London – and their design talent.' Among those included in the story were Serbian Roksanda Ilincic and Erdem Moralioglu, whose parentage is Turkish-English and who was raised in Canada. Thanks to an international reputation for excellence enjoyed by London's third-level institutions – particularly the Royal College of Art, Central St Martins and the London College of Fashion – aspiring designers from around the world have made a point of coming to study fashion in England in ever-growing numbers. In 2002 the Malcolm Newbery report on the British Fashion Designer Industry found there were ninety-one fashion courses available across the country, producing around three thousand graduates every year. Even designers who did not necessarily attend one of these colleges have found London to be the most sympathetic place from which to launch their careers. 'We are multi-cultural nomads,' Peter Pilotto told Avril

Nicholas Coleridge, Claudia Crow and the Prince of Wales discussing Fashion Rocks, the fundraising night held at the Royal Albert Hall in October 2003 to benefit the Prince's Trust.

Groom of *The Times* in September 2008, speaking of himself and his design partner, Christopher de Vos. 'I'm Austro-Italian, Chris is Belgian-Peruvian, but since we both worked for Vivienne Westwood, London has been home.'

This diversity of origin had an interesting effect on British fashion, making it far less homogeneous than that produced in France, Italy or the United States. London seems to thrive on eclecticism. 'British designers have such a huge range of references,' commented Andrew Bolton, curator of the Anglomania fashion exhibition that opened in New York's Metropolitan Museum of Art in May 2006. Interviewed by *Vogue*'s Harriet Quick that same month, he further observed of British designers, 'They draw on such an eclectic array of sources, but it always seems to come together so poetically. I'm always awed by the way these designers keep their creative vision intact, without undue compromise.' Britain's designers are also now more likely to produce clothes of a quality comparable to that coming out of any other fashion capital; the days of London being creative but incompetent are definitely in the past. 'Ten years ago, what London designers did was pretty approximate,' Paris boutique owner Maria Luisa told Sarah Mower, writing in the *Observer* in February 2008. 'It is no longer that. Everything they do is very carefully considered, and each one is different. They deserve as much as the bigger labels.'

Another of London's attractions for new designers has been that it offers them a warmer welcome than they could expect to find elsewhere. As a British Fashion Council spokesperson told the *Independent*'s Susannah Frankel in February 2002, 'London has never tried to compete with the other fashion capitals. We are very different. What we give designers, more than anywhere else, is the space to grow and be different. We expect the unexpected.' This point is made over and over again by designers and others involved in the British fashion industry. 'I couldn't imagine working anywhere but London,' Jane Shepherdson, chief executive and co-owner of the Whistles chain of stores told *The Times* in September 2008. 'The rawness, energy and dynamism are unique. We take more fashion risks and we're more irreverent. British people are not afraid to be different, try new silhouettes, even look a bit silly.' The city itself – in all its multicultural, polyglot, globally connected glory – is also often cited as a source of inspiration and a reason for remaining in London. In *The Measure*, a book published in 2008 to mark the centenary of the London College of Fashion, designer Giles Deacon commented, 'I find London one of the

Hilary Riva and Harold Tillman with Sarah Brown at 10 Downing Street in September 2008. A successful businesswoman, Riva served as a dynamic chief executive of the British Fashion Council from December 2005 to March 2009, when she took on a new role with the organization, focusing on its future development projects. A graduate of the London College of Fashion (where he established a £1 million scholarship fund in 2006) and the owner of Jaeger since 2004, Tillman was appointed chairman of the British Fashion Council in February 2008.

Scottish-born designer Jonathan Saunders launched his own line in 2003 after graduating from Central St Martins with an MA in printed textiles. Prints feature strongly in his collections, as is evident in this design from his autumn/winter 2004 range. Since that time, Saunders' silhouettes have become less sharply defined and more fluid.

most culturally and artistically diverse and exciting cities in the world – of all the places I have worked and travelled in I am constantly excited by the city.'

It was only after 2000 that the full significance of Britain's indigenous fashion industry began to be appreciated at home. In December 2002 the Malcolm Newbery Consulting Company published a report on the UK Designer Fashion Industry jointly commissioned by the Department of Trade and Industry and the British Fashion Council. Among its most significant findings was that the performance of the fashion sector had grown markedly over the previous decade, with turnover from sales of designer clothing rising from £75 million in 1990 to £700 million in 2001. This represented compound growth per annum of 22.5 per cent and as clothing inflation during the period had been effectively zero, real growth achieved the same percentage. Designer clothing sales provided employment for around 8,500 people – by then six per cent of the total clothing industry workforce in Britain – and, the report commented, 'When classic brands and top end contemporary brands are added to the designer figures, they account for 14 per cent of the UK retail clothing industry.' Furthermore, those classic brands and independent designer labels combined were responsible for 75 per cent of British clothing exports, worth £2 billion per annum. No wonder the Newbery report could reach the conclusion, 'The Designer sector has performed economically very well, in both the UK and export markets, in comparison with the UK clothing industry, and also with UK industry generally.'

And fashion not only continued to attract ever-greater numbers of would-be designers but also remained of abiding interest to the general public, as evidenced by new publications entering an already congested market. *Glamour*, a well-established Condé Nast American title, was launched in Britain in April 2000 in a convenient 'handbag-size' format; within three years it had become the country's best-selling monthly magazine, with an average circulation of more than 605,000 copies. Then in February 2005 British publishers Emap launched the country's first weekly glossy magazine, *Grazia*, which within a year was selling more than 170,000 copies per £1.70 issue (a figure which, when multiplied by weeks in a year, gave the newcomer the highest retail

Conceived by fashion writer and historian Colin McDowell in 2004, Fashion Fringe is an annual project intended to identify and nurture British fashion talent. Each year four designers are given the backing to produce a capsule collection of twelve 'looks', which are then shown during the September London Fashion Week. Basso & Brooke was the first winner; the example shown here is from its spring/summer 2005 collection.

sales value of any publication in its sector). By 2008 British publishers were offering consumers more than thirty weekly women's magazines including *Hello!*, *OK!*, *New* and *Look*, all of them featuring fashion as a key component, whether discussing the clothes worn by celebrities or proposing how readers could emulate the dress styles of the famous.

At the same time the nation's high street chains continued to prosper; in October 2008, for instance, although parent company Arcadia posted a slight dip in operating profits (down to £275.3 million from £293.3 million the previous year), its Topshop division announced a record turnover, with the group's owner, Sir Philip Green attributing much of the success to the collections produced for the chain by model Kate Moss. Overall the health of the Britain's designer fashion industry has never looked better.

Which is not to suggest that old problems had disappeared at the start of the new millennium, or were speedily resolved. Chief among the ongoing difficulties is the loss to London of British designers, who, once their careers reach a certain point of development, feel obliged to present new collections somewhere else, usually Paris or New York. In 2001 after his first show in New York, Matthew Williamson explained his decision to Susannah Frankel: 'I have shown to the same audience for nine seasons. It's time to spread my wings and go global. I want a bigger business, a piece of the action. It's happened for Alexander McQueen, Stella McCartney and Julien Macdonald. Now I'm at the top of the queue.' (However, in June 2009 Williamson announced that the following September he would once again be participating in London Fashion Week).

The reasoning behind Williamson's departure (and that of others like him) is that cities such as New York and Paris attract more international press and buyers. At the same time, it could be argued that by moving away from London, designers help to make this a self-fulfilling prophecy. During London Fashion Week in February 2002, Paul Smith denounced those of his fellow countrymen who staged their shows abroad; this came in the aftermath of an attack launched in the *Sunday Times* by Nicholas Coleridge, then chairman of the British Fashion Council, on 'petulant British commentators' who

Following his graduation from Central St Martins, Giles Deacon worked for a diverse range of fashion houses including Jean-Charles de Castelbajac, Bottega Veneta, Gucci and Louis Vuitton before showing under his own name for the first time in spring 2004. The work was immediately acclaimed, not least for its combination of technical expertise with the sort of whimsical irreverence apparent in this dress from his collection for autumn/winter 2006, when he was named Designer of the Year. 'Hopefully, if you saw someone wearing one of our frocks,' Deacon has commented, 'you'd think she looks quite interesting to have a chat with and say hello to.'

Even while still a student at Central St Martins, Christopher Kane was winning awards and on graduation in 2006 he established his own label with his sister, Tammy. His first show that September featured extremely short bandage dresses such as this one, all of them in brilliant neon shades. In November 2007 he was named New Designer of the Year at the British Fashion Awards. Kane has worked with the Italian label Versace and designed clothes for a number of performers, including Kylie Minogue and Beth Ditto.

Right Erdem Moralioglu grew up in Montreal and after studying at the Royal College of Art he worked for Diane von Furstenberg in New York before setting up his own label in 2005. He describes the client he has in mind when designing as 'A clever person who probably cares little about seasons. She has a lot of conviction and marches to her own drum.' He received British Fashion Council Fashion Forward sponsorship for spring/summer 2009. This dress of tiered ruffles is from his autumn/winter 2007 collection.

failed to do enough to support their own industry, and an equally trenchant response in the *Evening Standard* from writer and fashion historian Colin McDowell, who declared that Coleridge's article had made his blood run cold, 'because it sounds a formula for a rerun of the past when, in the eighties and early nineties, crude "my country, right or wrong" jingoism nearly destroyed London fashion.' Jingoism was obviously never going to be of any lasting help, but it remains indisputable that without adequate support from all possible sources British designers will continue to look at the option of showing elsewhere. That is particularly so because of the status they enjoy globally: British designers bring with them a kind of excitement unmatched by their counterparts elsewhere. This makes them very attractive to other cities where the inherent thrill-quotient is lower.

In any case, not everyone who leaves necessarily stays away. Luella Bartley, a key name in British fashion in the late 1990s, caused an upset at home in 2001 when she moved her runway show to New York. But in September 2007 she returned to London, subsequently telling Jess Cartner-Morley of the *Guardian* that her work had always referenced the city, 'so the label fits here. When people see the clothes in London they

make more sense … I was really nervous about coming back to London, not just because of worrying how it would affect the business, but also because London is so much more creative as a fashion capital than New York that people here are really tough on you. But I enjoyed myself so much more – it felt like a real homecoming.' John Rocha showed for three years in Paris during the mid-1990s. In retrospect, he says, 'I feel much more at home in London. I tried Paris and felt quite uncomfortable there. … So one day I said to everyone, "We're going home; this is getting me down."' Rocha has remained faithful to London ever since.

What also has to be considered is the possibility that there may be advantages to some designers moving away from the city, if only because it frees

Above Two of the latest generation of design names to emerge in London are Sinha Stanic (left) and Roksanda Ilincic (right); these images are from their respective spring/summer 2007 collections. When the first Sinha Stanic show was staged in February 2005, Colin McDowell called it 'one of the most beautiful seen in London for some time' and the label soon attracted a celebrity clientele including Keira Knightley, Jennifer Lopez and Amy Winehouse. Roksanda Ilincic says of her work, 'Concentrating mainly on cocktail and occasion dresses, for which I'm best known, my collections conjure up the romantic and feminine feel of the past. Their execution … provides a sharper, modern twist.'

up space for newer, younger names. Some young birds may have to fly the nest so that other chicks can hatch and grow. As Roland Mouret, by then showing in New York, told *Vogue* in September 2004, 'London is an amazing place to start in fashion – it has allowed me to be and do everything I've ever dreamt of. I did my time here but it was important to make way for the new generation.' In this respect, London might be viewed as an incubator in which new talent is helped to develop before emerging into the international fashion industry. 'We're a sort of petri dish,' says *Vogue* editor Alexandra Shulman, who argues, 'more and more I think it's about how you view the situation rather than whether there's a problem or not.' She points out that many of the city's so-called problems – the departure of established designers, the absence of key international buyers and press, the jostling for adequate space on the global fashion calendar – are cyclical: they seem to be resolved and then emerge again, 'but when London Fashion Week does work out, probably around 60 per cent of the time, you will see more interesting things here in a day or a week than in any of the other territories.'

While some of London's difficulties are peculiar to the place, incapable of resolution without fundamental alteration to the city's DNA, others have been successfully tackled in recent years. In 1998, at the request of the Department of Trade and Industry, Susi Cheshire produced a report analysing the state of British Designer Fashion. Her findings only confirmed what was already well known: that the designer industry in Britain was made up of mainly small companies, only a couple of which could compare with the major brands found in centres such as Paris or Milan; that while the British designer industry was worth approximately £600 million, that in France was worth £900 million, Italy's £1.5 billion and that of the United States £5.2 billion; that fashion businesses in Britain were under-capitalized, slow to adopt product licensing and lacking identifiable brands; that the domestic market was relatively small; and that designers were lacking in adequate business training and generally support in this area. In late November 1998, these findings were discussed at a conference organized by the British Fashion Council (and chaired by the organization's chairman at the time, Sir John Hoerner) and attended by 246 delegates including 82 designers. It was agreed that practical measures, rather than further dialogue, were needed if real change were to be effected. The time for merely mulling over London's woes had come to a close – now was the moment for action.

Some of the measures taken would come not from official organizations but courtesy of private initiatives. As a rule, their focus was on providing support for emerging designers, who were especially vulnerable to even the slightest shift in market forces. The Malcolm Newbery report of December 2002 warned in particular that 'It is not a viable proposition for a young and possibly inexperienced designer to embark on a catwalk show at London Fashion Week. Should the individual put themselves [sic] in potential financial jeopardy, without proper financial support and the business infrastructure to do so?' A partial answer to this hypothetical question had already been provided by Fashion East, a philanthropic enterprise created in September 2000 by fashion impresario Lulu Kennedy. Each season Fashion East provided the necessary funding and support to allow three young designers to show their collections at London Fashion Week. Among those so aided have been Gareth Pugh, Jonathan Saunders, Emma Cook, Roksanda Ilincic, Marios Schwab and Henry Holland of the House of Holland. 'Kennedy is the Dr Sebagh of London's fashion scene,' wrote *Vogue*'s Emma Elwick in May 2008, 'giving a staid London landscape back its youth and vitality, with the unknowing ease of a Botox needle.' As a not-for-profit organization,

Fashion East, which is sponsored by Topshop, channels any money made during one season into the next.

Another question raised by the Newbery report was how designers, 'can be helped to fire fight day to day issues, where to buy cloth, who to make the samples, how to find enough money to make the samples etc. ... Designer support should include business advice and mentoring in order to improve commercial acumen, as well as the more glamorous aspects.' Precisely these issues were addressed by the establishment in 2004 of Fashion Fringe. Conceived by Colin McDowell, Fashion Fringe is an annual project intended to locate and nurture undiscovered British designers; funding for the scheme comes from sponsors and not from any public source. 'It's my response to what I have seen as a dangerous weakness in London fashion,' McDowell wrote in *Elle* magazine in October 2008, 'a lack of support at the beginning of designers' careers.' Under the Fashion Fringe format, during May each year four finalists are selected and provided with a budget to cover the following three months' living expenses, the purchase of fabric and payment of technical staff. They also receive studio space and help from mentors. At the end of the period, the finalists are expected to have created a capsule collection of twelve 'looks'; which are then shown during the September London Fashion Week. At that time an overall winner is chosen, the prize being a bespoke package of mentoring, business advice and planning, marketing, studio space and development grants worth some £100,000 – and all leading to the presentation of a full collection at the following February's London Fashion Week. Previous recipients of this award include Basso & Brooke (the very first), Erdem Moralioglu and Gavin Douglas.

A third significant private initiative was the establishment in January 2006 of a £1 million-plus scholarship programme to support new design talent at the London College of Fashion. The funding for this was provided by one of the college's alumni, entrepreneur Harold Tillman (who two years later would become chairman of the British Fashion Council). At the time Tillman told the *Financial Times*, 'Fashion is worth around £10 billion a year to Britain but it is only based around a very small network of businesses and I don't think those are aware of how much they rely on students coming through the system. We are not talking about the world class British designers ... but about the general design pool that most businesses need.'

At the same time as projects like Fashion East, Fashion Fringe and the LCF's scholarship scheme were getting underway, the British Fashion Council underwent some changes in order to make it more effective in providing support to designers and their industry. In 2004 Sir Stuart Rose assumed the position of the Council's chairman only months before he was appointed chief executive of Marks & Spencer; despite the heavy demands of the latter position, he still managed to devote considerable attention to the BFC. One of his most important initiatives was to separate the organization from the British Clothing Industry Association, which for some twenty years had financially supported the Council. Throughout that period, John Wilson had acted as chief executive of both organizations and deserves credit for consistently encouraging the BCIA to support the BFC. While this aid had been of help to the BFC in the short-term, ultimately it tended to hinder its independence – and proved a drag on the BCIA's own resources. A break between the two bodies was necessary and inevitable, but the Council needed alternative funding.

London Fashion Week already raised a larger sum of money through commercial sponsorship – more than £1 million per season – than any other such event around the world. In addition, the Council had begun to receive some financial aid from Creative London, a division of the London Development Agency, the Mayor of London's office responsible for encouraging sustainable economic growth throughout the capital. Criticized for not doing enough for the fashion industry, in September 2004 then-Mayor Ken Livingstone told Fleur Britten of the *International Herald Tribune*, 'We are not complacent … We are working to rebuild London as one of the world's fashion capitals.' But much of the London Development Agemcy's work in this area was piecemeal and lacked a coherent strategy that could lead to tangible and permanent results. Change came with the intervention of Rose, particularly after he had appointed Hilary Riva as chief executive of the British Fashion Council.

Riva, who took up her new job at the BFC in December 2005, is an experienced businesswoman who, four years before, as managing director of the Rubicon Retail group, had led a management buyout of high street chains Warehouse, Hawkshead, Principles and Racing Green from their parent company, Arcadia. By 2004 she had turned a £9 million operating loss into a £20 million profit, and in February 2005 she and her business partner,

Right Henry Holland started his business with a line of cheeky T-shirts carrying slogans such as 'I'll tell you who's boss, Kate Moss.' He has since extended his collection to include clothes such as this tartan suit from his autumn/winter 2008 range, worn by his friend and muse, model Agyness Deyn.

Below According to Luella Bartley, ex-*Vogue* and newspaper journalist, her first collection was almost an accident. 'I think we just got a bit drunk one night and my friends were like, "Just do it! Just make your own fashion label!" and I was like, "All right then! Yeah!"' The Luella label launched in 2000 was described by *New York* magazine as embodying 'the British "It" girl, with punk and frilly accents, pearls adorning layered party dresses, and tastefully cropped jackets'. Bartley moved her shows to New York for a period in the early 2000s but has since returned to London to present collections like this one of spring/summer 2008.

Peter Davies, sold Rubicon to The Shoe Studio Group for £140 million. As Stuart Rose told Imogen Fox of the *Guardian* in September 2006, Riva 'brings energy and relevant business experience to the BFC and a determination to move it on.' In the same feature, *Vogue*'s Alexandra Shulman observed of Riva, 'She takes a commercial view, which I applaud. Fashion cannot work in parallel to the rest of the world and exist on some rarefied level. It has to make money and the industry should be run as a business.'

But the organization Riva had taken on could only be run as a successful independent business if it had the backing necessary to survive a clean break from the British Clothing Industry Association. That alternative backing ultimately came from the London Development Agency which in September 2007 announced it had designated designer fashion as one of the city's specialist sectors with the biggest potential for growth; not only did the industry make a significant direct contribution to the economy of London, but it also brought in considerable extra revenue through tourism and retail sales. Three months later the London Development Agency confirmed it would support the British Fashion Council with a three-year funding package worth £4.2 million in order to provide business support to designers and to raise the profile of London Fashion Week across international markets. As Hilary Riva declared at the time, this funding, 'reaffirms and recognizes the British Fashion Council's role in promoting British-based designer business as well as identifying, showcasing and supporting exciting and emerging new talent. London has become the world's most creative and dynamic fashion centre and this funding will allow the British Fashion Council to build on this reputation.'

In March 2009 it was announced that Riva would step down as the British Fashion Council's chief executive, this position thereafter to be jointly held by Caroline Rush and Simon Ward; Rush had supported the BFC on communication and strategy for two years and Ward had worked for the BFC for eighteen years, supporting Riva as head of operations for the last three. Riva meanwhile was to chair a new development committee charged with focusing on future projects, including the BFC's funding and its role within the industry.

The British Fashion Council has long supported new designers through programmes such as the New Generation scheme, running since 1993 and providing recipients with a launch pad during London Fashion Week. Beneficiaries originally received funding for either a runway show or an exhibition space; by 2008 New Generation also included sales seminars, international market seminars and business advice specific to the designer fashion business, all of it intended to sustain new companies and give them a better opportunity to grow and survive. New Generation could only back designers for four successive seasons, but clearly some fledgling businesses require additional assistance, so in 2006 the BFC created a post-New-Generation fund called Fashion Forward which, as well as providing direct aid, also

addresses commercial needs in a more specific way. Among those who have been helped by Fashion Forward are Giles Deacon, Jonathan Saunders, Richard Nicoll, Christopher Kane and Marios Schwab. Additional programmes include the Council's MA scholarship, which was reinstated by a cash injection to the British Fashion Council's Princess of Wales Charitable Trust to mark the tenth anniversary of the Princess's death. In August 2008 this award went to Nabil El Nayal, allowing him to study at the Royal College of Art. The BFC's Colleges Council also launched an internship scheme with Italian fashion label MaxMara, which offered the recipient a four-month paid internship with the company.

As we mentioned at the start of this book, in mid-September 2008 Sarah Brown, the Prime Minister's wife, hosted a reception at 10 Downing Street for the British Fashion Council. The BFC used the occasion to announce its plans for the next twelve months, during which the Council would celebrate the twenty-fifth anniversary of its foundation. Among the projects outlined was the commissioning of a report to look at the scope and scale of the domestic fashion industry, with information on its impact on Britain's economy and on the country's international reputation as a creative centre. The BFC also declared its intention of launching an internet portal to provide a comprehensive online resource for anyone either working in the fashion world or aspiring to do so, while a careers initiative would outline the breadth of roles and encourage a new generation to join the industry. But the most important element of the BFC's

Above left Chief executive of Marks & Spencer Sir Stuart Rose (seen here with designer Giles Deacon) was responsible during his term as chairman of the British Fashion Council for severing that organization's long-standing link with the British Clothing Industry Association, a necessary move if the British Fashion Council was ever to be a fully independent body. Rose also appointed Hilary Riva as chief executive of the British Fashion Council in 2005.

Above right Simon Ward has worked for the British Fashion Council for over twenty years, first as administrator and more recently as head of operations. In March 2009 he became joint chief executive.

anniversary celebrations was the creation of a British Fashion Council Fashion Fund, a new trust designed to support designers and their businesses into the future and thereby create a sustainable British fashion industry. Thanks to the Fashion Fund, and as a result of a selection process conducted by a committee of key industry players, one business each year – not necessarily one established by a recent graduate – would henceforth enjoy significant support, while smaller awards would also be allocated to assist emerging talent. The first awards were to be launched in the BFC's twenty-fifth anniversary year. Predicted to be larger than the New York Fashion Fund jointly sponsored by Council of Fashion Designers of America and *Vogue*, the BFC Fashion Fund, according to Harold Tillman, 'is set to become the single most significant thing to hit British design in my lifetime. This will allow us to make a real difference to exciting businesses, assisting them to grow and develop here.' The British Fashion Council had certainly come a long way since its foundation in 1983.

Writing in the *Daily Telegraph* in February 2008, Hilary Alexander, noting the proliferation of fashion weeks around the world, commented, 'If you were so inclined, you could spend the entire year flitting from one catwalk week to another: Tobago, Accra, Costa Rica, Reykjavik, Montevideo, Istanbul, Kiev and Kuta in Bali all have fashion weeks now, as do Australia, New Zealand, Portugal and Spain. Some countries even have two – São Paolo and Rio de Janeiro in Brazil; New Delhi and Mumbai in India.' But, Alexander emphasized, only four such events could be considered of truly global significance: those taking place in Milan, Paris, New York and London. Of that quartet the last is, in strictly commercial terms, the smallest. But commercial considerations have never been so important to London as they have to its three counterparts. To some extent, the city has suffered from not placing enough emphasis on mercantile matters; it has had to watch as store buyers, when short of funds, opt to skip London but still visit the other centres. Nevertheless the city knows those buyers will be back, and so too will the fashion journalists, style monitors and trend forecasters. Because London has something that cannot be found in Paris or Milan or New York: a superabundance of design originality. As Colin McDowell wrote in the *Sunday Times* Style supplement in September 2008, 'On every level, London is the most extraordinary fashion city in the world. Our young, avant-garde designers exert huge influence on world creativity, even when they are selling clothes in very small numbers …' In the twenty-first century, London is the fashion world's crucible of creative energy, the place from which more exciting young designers emerge than anywhere else. No doubt there will be further problems ahead – they seem to be almost an essential part of the city's make-up – but they will be overcome. Unquestionably, for the foreseeable future London is going to remain a global fashion capital.

Caroline Rush has worked with the British Fashion Council since 1998. In March 2009 she became its joint chief executive (with Simon Ward).

Bibliography

In addition to a large range of archival material from newspapers, magazines and other publications of the period covered, the author also consulted the following works.

Agins, Teri, *The End of Fashion: The Mass Marketing of the Clothing Business* (William Morrow and Company, 1999)

Baudot, Francois, *A Century of Fashion* (Thames & Hudson, 1999)

Blanchard, Tamsin, *Antonio Berardi: Sex and Sensibility* (Thames & Hudson, 1999)

Blow, Isabella; Treacy, Philip; Bowles, Hamish, *Philip Treacy, 'When Philip Met Isabella'* (Assouline, 2002)

Bolton, Andrew, *AngloMania: Tradition and Transgression in British Fashion* (Metropolitan Museum of Art, 2006)

Breward, Christopher; Gilbert, David; Lister, Jenny, *Swinging Sixties* (V&A Publications, 2006)

Breward, Christopher and Gilbert, David (eds), *Fashion's World Cities* (Berg, 2006)

Breward, Christopher; Conekin, Becky; and Cox, Caroline (eds), *The Englishness of English Dress* (Berg, 2002)

Breward, Christopher; Ehrman, Edwina; Evans, Caroline, *The London Look: Fashion from Street to Catwalk* (Yale University Press, 2004)

Brown, Tina, *The Diana Chronicles* (Century, 2007)

Callan, Georgina O'Hara, *The Thames and Hudson Dictionary of Fashion and Fashion Designers* (Thames & Hudson, 1998)

Cargill Thompson, Jessica and Derbyshire, Jonathan, (eds), *London Calling: High Art and Low Life in the Capital since 1968* (Time Out, 2008)

Cheshire, Susi, *British Fashion Designer Report* (Department of Trade and Industry, 1998)

Clarke, Louise, editor, *The Measure* (London College of Fashion, 2008)

Coates, Caroline, *Designer Fact File* (British Fashion Council, 1997)

Coleridge, Nicholas, *The Fashion Conspiracy* (Heinemann, 1988)

Connickie, Yvonne, *Fashions of a Decade: The 1960s* (B.T. Batsford, 1990)

Craik, Jennifer, *The Face of Fashion: Cultural Studies in Fashion* (Routledge, 1994)

de la Haye, Amy, *The Cutting Edge: 50 Years of British Fashion 1947-1997* (V&A Publications, 1996)

Doe, Tamasin, *Patrick Cox: Wit, Irony and Footwear* (Thames & Hudson, 1998)

Emanuel, David and Elizabeth, *A Dress for Diana* (Collins Design, 2006)

Frankel, Susannah, *Visionaries: Interviews with Fashion Designers* (V&A Publications, 2001)

Gaines, Steven and Churcher, Sharon, *Obsession: The Lives and Times of Calvin Klein* (Birch Lane Press, 1994)

Glynn, Prudence, *In Fashion: Dress in the Twentieth Century* (George Allen & Unwin, 1978)

Goodrum, Alison, *The National Fabric: Fashion, Britishness, Globalisation* (Berg, 2005)

Gorman, Paul, *The Look: Adventures in Pop and Rock Fashion* (Sanctuary Publishing, 2001)

Gross, Michael, *Model: The Ugly Business of Beautiful Women* (Bantam Press, 1995)

Gross, Michael, *Genuine Article: The Real Life of Ralph Lauren* (HarperCollins, 2003)

Herald, Jacqueline, *Fashion of a Decade: The 1970s* (B.T. Batsford, 1992)

Howell, Georgina, *Sultans of Style: Thirty Years of Fashion and Passion 1960-1990* (Ebury Press, 1990)

Howell, Georgina, *Diana: Her Life in Fashion* (Pavilion, 1998)

Hulanicki, Barbara, *From A to Biba* (V&A Publications, 2007)

Jones, Dylan, *Paul Smith True Brit* (Design Museum, 1996)

Kawamura, Yuniya, *The Japanese Revolution in Paris Fashion* (Berg, 2004)

Kingswell, Tamsin, *Red or Dead* (Thames & Hudson, 1998)

Kurt Salmon Associates, *Survey of the UK Fashion Designer Scene* (Prepared for the British Fashion Council, January 1991)

McDermott, Catherine, *Street Style – British Design in the 80s* (Design Council, 1987)

McDermott, Catherine, *Made in Britain: Tradition and Style in Contemporary British Fashion* (Mitchell Beazley, 2002)

McDowell, Colin, *Fashion Today* (Phaidon, 2000)

McDowell, Colin, *Galliano* (Weidenfeld & Nicolson, 1997)

McDowell, Colin, *Manolo Blahnik* (Cassell & Co, 2000)

McDowell, Colin, *Forties Fashion and the New Look* (Bloomsbury, 1997)

McRobbie, Angela (ed), *Zoot Suits and Second-Hand Dresses: An Anthology of Fashion and Music* (Macmillan, 1989)

McRobbie, Angela, *British Fashion Design: Rag Trade or Image Industry?* (Routledge, 1998)

Malcolm Newbery Consulting Company, *A Study of the UK Designer Fashion Industry* (Prepared for the Department of Trade and Industry and the British Fashion Council, December 2002)

Marr, Andrew, *A History of Modern Britain* (Macmillan, 2007)

Marwick, Arthur, *British Society since 1945* (Penguin, 1982)

Mendes, Valerie and de la Haye, Amy, *20th Century Fashion* (Thames & Hudson, 1999)

Morgan, Kenneth O., *Britain since 1945: The People's Peace* (Oxford University Press, 2001)

Mulvagh, Jane, *Vivienne Westwood: An Unfashionable Life* (HarperCollins, 1998)

Mulvagh, Jane, *Vogue History of 20th Century Fashion* (Viking, 1988)

Oldfield, Bruce, *Rootless* (Hutchinson, 2004)

O'Neill, Alistair, *London: After a Fashion* (Reaktion Books, 2007)

Polhemus, Ted, *Streetstyle* (Thames & Hudson, 1994)

Rhodes, Zandra and Knight, Anne, *The Art of Zandra Rhodes* (Zandra Rhodes Publications/Michael O'Mara Books, 1984)

Rhodes, Zandra, *Zandra Rhodes: A Lifelong Love Affair with Textiles* (Antique Collectors Club, 2005)

Rocha, John, *John Rocha: Texture, Form, Purity, Detail* (Conran Octopus, 2002)

Rous, Henrietta, *The Ossie Clark Diaries* (Bloomsbury, 1998)

Saunders, Gerry, *The UK Fashion Industry* (Emap Fashion, November 1998)

Smith, Paul, *You Can Find Inspiration in Everything* (Violette Editions, 2001)

Steele, Valerie, *Fifty Years of Fashion: New Look to Now* (Yale University Press, 1997)

Steele, Valerie, *Paris Fashion: A Cultural History* (Berg, 1998)

Steele, Valerie, *Fashion, Italian Style* (Yale University Press, 2003)

Stemp, Sinty, *Jean Muir: Beyond Fashion* (Antique Collectors' Club, 2007)

Storey, Helen, *Fighting Fashion* (Faber & Faber, 1996)

Tucker, Andrew, *The London Fashion Book* (Thames & Hudson, 1998)

Tungate, Mark, *Fashion Brands: Branding Style from Armani to Zara* (Kogan Page, 2008)

Turner, Alwyn W., *The Biba Experience* (Antique Collectors' Club, 2004)

Watson, Linda, *Vogue Twentieth Century Fashion* (Carlton, 1999)

Watt, Judith, *The Penguin Book of Twentieth Century Fashion Writing* (Viking, 1999)

Wilcox, Claire, *Radical Fashion* (V&A Publications, 2001)

Wilcox, Claire, *Vivienne Westwood* (V&A Publications, 2004)

Wilcox, Claire, *The Golden Age of Couture: Paris and London 1947-57* (V&A Publications, 2007)

Wilson, John, *The UK Fashion Designer Scene* (Report for the Department of Trade and Industry, February 1986)

Picture Credits

Every effort has been made to contact holders of copyright works. Any copyright holders we have been unable to reach are invited to contact the publishers so that a full acknowledgment may be given in subsequent editions. For permission to reproduce the images below, we wish to thank the following.

© Billa Baldwin 244 top right

© Manolo Blahnik 256 ('Campari' – the Mary Jane shoe that was first made in 1994 and became iconic thanks to *Sex and the City*)

Camera Press, London 25; Andy Kyle 67 above; Stewart Mark 111; The Sunday Times 120; Terry Smith 129; Jonathan Player 206; Tim Douglas 215

Catwalking 4–5, 119, 155, 160–61, 163, 168, 191, 193, 195, 198, 199, 200, 204, 207, 210, 216, 217, 218, 219, 224, 225, 227, 229, 230, 234, 235, 236, 237, 238, 239, 240, 241, 242, 243

The Condé Nast Publications Ltd/Willie Christie/Vogue 34; Patrick Lichfield/Vogue 39; Barry Lategan/Vogue 40; Paul Lange/Vogue 93 left; Albert Watson/Vogue 93 right; Sudhir Pithwa/Vogue 100; Diana Cochrane/Vogue 101 above; Barry Swaebe/Vogue 101 below; Jean Pierre Masclat/Vogue 118; Michael Roberts/Tatler 126; Alex Chatelain/Vogue 150; Sean Cunningham/Vogue 176–7; Chris Crymer/Vogue 179; Terence Donovan/Vogue 186 above; Jean Pierre Maslat/Vogue 205

© Corbis/Richard Frank Smith/Sygma 196 below; Stephane Cardinale/Sygma 220–21

© John Galliano 131

Getty Images/Hulton Archive/Justin de Villeneuve 35 (56013790); Hulton Archive 66 (3065606); Getty Images Entertainment/Dave M. Bennett 244 above left (81417524)

© Dafydd Jones 104, 157, 202 above

© www.justinephotography.com 135

© Nick Knight 86, 87

© Barry Lategan 42–3

© Mark Lebon/ i-D 136

London Designer Collections 32, 48, 49, 50, 52, 209; David Bailey 58–9; Tony McGee 69, 94, 95, 96

London Fashion Week 86 below (designer Nathan Church)

© Eamonn J. McCabe 128

© Niall McInerney 1, 2–3, 28, 29, 36–7, 46, 47, 56–7, 74, 75, 76, 77, 78–9, 81 below, 90–91, 108, 110, 112, 113, 114, 115, 116, 122, 123, 125, 132, 133, 142, 158, 159, 164, 166, 172, 185, 192, 194, 196 above, 201, 226

© Andrew McPherson 121

© Will Matthews 233

Mirrorpix 27

© Norma Moriceau 54

© Sarah Morris 212 (Photo: Jörg + Philipp von Bruchhausen, Courtesy White Cube/Jay Jopling)

© Morgan O'Donovan 245

© Ted Polhemus/PYMCA 82 above

© Jonathan Postal 144

Press Association Images 70, 72 below, 98, 139, 182, 186 above, 187

© Hugrun Ragnarsson 223

© Reuters/Paul Hackett 214

Rex Features/Stevens/Daily Mail 6–7; Sheila Rock 26, 30, 84–5; Jon Lyons 60 above; Richard Young 63 above, 67 below, 83, 180, 203, 207; Fraser Gray 80; Eugene Adebari 82 below; John Rogers 140; Simon Townsley 156; Rex Features 171, 173, 197, 228; Clive Dixon 175

John Swannell 33 above, 147

© Topfoto 60 below, 64, 73, 81; PA 63 below left, 72 above; UPP 146, 188, 189

© Max Vadukul 106

© James Wedge 92

Index